THE
COOKBOOK

THE
COOKBOOK

Coming of Age in Turbulent Times

William Powell

THE COOKBOOK

Published by Reputation Books, LLC
www.reputationbooksllc.com

Copyright © 2019 by William Powell
All rights reserved.

Book Design: Lisa Abellera

ISBN 978-1-944387-21-1 (hardcover)

ISBN 978-1-944387-20-4 (paperback)

ISBN 978-1-944387-22-8 (ebook)

First Edition: June 2019

10 9 8 7 6 5 4 3 2 1

Reputation Books

How is it, Rollin, that the body has eyes in the front to see the way, our consciousness has its eyes behind? Fate carries us on the back seat of a cart, so that we only see things after they have passed, and the road speeds dizzily away beneath us. Humanity is an explorer who advances backward.

—Henri Fauconnier,
The Soul of Malaya, 1931

Contents

PREFACE

MANY PEOPLE HAVE HEARD OF *The Anarchist Cookbook* and some may be curious about who the author, William Powell, was in real life. The notoriety of the book and its associations with violent acts will have led some to develop vivid, and perhaps unkind, assumptions about him. In fact, unless you'd met Bill personally, little public information existed about the person who had written *The Anarchist Cookbook*. After the rise of the internet, journalists tracked him down and despite repeated requests for interviews, Bill declined most. In life, he was a very shy man.

I met Bill in the fall of 1976 when we were teachers at a private school for learning disabled and emotionally disturbed children in the suburbs of New York City. At the start of the school semester, we were both on bus duty at the end of the school day when one of my second grade charges ran out into moving traffic and attacked the side of a school bus as it pulled away from the curb. This little girl had had a bad day and, spotting the source of her frustration inside that bus, she flew off the sidewalk without a second thought. I ran to bring her back, and it turned out that the gentleman who came after us to make sure we were all right was none other than

Bill. The three of us rolled around in the gutter and, fortunately, no one was hurt. Bill introduced himself. Later, we would tell our students that we had met under a bus, and the rest was history. They told us that was a cool story.

There were so many points of connection it seemed like fate that Bill and I should meet, fall in love, and marry. Both our fathers worked for the United Nations and we had each spent time growing up outside the United States. Now, enrolled in the same masters program in education, we developed a growing passion for learning and teaching. When we met, not even a year had elapsed since the passage of Public Law 94-142 in the United States: the Education for All Handicapped Children Act. We didn't know then how a lifetime of thinking about inclusion would be influenced by this new law, one of the first in the world to protect the rights of children with handicaps and learning differences.

It wasn't long after we met that Bill told me about *The Anarchist Cookbook* and shared the many newspaper articles and reviews that had been written about it. While there had been a big splash after it was just published, media attention moved on to other issues. We were consumed by news of the Watergate scandal, the end of the Vietnam war and reintegration of US soldiers, the Soweto riots, and the election of Margaret Thatcher as first female Prime Minister in the United Kingdom. *The Anarchist Cookbook* was quietly forgotten by the fall of 1976. Or so we thought. Who could have predicted that the book would make a resurgence with the rise of the internet and that many copycat models would also be produced.

People may wonder how it is possible that the person who wrote *The Anarchist Cookbook* could also be the well-loved teacher of so many young people and adults alike? How could he be the inspiring international school leader who devoted his life to supporting the education of children with special educational needs and who then continued his advocacy in teaching adults?

Such a question has no simple answers. Those who knew him would say that Bill was a driven man, one who could fill the unforgiving minute like no one else. An avid learner, he was most suspicious of dogma. In his later years, he would say "There is learning in every experience; we have only to recognize it." Bill developed serious reservations about *The Cookbook* in the years after its publication, and disavowed the premise that violence can be used to correct the wrongs of society. Although Bill never owned the rights to the book and was not successful in pulling it out of print, he also never allowed *The Cookbook* to define who he was or who he became.

Although it isn't mentioned within this book, Bill's graduation from university came with the highest of distinctions, *Magna Cum Laude.* I would venture to guess that after years of struggle in grade school, this award proved to him his own capacity for learning. It is probably also one of the experiences that began to suggest to him the inherent worth of students who don't do well in school: They *all* have the potential for growth and success that traditional schooling may not support or encourage. This belief was a driving force in establishing the *Next Frontier: Inclusion.* NFI is the organization we founded with Kevin Bartlett and Kristen

Pelletier to support international schools in becoming increasingly inclusive of children with special educational needs.

Throughout his life, Bill persistently questioned what might have been accepted 'truths' and always sought to find connections. A favorite query for exploration was, "I wonder what we believe in today, what practices we engage in and are proud of, that will embarrass our grandchildren tomorrow?" His conviction that all knowledge is tentative served as a model to me and our sons that inquiry never stops.

Bill's sudden and unexpected death in July 2016 cut short a very rich life filled with thinking, learning, and loving.

I will always love you, Bill.

—Ochan Kusuma-Powell
Kuala Lumpur, December 2017

FOREWORD
"According to the Best Authorities..."

IN 1971 I WAS LIVING IN Putney, Vermont and attending Windham College as an undergraduate. I had just turned twenty years old. In January of that year, my first book, *The Anarchist Cookbook*, appeared in bookshops across the US. On April 19th, I found the following letter in my mailbox.

> *"Dear Anti-Christ,*
> *You are a foreign commie bastard! We hate you and*
> *your fucking book. We will burn your book and you.*
> *Prepare to die you bastard!"*

The letter was unsigned, but was postmarked from Brattleboro—some ten miles away. It was the first of a dozen such letters and phone calls.

The "fun" had begun.

The letter includes four factual errors: I am not foreign. I was born on Long Island, New York in December, 1949 and I carry a US passport. I am not a communist. In fact, the tedium of Marxist rhetoric drives me nuts. I am not a bastard. My father and mother were legally married well before I was conceived. And finally, some popular opinion notwithstanding, I am not the Anti-Christ.

Despite the errors, it was easy to appreciate the letter's underlying sentiment.

I wrote *The Anarchist Cookbook* when I was nineteen. It is a collection of how-to recipes for a variety of illegal activities— from growing pot plants on your windowsill to making homemade bombs in the bathroom.

As I was writing *The Anarchist Cookbook (The Cookbook)* I had a notion that it would be controversial, but I had no idea then of how much of a stir it would create. I also had no idea that it would become a staple of the internet sub-culture, have a film named after it, be featured in a number of best-selling novels, and still be in print nearly fifty years later selling over two million copies.

I do not now agree with many of the premises of *The Cookbook*; most notably that constructive political change can emerge through violence. While I regret writing the book, I also recognize that *The Cookbook* is part of my past and has contributed to who I am now. I would like to distance myself from it and dismiss it as the folly of an angry adolescent, but somehow that seems to me to be a cop out. Having said that, I have not owned a copy of the book for the last thirty years and only rarely spoke about it. Perhaps it is this uncomfortable paradox that now causes me to put pen to paper.

At the time, *The Cookbook* was a personal statement of what I held to be true. It was received with near universal condemnation. Critics on the right held it to be communist inspired. Some equated the contents of the book to fascism. Critics from the so-called New Left described me as a "phony" and said that the book was exploitive of the "revolution." I take issue with the word "phony" because it suggests that I didn't actually believe in what I had written. I am many things that I am not proud of, but I rarely lie—most of the untruths that I have spoken I have believed in. *The Cookbook* is a case in point.

The most vociferous criticism focused on the irresponsibility of placing destructive and dangerous recipes in the public domain. This criticism I find interesting because the recipes for the most controversial content (bomb-making instructions) were in no way original with me. I have never built a bomb. I researched bomb-making by reading US Army field manuals. So, for these critics it was apparently acceptable for the military to publish such instructions, but not so when the same content was placed between the covers of *The Anarchist Cookbook*. Presumably, this distinction is based upon the assumption that the military (and the political leadership that instructs it) is seen to use the destructive content in a reasonable and responsible fashion. While in no way trying to defend *The Cookbook,* I don't believe history supports this assumption.

Reading passages of *The Cookbook* forty-five years after it was first published makes me cringe. The tone of the prose is supremely self-confident and the content is embarrassingly self-aggrandizing.

So what is it about the book that has resulted in its popular endurance?

By rights it should have been a temporary fad that had its splash in the media pan and then disappeared from public consciousness.

This doesn't seem to be the case with *The Cookbook.* I personally don't think the long publishing history of the book is the result of the recipes. These are available in any large library and now, of course, are readily accessible in a multitude of contexts on the Internet. I suspect that the endurance of *The Cookbook* may have to do with the dreadful prose that I now find so embarrassing. The book's "voice" may capture in some perverse way the voice of alienated, angry, self-absorbed adolescence.

Soon after its publication and the subsequent spat of media attention, my father said to me: "Everyone has a dark side of their soul, but not everyone puts theirs in print for thousands to view."

Ironically, publishing a best-selling book full of ideas that I now find repugnant has served me in a number of different ways. It has made me acutely aware of the enormous potential people have for cognitive and emotional growth. I am humbled and comforted to recognize that I was not finished product at nineteen years old.

The Cookbook has been my companion for the past forty-five years and has served as a reminder of how vulnerable we may be to the self-deceptive allure of certainty. At nineteen, I had many more answers than I had questions. The opposite is now the case. The book has hovered like an awkward question on the rim of my consciousness for years and has the annoying habit of popping into mind every time I am about to be absolutely certain about something. It was Hamlet who said: "I could be bounded in a nutshell and call myself king of infinite space, but that I have bad dreams."

In the years that followed the publication of *The Cookbook,* I gradually grew uncomfortable with its contents. I found the demands for justification increasingly difficult to address.

While there are some very simplistic and inane ideas presented in *The Cookbook* (e.g. "respect is only a product of power and fear and achieved through the spilling of blood") there are also some other ideas that are more subtle and enduring. For example, implicit in *The Cookbook* is that we have much greater reason to have faith and trust in the integrity, compassion, and courage of individuals than we do once those individuals have come together into governing bodies. Despite what we read about in the newspapers regarding individual acts of carnage, the greatest perpetrators of mass violence remain governments—in which individuals, under the guise of patriotism or tribal loyalty, vested self-interest couched as "realism," religious fervor or fear-mongering about "national security" abrogate personal responsibility. This has been an all too regular feature of our modern life. From the killing fields of Cambodia, Bosnia, and Rwanda, from the oppressive autocracies of the Middle East, from the Soviet gulags to Guantanamo, we have seen over and over again that in the collective governing mind, the ends more often than not justify the means.

I continue to have a great faith in individuals and their potential for development. This is one of the reasons that I have devoted the last forty years of my life to the education of children, especially children with special educational needs.

For better or for worse, *The Cookbook* is part of my past and my past has a powerful influence on whom I have become.

Why forty-five years later would I consider writing on the subject of *The Anarchist Cookbook*?

Let me address the question by making an analogy to my favorite hobby: collecting antique maps. Contemporary maps are valuable because of their accuracy and precision. They guide us as we navigate and explore unfamiliar terrain. An inaccurate contemporary map would be worse than useless—it would be misleading.

Antique maps, on the other hand, are interesting because of their inaccuracies. There is a wonderful 18th century map that boldly displays California as an island off the west coast of America. There are also many old maps that show Australia as an appendage connected to Indonesia. Antique maps provide us with a fascinating window into the thinking of an earlier age: their discoveries, illusions, and beliefs. We see in antique maps what the cartographers of the age believed to be immutably true. We see their prejudices and their cultural myopia.

On the wall of my living room hangs a copy of the so-called "slug map" of Africa drawn in 1771. The depiction of West Africa is reasonably accurate. European explorers and slave traders had made frequent visits and had brought back to the great cartographers of Europe detailed geographical descriptions. However, the map of the East Coast of Africa is a mass of inaccuracies. In fact, the map that hangs on my living room wall has merged all the great African lakes (Victoria, Albert, Tanganyika and Nyasa) into one slug-shaped body of water—hence the nickname of the map. The elaborate and rather pompous cartouche in the upper right hand corner announces that the map has been drawn "According to the

Best Authorities." Presumably the best authorities did not include the Africans who were actually living on the edges of the lakes.

Each generation suffers the arrogance of presentism—that unfortunate combination of having our perspective limited to the present moment coupled with the sense that we have reached an enduring pinnacle of knowledge, understanding, and wisdom.

We rarely hear people asking: In what ways will my great-grandchildren be ashamed of me? Or, what am I currently embracing that future generations will scorn?

The Cookbook was a product of such arrogant certainty. Like an antique map, it was written in an earlier age both in terms of the cultural context out of which it came, and in terms of the development of its author. Over the years, I have come to have a profound mistrust of certainty and those who claim it.

The reflections that are contained in this book are similar to the investigations into an antique map. I am writing not to explain, excuse, or apologize, but rather to develop a greater understanding of myself and the world that I inhabit. Hopefully my story may also contain an insight or two that will be helpful for others.

My story starts on top of a historic hill in north London.

Part One: My Life as an Idiot

CHAPTER 1
Mis-Education, British Style

WHEN I WAS ABOUT THREE years old, my American father was transferred from the United Nations Headquarters in New York to London. My mother is British and they had met in London during the War. For my mother, the transfer was a return home to all that was familiar. For me, it was a journey into a strange new world.

I don't know why my father chose to live in Harrow-on-the-Hill. Perhaps it was because of the presence of the famous school by the same name. Perhaps he was under the illusion that one day I would sit in the same classroom as had Churchill, Palmerston, or Nehru. If this was his dream, he would be disappointed.

My father was an Anglophile of the first order and I am sure Harrow-on-the-Hill appealed to his desire to be immersed in English history. There was the school dating back to the 16th century, a church that was built by St. Anselm and consecrated at the Feast of the Epiphany, and a charming Tudor pub, which allegedly had served as King Henry VIII's hunting lodge. My father and I would often walk through Harrow-on-the-Hill stopping in St. Mary's Churchyard where he would point out to me the gravestone upon which Lord Byron reclined while composing "Lines Written Beneath an Elm in the Churchyard of Harrow."

In the 1950's, Harrow-on-the-Hill was a leafy English village that hadn't changed a great deal since the turn of the century. There was a green grocer shop, a tobacconist, a chemist, and a sweet shop that displayed enormous glass jars of toffees, boiled sweets, liquorice, and sherbert fountains, and sold multi-colored gobstoppers for a penny a piece. The old world atmosphere of the village was further enhanced by the presence of Harrow school boys who wore a uniform of grey trousers, a dark-blue woolen jacket, black tie and a straw boater-style hat with a blue band around it. On Sundays the boys wore their morning suits: a black tailcoat, pinstriped grey trousers, and black waistcoat and tie. The monitors wore top hats and sported personalized canes.

It could have been a movie set, but it wasn't.

Harrow was a good place for walking and we did a good deal of it. Except, that is, for Piggy Lane. Piggy Lane was a dirt track that ran from Harrow-on-the-Hill to the Sudbury Hill Underground Station. It was a shortcut that children were forbidden use. I can remember on numerous occasions my mother warning me not to go down Piggy Lane. She told me that something not very nice had happened there. When she spoke about Piggy Lane her eyes would grow to the size of silver shillings and I would get gooseflesh. When I asked her what had happened in Piggy Lane, she just shook her head and repeated her dire warning. I remember lying in bed at night going through a catalogue of possible Piggy Lane horrors. In my imagination, there were robberies, muggings, kidnappings, and grizzly murders of young children.

All my playmates were also forbidden to go into Piggy Lane. So, of course, Piggy Lane was a major feature of our conversation and curiosity. None of us knew the terrible secret that the adult world shared. And so, we did what curious children do, and mounted a secret early evening foray into Piggy Lane. We had a marvelous time, scared ourselves silly, but discovered nothing more ominous than a dead garter snake. (Years later, I learned that a man had jumped out from behind a bush and exposed himself to the wife of the local butcher and the lane became contaminated by association for years thereafter).

In many respects, my childhood and adolescence were a series of forbidden Piggy Lanes—almost none of which I could resist the temptation to explore.

I believe I was a disappointment to my father. I know he had dreams for me that I never fulfilled. Within a week of my birth my father had entered my name on the admissions waiting list for St. Paul's School, one of the most prestigious boys prep schools in London. At seven, I took the entrance examination and failed miserably.

My father also had a love affair with Cambridge and we spent many holidays staying at the Old Vicarage in Grantchester next to the Orchard Tea Garden. I can still recite by heart some of the poetry of Rupert Brooke who lived in the Old Vicarage for a number of years before World War I. We would punt along the River Cam and my father would point to King's College Chapel, a masterpiece of gothic perpendicular architecture, and announce that was where I would go to university. In this too, he would be disappointed.

Before joining the United Nations, my father had been a university professor. So we didn't take holidays like normal people, we went on field trips. I have fond memories of listening to my dad recount Arthurian legends in Glastonbury and Tintagel or describing how the hypocaust (Roman heating system) worked in Bath. We spent Easter in Llandudno in North Wales. We stayed in the Gogarth Abbey Hotel where Lewis Carroll had put the finishing touches on *Alice in Wonderland.* In the summers, we explored Hardy-country in and around Dorchester.

It would have been a pleasant childhood had school not interfered.

At the age of four, I was admitted to one of the most peculiar establishments ever to call itself a place of learning. Its official name was the Langdale House School, but everyone called it Miss Gordon's after the Scottish harridan who ran it. One of the most intriguing things I learned from this school was how differently teachers behaved when parents were around. They were situation sensitive. They actually smiled and appeared human when the parents were dropping off or picking up their children. Once the parents were out of sight, they would revert to being aliens— unpleasant, unkind, morose, and, at times, cruel.

Miss Gordon was very old and looked like the witch in *Hansel and Gretel.* She had a large hooked nose, a huge wart on her neck, and had lost all but two of her front teeth. She practiced discipline by glaring and she was very good at it. One morning, she read a garbled version of Genesis to us in which Lot's wife looks backward and is turned into a pillar of salt. My classmate, Sumner, said to me afterwards that was what Miss Gordon did. If she stared at you long enough you'd turn into a pillar of salt. There were very few disciplinary problems at her school.

Some of the parents said Miss Gordon had a heart of gold, but you certainly couldn't tell that from her manner.

The school was housed in a large Victorian house that was desperately in need of repairs. Not even the French would have approved of the antiquated plumbing. There was no known curriculum and I doubt any of the teachers were qualified. The lessons were eclectic and idiosyncratic. One day we would learn about Bulgarian agriculture and the next how King Harold took an arrow in the eye at the Battle of Hastings. The scope and sequence of learning was spontaneous and fragmented. I'm sure the school would now be closed by any education authority worth its salt, if the health inspectors hadn't shut it first.

Children at Miss Gordon's school were motivated by trying to avoid the wrath of the teachers or at least to deflect it onto others. It wasn't always possible. The worst wrath of all was that of the dragon empress herself, Miss Gordon.

When I was six, Miss Gordon decided that she was going to teach us math and instructed me to go to the blackboard and solve a long division problem involving the British currency that was in circulation at the time, namely pounds, shillings, and pence. This was a fairly complex procedure since Britain had not yet moved to the decimal system. There were four farthings in a penny, twelve pence in a shilling, and twenty shillings in a pound. In front of the class, I remember struggling unsuccessfully with the problem. After a few minutes, a red-faced Miss Gordon came to the front of the classroom and announced that she would put a problem on the board that was so simple that even Billy could solve it. She wrote up a three-digit addition problem. However, by this point I was feeling such intense anxiety that concentration was impossible. To the amusement of the rest of the class, I was unable to perform even the most basic calculations.

"Don't just stand there like an idiot," she roared.

I didn't. I wet my pants.

It was the first inkling I had that I might be an idiot. It wouldn't be the last.

Miss Gordon collected foul-smelling stray dogs, most of whom hated children. Not a week went by when a student wasn't bitten by one of her dogs. I still have the scars on both legs. Her reaction was always the same. She accused the child of teasing the dog.

There was a large open space behind the school that was referred to as the "playground." I say it was an open space, because the term "garden" might be misleading. The only living things, other than children, were twenty or thirty filthy rabbits that Miss Gordon kept in vile-smelling hutches against the rear wall. There were no trees or bushes and the last blade of grass had been beaten into extinction in a previous century. The "playground" looked like a disused builders' yard. There were hundreds and hundreds of loose bricks scattered around the ground—as though someone had planned to build something and then had run out of money or had otherwise abandoned the project.

These bricks were marvelous playthings and every recess the playground was turned into a war zone. We boys used the bricks to build all sorts of fabulous castles and then spent the rest of recess hurling bricks at each other from within our prefabricated fortifications. Every two or three days, a child would be injured, some even required stitches, but no effort was made to stop us from this pastime. It was marvelous sport: the second best thing about Miss Gordon's school.

The best thing about the school was a curious notion that the teachers had that after lunch little children needed to sit still in order to digest their food. So to keep us still, the teachers read us stories. This was my absolute favorite part of the day. The teachers read us children's versions of Homer's *Odyssey* and Bunyan's *Pilgrim's Progress*.

I had a difficult time learning to read. I now suspect I had and have an auditory processing problem. I simply couldn't associate letter configurations with sounds. The phonemic approach to reading just didn't work for me. To this day, when reading Russian novels I will not attempt to pronounce the character's names, I simply memorize the letter configurations. But my slow development in reading worried my parents, particularly my dad who was an avid reader. And so they did what caring parents do. We read together in the evenings. I got to choose the books and we would read alternate pages aloud. How I looked forward to those times! We read the entire Dr. Doolittle series and most of Enid Blyton's *Secret Seven* series. My father and mother managed to turn something that I dreaded into a nightly event that I looked forward to with relish.

My other memories of Miss Gordon's school include being falsely accused of stealing a knob from a portable heater. Why anyone would want to steal such a knob is anyone's guess. But that was the sort of place Miss Gordon's was. Something didn't need to make sense in order to be true.

Every summer Miss Gordon would take a small group of children on holiday with her to Broadstairs on the southeast coast of Kent. She did this to augment her income, because she certainly didn't show any interest in the children once we arrived. There were no planned activities, excursions, or outings for the children. We were simply left to our own devices. I liked to go to Broadstairs because there was virtually no supervision and we could get into all sorts of wonderful mischief. I recall one afternoon when three of us returned from exploring the caves that riddled the limestone cliffs that overlooked the sea. Miss Gordon asked us what we had done. My friend Sumner replied that we had seen the army shoot a man on the beach. Miss Gordon took a ruler to Sumner's knuckles for making up stories. The lead story in the following days' newspaper was how the army had shot and killed an escaped lunatic on the beach. There was always something to do in Broadstairs.

I often spent weekends at the home of my English grandparents. Grandma and Grandpa Newman lived in a large suburban house in North Ealing. Grandpa was a dentist and had his surgery on the ground floor of his home. Grandma was a respectable British housewife who ran a neat house, paid her debts on time, and weeded her garden regularly. I say that she was "respectable" because this seemed to be her primary goal in life.

My grandmother was from rural Devon and her father had managed a pub (although my grandmother would always refer to it as a "hotel"). My grandfather was from just outside London.

When they migrated to London after World War I to set up a dental practice, they moved both across county lines and class boundaries. They entered the professional class. I have a sense that my grandmother's claim on the professional class was always a little tenuous as though there was always a nagging fear that something would occur that would expose the peasant stock she so desperately wanted to leave behind.

In terms of my upbringing, this almost single-minded focus on middle class respectability manifested itself in obsession with having the proper accent and table manners.

When I turned six, my father and mother took me for an interview at Orley Farm School. I am sure that there must have been some excellent schools in Britain in the 1950's, but Orley Farm wasn't one of them. (The school is still in existence and I'm sure has evolved into a more child-centered and humane establishment). The main school building had been the family home of the author Anthony Trollope who wrote a novel in 1862 called *Orley Farm*.

I remember entering the headmaster's study. It smelled of over-brewed tea and stale tobacco smoke. Against the far wall was a bookshelf full of tarnished cricket trophies. A threadbare Middle Eastern carpet covered the center of the room. Mr. Ellis sat behind a large desk. He was a formidable figure, balding with bushy eyebrows and penetrating eyes that seemed to suggest that he was a master of reading the thoughts of little boys and highly adept at identifying those that were naughty.

After a few minutes of small talk, Mr. Ellis nodded in my direction and announced that he would personally instruct young William in classical Greek.

"You'd better teach him English first," my father quipped.

Orley Farm was primarily a boarding school, but I attended as a day student. This was both an advantage and disadvantage. It meant that at about five o'clock in the afternoon I could escape the terror and the trauma that were part of my daily life at school, but it also meant that I never really developed a sense of membership or belonging with the other boys.

The students at Orley Farm School had nicknamed Headmaster Ellis, "Elijah" because of his resemblance to the Old Testament Prophet. According to the Bible, Elijah raised the dead, brought fire down from the sky, and ascended into Heaven in a whirlwind—all of which we witnessed Mr. Ellis do daily before morning chapel.

My years at Orley Farm School were unhappy ones. The curriculum was as bizarre as the teachers. At seven, I was studying French, Latin, classical Greek, and a class on Scripture that was taught by Elijah himself. We had compulsory boxing every afternoon during the winter term. I always tried to pair up with my classmate, Greensbury Minor. (Boys were always referred to by their last name. If a boy had an older brother in the school, the masters would distinguish between them by adding the appellation "major" and "minor" respectively). Greensbury Minor and I had a secret understanding that we wouldn't attempt to bash each other's brains out. However, the boxing master was no fool and he soon saw the pattern and separated us. He seemed to take pleasure in pairing me with emerging sadists. Just about every other afternoon for a month, I left the gym with a bloody nose.

Our history master, Mr. Hastings, kept a copy of Gibbon's *Decline and Fall of the Roman Empire* on his desk, which he would hurl at little boys who were not perceived to be paying attention. I remember clearly one day when Greensbury Minor was daydreaming and the veritable tome came flying in his direction. However, Greensbury Minor saw it coming, ducked, and Gibbon's legacy smashed through the window beside him and came to rest in a rhododendron bush. It was a red-letter day.

The most terrifying class was our weekly Scripture session with Elijah. Each week the lesson was exactly the same. Our homework was to memorize a portion of the Bible and the entire class period was consumed by each of us reciting the same passage from memory. I suppose you could argue that this served to improve our memory. However, I suspect the real motivation was the absence of any need for lesson planning on the part of the headmaster.

The psychologists tell us that we have so-called "flashbulb" memories. These are memories that are acute and enduring because they are connected to strong emotional associations or physical sensations. For example, most of us can remember exactly where we were and what we were doing when we heard that the Twin Towers had been attacked on September 11th, 2001. My recollections of the time I spent at Orley Farm School are similarly flashbulb memories that focus on physical pain and the fear that it produced. I was caned three times during my tenure at Orley Farm School. I remember each incident vividly. The first time was for something I didn't do in Elijah's Scripture class. The incident puzzles me to this day.

About halfway through the seemingly endless recitations of the 23rd Psalm, Elijah was called out of our Scripture class for a telephone call. He ordered us to sit in silence. According to my memory, this is exactly what we did. However, when he returned he demanded to know who had spoken during the time he was out of the room. To my knowledge, no one had. I certainly hadn't and yet I had a compelling urge to confess. I have no idea why. Perhaps I was seeking the attention of the other boys. Or perhaps this was a precursor to later problems I would have with idiotic authority figures. Or maybe I was just curious to see what would happen when one disobeyed an Old Testament Prophet. Or maybe I was bored. I always manage to get into trouble when I'm bored.

I raised my hand and announced that I had been talking. I registered the puzzlement of my classmates. I was removed from the class and taken to the headmaster's study. Elijah then ordered me to drop my trousers and bend over his chair. The chair had a leather seat into which I buried my face. I still associate the smell of leather with excruciating pain. The welts on my rear end lasted for ten days. The fear lasted much longer. His rod was definitely not comforting.

The second time I was caned it was for being "revolting" at table. The dining hall at the school consisted of four very long rectangular tables. Each "house" sat at a different table and ate the midday meal in silence. A master sat at each end of the table. The school had its own kitchen garden and grew most of its own vegetables. One lunchtime we were served a lettuce salad and I discovered on the underside of a lettuce leaf a small garden slug.

I politely raised my hand and informed the master at the end of the table about the presence of the slug. I was told to put the slug on the side of my plate and to say no more about it. I did as I was told, albeit not relishing the idea of eating a lettuce leaf that I had shared with a slug. The slug, however, had other plans. He much preferred the lettuce leaf to the side of my plate and soon began his slow journey back to the lettuce leaving a trail of glistening, iridescent slime across my plate.

I cast surreptitious glances in either direction and seeing that both masters' attention were occupied elsewhere, plucked the lettuce from my plate and shoved it in my pocket (we were required to eat everything on our plates). I then took my index finger and thumb and flicked the offending slug off the side of my plate. Perhaps I used too much force because Spottiswood, the boy sitting opposite me, suddenly screamed. The slug was attached to his cheek.

I received three strokes of the cane for this infraction.

Although I firmly disagree with the use of corporal punishment, I do admit that the third and most serious caning, I thoroughly deserved. It took place just before Christmas. One Saturday morning, my classmate Martin and I went Christmas shopping in the high street of Sudbury Hill. We entered Woolworths and were immediately drawn to the Christmas decorations. There was a counter that was full of miniature plastic crèche figures. There were shepherds, camels, wise men, donkeys, and, of course, Mary, Joseph, and the baby Jesus. I can't remember who put a figure in his pocket first, but Martin and I both left the shop with our pockets bulging with unpaid-for nativities. I recall the experience being rather exhilarating.

The following Monday morning I was summoned into the prefects' lounge and was interrogated about the incident. I don't know if Martin had boasted about the shoplifting to a classmate or whether he had felt remorse and confessed. Either way we stood accused and the Elijah was summoned. When questioned, I told the truth and was again caned. Our crime was exacerbated by the fact that our loot comprised religious figurines. I say this because Elijah kept shouting about how outrageous it was to steal the baby Jesus. This time I received "six of the best," a letter was sent home to my father and mother, and Martin and I were taken back to Woolworth's to apologize to the manager. This was definitely not my finest hour.

Even more troubling was the phone call my father received from Martin's father, who was the vicar of St. Mary's. Martin's father stated that he considered me responsible for leading Martin astray. I was a bad influence on his son and that in the future Martin would not be permitted to play with me. And we never did.

Thinking back on the incident, I suspect that being forbidden to play with Martin may have had a more long-lasting influence than the caning. Although I don't think I led Martin astray, this was what the rest of the world seemed to accept.

We lived in an apartment block called Herga Court that was next door to a convent with huge grounds. I learned that by climbing onto the flat roofs of the garages you could jump over the fence into the expansive convent grounds. It was a latter-day

Piggy Lane. I spent many, many solitary hours exploring the woods behind the convent, climbing in their apple orchard and pinching sweet peas from their vegetable gardens. The adventure was made all the more exciting because there were "strictly no trespassing" signs on all the interior walls and the nuns had hired a gamekeeper who patrolled the grounds with a shotgun.

It was about this time that my mother began to worry about me socially. I was an American in a solidly British school and I was teased and bullied fairly regularly. I suspect I was also fairly socially awkward. Outside of school, I preferred to be on my own. I had a large collection of tin soldiers and I was content to play with them by myself for hours on end. I remember making long and complex stories about the heroes and the battles that were fought on my bedroom floor. I know my solitude had begun to worry my parents. It was my mother who suggested that I join the Cub Scouts.

My experience with the Cubs lasted three very surreal weeks. My parents decided that I should join, but nobody explained why. Nor did anyone provide any background for this decidedly odd organization. In fairness, I don't think my father had a clue. Like me, he wasn't a joiner. The Cubs met at a church that we did not attend, so I knew no one in the pack. My first impression was confusion. I was outfitted in a uniform and was greeted by a fat woman who claimed to be a wolf named Akela. I soon realized that everyone had code names—just like spies on TV. During the meetings, Mr. Betts, the local librarian, was called "Baloo" the bear and Jeremy's mother was "Bagheera" the panther. Even the kids had weird names. A skinny boy with bright red hair and a million freckles was called "The Black Plume," and a pasty-faced boy with a pronounced lisp answered to "Red Fang." I was taught a two-finger salute and was made to memorize the scout promise and the scout law. Our meetings began and ended with something called the "Grand Howl." It was all too strange. It took me three weeks to convince my mother that I wanted out of this paramilitary cult.

It was at about this time that my brother, Chris, was born. I was thrilled to have a brother, but probably somewhat jealous of the attention that the baby attracted.

My British family had its share of black sheep of which I am perhaps the most recent incarnation. However, in the 1950's eccentricity was not appreciated. Uncle Donald, my grandfather's younger brother, disappeared to Australia. Rumor had it that he might have been queer. Others disappeared to Canada. The unspoken rule was: do nothing to disturb the respectability of the family. Unfortunately, Aunt Margaret did exactly that.

My Aunt Margaret was a "little odd" or at least that was how she was described to me as we drove out to the mental institution in which she had been confined. I didn't find her odd at all. I liked Aunt Margaret immensely. She played cards and board games with me. She was gentle, kind, and very intelligent. She was also a remarkably good listener and seemed genuinely interested in what a six-year-old boy had to say. I visited Aunt Margaret at her asylum a number of times and we took long walks in the grounds. She enjoyed the flowers and knew an incredible number by name. I recall the two of us feeding the fish in the ornamental pool behind the administration building.

But Aunt Margaret was a family embarrassment. She failed to understand that women should be seen and not heard. She had opinions that she did not keep to herself. She read voraciously, loved classical music, painting, and sculpture, and often made strange and unpredictable connections. In a different milieu, she might have been perceived as creative—a poet or an artist. But her "odd" behavior was drawing unwanted attention to the family. The final straw occurred when my mother first brought my father to the family home in Ealing to meet his future in-laws. The clan had gathered in all its tedious respectability to meet the American naval lieutenant. It would be a proper English tea with cucumber and tomato sandwiches and scones. Aunt Margaret appeared in the doorway of the drawing room dangling a used sanitary napkin from her right hand.

Aunt Margaret was confined in the sanatorium outside London, under medication (a chemical straightjacket) for more than twenty years. She was over sixty when she was finally released. The story, however, has a wonderful ending. I liked Aunt Margaret and even as a child I had a sense that she had received very unfair treatment. In a different age, she would have simply been a bohemian. We stayed in touch over the years and exchanged three or four letters each year.

In her eighties, Aunt Margaret met her prince charming, a gentleman several years her senior, who shared her passion for music, art, and poetry. They traveled on the continent together and they fell hopelessly in love. I received postcards from Florence, Rome, and Venice. Her letters to me could have been written by a starstruck sixteen-year-old. They were a joy to read. It was as if all the passion that had been chemically dormant during her years in the asylum had sprung to life. She debated whether to marry her beau or simply to live with him. In the end, she married—she was eighty-eight and he ninety-two. They had to be driven to the church because both had lost their driver's licenses due to old age. They had six wonderful, loving years together.

When I reflect on the time I spent growing up in Britain, the predominant impression is that of disassociation. I was somehow out of time and place. In my corner of Britain in the 1950's there was still a commonly held understanding of what it was to be British. There was still a shared idea of common national identity. This was before the Caribbean, Indian sub-continent and Asian ex-colonials came home to roost. The English gentleman was still very much an archetype. His quintessential Englishness was demonstrated by dress, manners, and accent—and was openly idealized by my family. Every waking minute I was being trained and conditioned towards this ideal, and yet I wasn't British and wasn't sure I wanted to be. I had the sense that I had walked into a movie set and had been handed a script that I was to act out. As I played this role, I watched others play their roles both from the perspective of actor and audience. I knew intuitively that what I saw in other people's behavior, didn't necessarily reflect what was actually going inside their heads. I wouldn't have used the words then, but now I think of it as an immensely fragile domestic comedy that nobody found in the least bit funny. I was looking at life from the outside.

And then one evening my dad and mom invited me into the living room for a "family conversation." My brother, Chris, was still too young to be a part of it. It was a conversation that would dramatically complicate my worldview.

My father began by explaining that he had just received the news that he was being transferred from London back to UN Headquarters in New York. He paused to let the information sink in. I assume he thought I would share his dismay at having to leave his beloved England because he went on to say that he knew this would disrupt my schooling and that if I wanted to I could stay at Orley Farm School as a boarder and spend weekends with my English grandparents.

I looked at him as if he was mad. There was no way that I was staying behind. I had been to America several times on holiday and there was no question in my mind that it represented a vastly more attractive prospect than continuing at Orley Farm. And so began the first of my many leaps out of the frying pan into the fire.

CHAPTER 2
Mis-Education, American Style

MY MOTHER, CHRISTOPHER, and I traveled to the United States in the May of 1959 on the *RMS Britannic*. The *Britannic* had plied the transatlantic passenger route from Liverpool to New York since 1929, with time out for troop transport during World War II. She was a truly elegant ship, with graceful circular staircases, wood-paneled dining rooms, a library with leather-covered writing tables, potted palms, and a circa Roaring 20's art deco interior. Passengers sat in deckchairs wrapped in plaid blankets against the breeze from the North Atlantic. A string quartet played Strauss waltzes in the promenade deck lounge daily during the service of afternoon tea. There was turtle racing in the swimming pool, shuffleboard, a movie theater, and the forbidden First Class (we traveled Cabin Class) to explore. She took seven days between Britain and New York—seven wonderful days outside the sight of land and outside the reach of teachers.

My father had gone ahead of us to New York to find a place to live. He had selected suburban White Plains, a town in Westchester that was a relatively easy commute into Manhattan and was reputed to have a good school system.

The neighborhood we moved into could have been the set for *Leave it to Beaver*. It was 1959 and be-freckled, crew cut boys really did deliver newspapers from little red wagons. Moms wore aprons and dispensed cookies and pink lemonade in the backyard. Cookouts were all the rage—as were dilly beans, madras shirts, hoola hoops, and Davy Crockett paraphernalia. It was a benign world that was overseen by benevolent Grandfather Ike and virginal Annette Funicello. Joe McCarthy had lured the domestic commies from beneath our beds and there was a hiatus between the carnage of Korea and Vietnam. Sex was something adults did, but didn't talk about and no one separated their garbage. Glass bottles, plastic bags, and food scraps fraternized unashamedly beneath the kitchen sink. There were Protestants, Catholics, and Jews in our neighborhood but they were all safely white. Black and brown people came to clean houses and mow lawns, but went somewhere else at night. Dogs didn't bite and cats didn't scratch. No one got divorced. Weirdos didn't embed razor blades in apples at Halloween and pot was something my mother planted geraniums in.

Thank god the 60's were just around the corner.

I didn't know it at the time, but there were subtle and not so subtle rumblings in this air-conditioned nightmare.

Rudolph Flesch had just published *Why Johnny Can't Read*. Very soon Arthur Bestor would write *Educational Wasteland* and Albert Lynd *Quackery in Public Schools*. Something was rotten in the kingdom of American education. Although I would not have understood the language of their criticism as a newly enrolled fifth grader, I could have told the experts exactly what was wrong.

Classroom learning, if you could call it that, was fragmented, trivial, and irrelevant. There was an almost total absence of thinking on the part of both the teachers and the students. The message was clear: When you come to school, leave your curiosity, passion, frontal lobes, and sense of humor at home. The class periods were dull and repetitious; the teaching unrelentingly tedious. It was like watching a bad movie in slow motion. British fear was replaced by American boredom. The fifth grade was excellent preparation for a monotonous factory job in Pittsburg or Detroit.

I suspect that my upper crust British accent irritated Mrs. Marzac, my fifth grade teacher. Perhaps she thought I was trying to put on airs or that I was arrogant, because she started to mimic my accent in front of the class. She delighted in correcting my British spelling and insisted that my cursive handwriting was all wrong. I spent hours re-learning how to form my letters. The most perplexing was our vocabulary lessons in which we were supposed to identify the accented syllables. I could never get them right.

The content was also entirely different from what I had been exposed to in Britain. Mrs. Marzac felt it her duty to have us memorize the names of the state capitals and mighty American rivers. Everyone had an entirely different frame of reference from my own. My classmates knew all about people I had never heard of: Paul Bunyan, Johnny Appleseed, Mickey Mantle, Roy Rogers, and The Three Stooges.

I do not mean to give the impression that I didn't learn anything useful in the fifth grade. I did, but most of it was out of school. Jonty Barnes and Robbie Brue taught me a lexicon of four letter words that I devoured with relish. This was how vocabulary should be taught! Unlike classroom vocabulary lessons, I learned these words seemingly without effort. Even their spelling came naturally. They were connected to everyday life. Excretory functions and male and female private parts were immediately relevant. There was also something very engaging and stimulating about learning words that one wasn't allowed to say in front of adults. These words have had enduring value for me throughout my life. I have employed them on five continents to express surprise, dismay, irritation, humor, delight, anger, and exaltation. They are truly words for all seasons! Perhaps Shakespeare's feral savage, Caliban, has it right when he tells Prospero and Miranda: "You taught me language; and my profit on't is that I learned to curse. . . ."(*The Tempest*, Act I, Scene ii).

Probably the most important thing I learned in the fifth grade was that friends were a luxury that I could live without—and for the most part I did. I wanted friends, but didn't have a clue as to how to make and keep them. I didn't understand American culture, sports, TV, or slang and I seemed to have very little in common with my classmates. Most of my free time was spent reading, playing with my dog, Cookie, or attempting to burn down the house with the chemistry set I had been given for Christmas (I came perilously close).

At Thanksgiving and Christmas we would drive down to Washington DC to celebrate these occasions with my American aunts and uncles. Auntie Grace was the matriarch of the family, a simpering passive-aggressive who would torment me by alternately making me drink warm milk and taking me clothes shopping. I hated both. Her husband, Uncle Jack, was from Texas and worked at the Pentagon. Uncle Jack had had mumps as a young adult and this had prevented them from having children. Everyone would say that it was such a shame that they were childless. From my point of view, it was one of the few shreds of evidence that there might be a merciful god. Uncle Jack would have preferred a hot lead enema to a Democrat in the White House.

Auntie Ruth was a self-made real estate millionaire who collected guns, and in comparison to Uncle Jack, was a flaming liberal. Having said that, her hero and frequent dinner guest for a number of years was G. Gordon Liddy of Watergate fame. I suspect they talked guns together. She had a soft spot for rogues of all political complexions.

Auntie Marion was divorced and was carrying on a rather obvious affair with Auntie Ruth's step-son—but nobody talked about that.

After Thanksgiving dinner at Aunt Grace's house, I had what I thought was a profound insight and got into serious trouble for it. Soon after the meal was over, all the men repaired to the front sitting room to drink coffee and, in the case of my father, smoke his pipe. The women, on the other hand, would troop into the kitchen to attack the mountains of dirty dishes that covered every inch of available space. I had seen this gender difference before, but it had never really made an impression on me. But I had been reading a book about the American Civil War and the Underground Railroad, and I made a connection. So, I addressed my question to Uncle Jack.

"Aren't women like slaves? They do all the work."

By way of reply, he caught hold of my ear and dragged me into the backyard where he told me that if I ever said anything like that again he would take a stick to me.

So much for inquiry. . . .

Actually, race relations in America confused me (I now recognize that I wasn't alone. Four years later the US Senate would spend 57 days of filibuster before passing the landmark Civil Rights Act of 1964). One evening, my Aunt Ruth hosted a large family dinner party at the Kennedy Warren. The conversation turned to the issue of race and my Uncle Fred from Virginia and my father were going at it tooth and claw. My father defined himself as a 1930's liberal and was an ardent supporter of Martin Luther King Jr. and the Civil Rights Movement. Finally, in frustration, Uncle Fred pointed to me and demanded to know what my father would do if "little Billy wanted to marry a Negra woman."

I was surprised by the sudden attention I had garnered and wondered if again I had done something wrong. However, I will never forget my father's response.

"I would sit the young couple down and talk with them about the difficulties of an interracial marriage in a country inhabited by bigots like you."

Uncle Fred and his family stormed out of the dining room. It was another red-letter day. I was really proud of my dad.

My confusion about race went further than hypothetical speculation about my future domestic life. My previous life in Britain in the 1950's had been racially monochromatic. There were a few Indian and Chinese in Soho who tended restaurants or laundries, but otherwise from Land's End to John O'Groats, it was pretty much wall-to-wall whiteness. Not so America.

My school appeared to be split into four distinct groups: the relatively wealthy white suburban kids, the African Americans who lived in something ominously called "The Projects," the newly arrived Hispanics, and the blue collar Italian Americans. I assumed that I was to feel a sense of belonging with the white suburbanites, but I didn't. The African Americans were scary and I didn't understand the Hispanics. For a while I tried to befriend the Italian Americans, but when all was said and done, I just didn't fit. Towards the end of the fifth grade, I made the discovery that being alone and being lonely were not necessarily the same thing. I discovered that it might be less painful to be alone than it was to be rejected and therefore lonely. The tension between solitude and loneliness would be a recurrent theme for years to come.

In the sixth grade I had a revelation about social status. The insight came in school during a humanities unit on the Soviet Union. Mr. Kakandis, a mad Greek with a violent temper, (who was ultimately fired several years later for taking a canoe paddle to a seventh grade boy) had spent six weeks putting on the blackboard every known fact about the Soviet Union. I have no idea why, but we were responsible for memorizing the per capita income, life expectancy, infant mortality rates, doctors per thousand, square miles of arable land etc. Periodically, Mr. K would give us a surprise spelling test. In order to avoid having to mark the papers himself, Mr. K. would have us exchange papers and mark each other's tests. Afterwards, he would call on each of us and we would publically announce how many words we had got wrong. I was not a good speller and was always at the bottom of the class ranking. This prompted me to think about other ways that we ranked ourselves and I realized that there was a social hierarchy among the students in the class. It was an invisible, but obvious structure that we all seemed to take for granted. It impacted every aspect of our social interaction and yet no one talked about it. Years later, I would read about "pecking order theory" and how an animal's dominance levels determine which individuals get preferential access to resources such as food and mates. I would also read about UCLA Professor Elizabeth Cohen's research on social status and its impact on student learning. Not surprisingly, she found that low status children learn far less and far less effectively than high status children. She also discovered that teachers could have a profound impact on a student's social status within the classroom—both negatively and positively.

I didn't know all this in sixth grade, but nevertheless the idea of social ranking fascinated me. As I thought about it, I realized that status was awarded on the grounds of popularity, physical attractiveness, academic achievement, and prowess in sports. What amazed me was how all of us seemed to understand and accept this social order without ever having discussed it or its larger implications. And so I amused myself by silently ranking every student in the class based on these criteria. Julie was number one. She was the Alfa female—pretty, a member on the dominant culture, popular, and consistently on the honor roll. She wasn't good at sports, but had great breasts. She also had a good sense of humor and everyone wanted to be invited to her parties. Bernard was probably the Alfa male. I put him as number two because he was cool and a straight-A student. Scott was stupid but really good in PE. He got slot number 16. It was an interesting exercise, far more interesting than Mr. K's endless trivia about the Soviet Union, which in case Mr. K. may have missed it, doesn't exist anymore!

I placed myself at number 27, second to the bottom of my social hierarchy. At the absolute bottom was a boy named Stewart Robbins who had recently arrived from Australia. Stewart was even goofier than I was. One day he stole tampons from his mother's purse, stuck them up his nostrils, and galloped around the school cafeteria trumpeting like a bull elephant.

As I entered junior high school, my understanding of social status became more sophisticated. I recognized that there were sub-cultures within ethnic groups and the status was actually determined differently in each sub-group. For example, in the Caucasian community there were jocks, nerds, and hoods. The Jocks were into sport, Nerds were into academics, and Hoods were into being tough. With a perversity that has followed me through most of my life, I decided that my best chance of acceptance was with the Hoods. This was probably because the Hoods were rejected by everyone else. I may have assuaged my social anxiety by believing that do-it-yourself rejection is a kind of double negative—a weird acceptance of sorts.

As a species we have an archetypical need for a sense of belonging and membership in a community. Abraham Maslow puts this sense of belonging just above physical security, food, and shelter as one of the most basic human needs. Nicholas Wade in his book *Before the Dawn* makes the observation that pre-historic homo sapiens were very ill-equipped to survive except when they formed small cooperative groups. Exclusion from such a hunting and gathering group meant almost certain death. Over the millennia, we humans have come to need a sense of community as much as we need food and water. Short of torture and capital punishment, the worst we can inflict on another person is solitary confinement. Ironically, at the same time as we desperately need to belong to a social group, we have also come to crave a sense of individuality and personal autonomy. This tension has certainly been a defining feature of my life.

I say my identification with the Hoods was perverse because I had none of the membership requirements. The primary attribute of a successful Hood was that you had to be tough; you needed physical strength and prowess (you needed to be able to beat the shit out of other people). This wasn't me. Out of the scores of fights I managed to get into, I never won one. I thought about carrying a knife, but I didn't really want to hurt people and I was scared that someone would use it on me. Because I was so dreadful at fighting, I developed exaggerated displays of aggression in hopes of getting the-would-be adversary to chicken out. My favorite threat was: "I'll tear out your goddam eyes and skull-fuck ya!"

Hoods were also associated with various law-breaking activities such as underage drinking and borrowing cars that didn't belong to them. To my parents' great disappointment, these were areas in which I would soon develop moderate proficiency.

If I was not very good at playing the part of the Hood, I compensated by looking the part. Hoods dressed in skin-tight pants, wore pointed shoes (we called them "Puerto Rican fence climbers" or "brothel creepers") and black parkas. We used Brylcreem to perfect our ducktails and we sported sullen, dismissive smirks. The more I looked the part, the more rejected I would become amongst the respectable families in the neighborhood we lived in. In fact, although I did not appreciate it at the time, I served the socially redeeming function of being the example of "the bad influence" that mothers could point to when warning their children about the perils of the teenage years. *Be careful or you could end up like Billy Powell.*

Hoods were also not supposed to do well in school. At this I excelled: my life as an idiot.

There was one other characteristic of Hoods. They were supposed to be sexually active. This was a problem for me. I was a virgin and was pretty confused about the facts of life. In fact, most of what I knew came from Butch Galluchi. Butch was a sixteen-year-old in the seventh grade. He had been held back twice because of his poor academic achievement. Butch owned a well-worn book entitled *The Diary of a Nymphomaniac*, but he couldn't read very well so I read it out loud to him; which was exactly what I was doing in the back of the science lab when we were interrupted by Miss Morgan, the science teacher. When she read the title her face turned the color of a toffee-apple. She did manage to confiscate the book, but was so mortified by the content that she forgot to inform the principal.

Towards the end of the seventh grade I went steady with Laurie Orama for three whole weeks. Laurie was Cuban and Roman Catholic. I would pick Laurie up from confession at Our Lady of Mount Carmel Church on Saturday afternoons and take her to RKO Keith's Movie House where we would sit on the balcony and make out. I gave her my ID bracelet and she rewarded me with what remained on her breath of the garlic she had eaten for lunch. I never went any further than French kissing. I didn't have a clue what was going on in Laurie's mind—partially because I guessed it was going on in Spanish and I didn't speak that language, but also because I was socially very obtuse and would miss even the most obvious social cues.

Home life was pretty tempestuous at this time, but there were periods of relative calm—curiously these often coincided the great global crises. For many years my father served as the press spokesman for the Secretary General of the United Nations and international crises followed him home. I recall being fascinated by the vast global game of chess that was played out at the UN. One of my earliest memories was sitting at the kitchen table in Harrow with my dad explaining the complexities of the Suez Crisis and how difficult it was being an American UN spokesman in Britain at the time. Dinnertime conversation in White Plains often focused on the Congo Crisis. Tshombe, Kasa-Vubu, Lumumba, and Mobutu were household names and our attention was even further galvanized when a close family friend and colleague of my father's, George Ivan Smith, was taken hostage in Katanga by white mercenaries. The Middle East was also a very frequent topic of conversation. I recall my father shaking his head sadly and announcing that while Israel won every war, it lost every peace.

The United States has a history of being an amazingly inward-looking country and, with the exception of a very few newspapers, the American news media is shockingly provincial. But our dining room table was a global oasis. We listened to the world service of the BBC. My dad read daily dispatches from Reuters, AFP, Pravda, and Xinhua and would bring those differing perspectives to our conversations. There were lively discussions of the national independence movements in Africa and Asia, Kennedy's Bay of Pigs fiasco, the Cuban Missile Crisis, and of course the growing American "police action" in Indochina.

It was during these wonderfully stimulating conversations that I first began to feel discomfort with displays of patriotism. Years later when I had first been appointed high school principal in Dar es Salaam, the wife of an American diplomat accused me of not being "a real American." She was right. I'm not a real American, nor do I know what it means to be a "real American." While I appreciate that we all need to feel a part of a community, nationalism doesn't fill that need for me. In fact, I am uncomfortable around people who find their identity in their citizenship papers. Many of them are filled with dangerous, unexamined and arbitrary platitudes. During the height of the Vietnam War, it was relatively common to see cars that sported bumper stickers that read: *America: love it or leave it* or *America: my country right or wrong*. New Hampshire ordered all of its residents, by way of its license plates to: *Live free or die.* The great Doctor Johnson had it right when he wrote: "Patriotism is the last refuge of the scoundrel."

As I mentioned before, I had caring parents who certainly didn't deserve the royal headache that I was rapidly becoming. Both my father and mother were deeply interested in human psychology. My father spent years in therapy—not because he was any more neurotic than the rest of us, but because he was fascinated by the complexities of the human mind, especially his own.

My mother also had a personal avenue into psychology. For years she suffered from a phobia of elevators. As my father climbed the career ladder at the United Nations, she was required to attend more and more diplomatic receptions—almost all of which were located in Manhattan skyscrapers that required her either to ride in terrifying elevators or climb hundreds of stairs. My mother went into therapy for her phobia and became so interested in the process that she became a phobia therapist herself, and ultimately served for many years as the Director of the Phobia Clinic at White Plains Hospital. She has written articles on phobia treatments, spoken at national conferences, and for years published a regular newsletter on phobia treatments. Not a bad track record for a woman who left school at sixteen to become a clerk typist.

In part, it was my parents' interest in the human mind that led me into psychoanalysis. I was midway through grade seven when Mom and Dad decided that I was lonely and unhappy and I needed to see a psychiatrist. So I did. Not once or twice, but *three times a week for the next three years!* With time off for vacations (there was little good behavior) that amounts 360 fifty-minute-hours of intensive one-to-one Freudian psychoanalysis. Surely that's enough to shrink anyone's head to the size of a raisin.

Although medical insurance paid a portion of the psychiatrist's bill, my parents also paid a huge amount themselves. It was a very significant financial commitment and an enormous waste of money.

I don't think Dr. Leonard Neff was a charlatan. He was a qualified doctor and had a degree in psychiatry. In other words, the shingle above his door was genuine. He was, however, one of the least effective therapists on the face of the earth. He would sit and stare at me in silence for long periods of time and then accuse me of giving him the silent treatment. Talk about transference! At the end of three years, Dr. Neff announced that there was little value in continued therapy. His diagnosis was that I was a bright boy who was socially isolated and awkward with a negative attitude towards authority figures. Any amusement park geek could have told us that, and guess my weight for fifty cents.

Having said that, there is such a thing as reality therapy. This is when situations spiral out of all control and one comes face to face with real, bone-shaking, pee-in-your-pants terror. About a third of the way into the ninth grade I encountered just such a situation and came away a changed (not better) person.

In White Plains there were a number of churches that would organize dances for teenagers on Friday or Saturday nights. The idea was that these well-chaperoned events would keep kids off the streets and out of mischief. Not so. A small group of us would visit the local liquor store before the dance (I had a fake birth certificate that I purchased at a novelty store on Times Square) and stock up on Thunderbird wine and Colt 45 Malt Liquor, which we would drink in the bushes across the street from the church. This is exactly what we did one Saturday night in November. I was with three other boys: Mitch, Angelo, and Danny. Mitch and Angelo were garden variety hoods—full of bravado, but essentially sane. But Danny was not. Danny was an absolute nutter—and not a nice one. He was, and perhaps still is, a violent psychopath who is almost certainly either dead or in prison. I didn't know this at the time or I might have behaved differently.

Danny was seventeen and had already spent a good portion of his life in juvenile homes, youthful offender lock-ups and police holding cells—usually for something that involved violence. Danny's chest had so many scars—he said from knife fights—that it looked like a ploughed field. I remember thinking that Danny was pretty cool, but scary. I had no idea how scary he really was.

Before the dance was over, the four of us went out to roam the streets and finish our Colt 45 malt liquor. Danny had had an argument with one of the chaperones and had been told to leave the dance. He was in a foul mood and stood in front of the church debating loudly with himself whether to go back into the church and "bust" the chaperone. At one point he withdrew a knife from his pocket that was large enough to skin a bear.

It was Mitch that talked Danny out of busting the chaperone. Anyway, the four of us roamed the streets for an hour or so, until Danny spotted a blue 1956 Chevie. The make and year of the car is significant because if the owner left the ignition in the "on" position, the car could be started without the key. This is exactly what happened and before I had a chance to say, *Holy shit we're stealing a car*, we were sailing down the Bronx River Parkway with Danny behind the wheel, heading for the George Washington Bridge. Danny's mood improved considerably and he took on responsibility for planning our adventure. Our destination would be Columbus, Georgia. He knew the owner of a pool hall in Columbus who would put us up. We combined our cash and discovered we had collectively just under twenty dollars. Danny didn't think it was enough for gas to get us to Georgia and suggested that we might need to hit a convenience store. I listened from the back seat with a combination of awe and disbelief.

Dawn saw us outside DC and I wondered to myself what Auntie Grace would think if she knew that little Billy was cruising in a hot car on the Beltway. We stopped for coffee and gas just across the Virginia line and Danny announced that he was sleepy and that someone else should drive. I remained silent. I'd never driven a car, but there was no way I could admit that.

By early evening we had crossed into North Carolina and were in the outskirts of Fayetteville. Danny pulled us off the interstate into a poor rural community and provided us with a choice. We could either find a gas station to hit or we would have to hitchhike. The fuel gauge was on empty. The prospect of having Danny lead us into the armed robbery of a gas station filled me with sufficient dread to overcome any intimidation I was feeling. I made a strong case for hitchhiking.

Danny used his knife to unscrew the license plates from the car and then buried them a little way off in the woods. He'd done this before. We then walked down a country road until we came to a highway. Dusk turned to darkness as we followed the highway to an intersection. On one side of the intersection was a gas station, on the other a row of dilapidated clapboard houses. Angelo was the first to recognize where we were.

A small cluster of black young men sat and stood in front of the ramshackle houses. It was Saturday night and they were drinking beer and listening to music. It sounded like Ray Charles "Hit the Road Jack." But if I thought we were going to slip away into the darkness unseen, I was very much mistaken.

One of the black men let out a shout and pointed in our direction. Seconds later a beer bottle came whistling in our direction.

Danny's response was instantaneous. He whipped out his knife, tore off his necktie and ordered Mitch to bind the knife into his right hand with the necktie. In the meantime, more rocks and bottles were raining down on us. Mitch hesitated and Danny shouted at him telling him to tie the knife into his right hand. Still Mitch hesitated and Danny turned the knife on him.

A rock hit Angelo in the leg and he cried out in pain. Danny threw the necktie aside and ran towards the black youths, knife in hand, screaming racial invectives at the top of his lungs.

My heart beat faster than Ray Charles' music. This was not a good scene.

Porch lights flickered on in the rundown houses and more and more black people poured into the street. I knew Danny expected us to follow him into the fight. The consequences of running away were dire, but the prospect of following Danny was even worse. Angelo and I exchange terrified glances. I'm not sure whether we were more terrified of the African American mob or Danny.

When Danny reached the other side of the intersection, he realized that none of us had followed him. He now became the sole target of the barrage of rocks and bottles. A rock struck him above the eye and cut his forehead.

I shouted at him to get out of there. I don't know whether he heard me or not, but he was soon running in our direction. Of course, the youths followed him. Having a white lunatic to throw rocks at was fine sport.

We took off at a dead run and didn't stop until we had crossed the interstate and we were deep in the woods on the far side. I collapsed into a panting heap.

Danny was predictably furious and berated our cowardly behavior. Angelo surprised me. He turned on Danny.

"I don't care if you've got a knife. You're a crazy bastard and you almost got us all killed. Now, shut the fuck up!"

Danny seethed but was silent.

We remained in the woods for quite a while, making sure that none of the youths had followed us. Finally, Mitch announced that he was hungry. In the excitement, I had forgotten that I hadn't eaten in more than twenty-four hours. Suddenly I was ravenous.

We crossed back over the interstate and picked up a county road going south, the opposite direction from where the trouble had been. We walked a mile along the road or so before we came to a truck-stop diner. Mitch once again announced the hunger that all of us were feeling. Angelo reminded us that we had spent the last of our money on gas.

Before we could come up with a plan, a middle-aged man came out of the diner and asked us if we were hungry. I didn't see it at the time, but it was a trap. Following Danny's insane attack on the black youth, someone must have called the police who in turn must have called the diner to see if any white teenagers had appeared.

We were halfway through our beef stew when two police cruisers pulled up outside with their reds and blues flashing. To my relief, Danny went quietly.

At the police station, we were questioned. None of us mentioned the stolen car. Danny, Mitch, and Angelo were put in a holding cell. Because I was not yet sixteen, I couldn't be put into a cell. To my surprise, the town sheriff took me home with him and put me into his guest bedroom. The following morning his wife made me pancakes and eggs. It was the last thing I expected. They were really kind people.

I spent the day playing in the garden with their five-year-old daughter. I told her bits and pieces of the story of Odysseus' return journey from the Trojan War. She drew a picture of Penelope weaving. She was really proud of it and ran into the house to show it to her mother. Together we composed a modern day adventure story. She dictated and I wrote out the words.

In the late afternoon, my parents arrived. I'm not sure what exactly they must have been feeling. The little empathy that I have managed to develop came late in life. I am sure it must have been some combination of worry, disappointment, relief, and rage.

No charges were filed and the little girl gave me her portrait of Penelope as a farewell gift.

In the car on the way home, my dad and mom told me that they were very worried about the group of kids I was hanging around with. I didn't tell them, but I was too. Danny had really freaked me out. And so when Dad told me that I would be going to a boarding school, I didn't argue. I simply asked where.

That's when I learned that I was being sent up the Hudson.

CHAPTER 3
Up the Hudson

"BEING SENT UP THE HUDSON" or simply "up the river" was an expression made famous in the gangster movies of the 1950's. It meant being incarcerated in the maximum-security prison called "Sing Sing" in Ossining-on-Hudson, New York.

Storm King School (SKS) in Cornwall-on-Hudson was not a prison, and other than my last night at the school, I was not under lockup. SKS is still in existence and has a delightful website that looks very inviting. There have been some significant changes. When I attended SKS, it was all boys. It is now co-educational. It now appears to be quite multiracial. When I attended, there was only one African American student, Rickie, who managed to get himself expelled six weeks before I did. Years later, David Schulman, a classmate a year ahead of me, would describe SKS in the 1960's as a school for wealthy delinquent boys. That's probably a bit of an exaggeration, but the Headmaster at the time, Mr. Leonard, was liberal in outlook and believed in giving youngsters a second chance; a value that I have also come to hold dear.

I had mixed feelings about going to boarding school. On the one hand, I was relieved to be out of White Plains and away from the guys that I had been hanging around with. The joyless joyride to North Carolina with Danny left an enduring impression on me. There were truly dangerous and frightening people out there. It was a relief to be away from that lunacy.

On the other hand, during the first year at SKS, as strange as it may sound, I was very homesick. How, you may be asking, could someone who had just run away from home in a stolen car, be homesick? I'm not sure I know the answer. Consistency has never been my strong suit.

The most difficult time was between study hall in the evening and lights out. It was the time we could call home. During the time between the end of evening study hall and lights out, the boys would line up in front of the one pay phone on campus to make calls home. Calls were limited to five minutes. I was filled with depression and anxiety.

During this time, I came to the revelation that I would probably never live at home again; I would always be a visitor in my childhood home. This came as a disturbing shock. If I followed the career trajectory of most of the SKS boys, I would finish high school and then enroll in a university. From university I would go to work. This map of the future never had me moving back "home." I found this idea very disconcerting.

I found myself thinking that there were two "me's"; one who wanted to be an autonomous adventurer and one who desperately wanted the security of parents and home. I suspect now that this isn't an uncommon tension in teenagers, but I didn't know that at the time. One of the remarkably poignant aspects of adolescence is that while everyone goes through it, many of us believe that we are doing so alone.

Researchers into the brain tell us that the neocortex, the home of executive function, conscious cognition, and good judgment, develops much later in boys than in girls. In fact, the frontal lobes of most individuals are not fully mature until about the age of twenty. This may explain a great deal about those free-wheeling, adrenaline-soaked, death-defying adolescent years.

Harvard psychologist Robert Kegan suggests that humans continue to develop throughout their lives. We don't stop growing cognitively or emotionally at twenty. Kegan suggests that the stages of adult development are correlated to the degree of complexity with which we make meaning out of the world around us. Some people see the world solely in terms of black and white, they are rule-bound and find external constraints comforting. Other more complex individuals see the world in shades of grey. They are able to see multiple points of view and entertain seemingly contradictory perspectives. We develop more complex ways of meaning-making by being in an appropriate "holding environment." A healthy holding environment provides appropriate supports and challenges for our level of development. We need both protection and provocation.

Like most boarding schools, SKS provided its students little "free" time. Accordingly, for the most part, we were protected from ourselves. I have always managed to get into trouble when I've had time on my hands. There was an understanding that boys needed to burn off excess energy and so we had sports daily. At the same time, there were just enough eccentric characters to make life interesting.

Take John Speed, for example. John was a nature-loving, survivalist senior who was rumored to keep a collection of guns, including an AK-47, beneath his bed. According to school mythology, he would go out in the woods around the school and blast tree stumps into oblivion. He was also rumored to be sleeping with the wife of his English teacher. Some of these rumors are almost certainly apocryphal. However, I did run across John years later in Tanzania where he was working as a game scout in the Selous (the largest wilderness preserve in the world). John had a deep and abiding passion for preserving the elephant population. This resulted in him declaring his own personal war on poachers. I don't know if he actually killed any, but his behavior was so concerning to both the Department of Wildlife Conservation and the US Embassy that he was deported. The last I heard of John, he was doing a doctorate in lepidoptera (butterfly collecting). John was the inspiration for the character Jack Perkins in my collection of short stories *During Mango Rains*.

Until I came to SKS, I had not had a schoolteacher worth writing home about. At SKS I had several that are worthy of mention. Each taught me something that I carry with me to this day; some by design and some by default.

Mr. Park was not a very effective math teacher. I suspect that Mr. Park, like many teachers, knew his subject well; he had developed a degree of expertise that actually made it difficult for him to understand the mind of a novice. Only the master teacher can step deliberately into the shoes of their students' misunderstanding.

Mr. Park taught us geometry or tried to. I struggled with trapezoids and rhombi, with different kinds of triangles and a plethora of formulas to memorize. I can remember thinking that with all the really useful stuff out there to learn, who cares how to find the surface area of a sphere. On a unit test, Mr. Park asked us how we would find the volume of a cone. I wrote that I would stuff it with ice cream, allow the ice cream to melt and pour it into a graduated cylinder. Mr. Park didn't appreciate my humor.

By November I was on the cusp of failing geometry. I was doing fairly well in the other subjects, but math was a problem. Mr. Park announced a major test and I knew that passing or failing for the semester depended on my performance on that test. I decided to study hard. However, as I immersed myself in the textbook, I realized how much I didn't understand. In desperation, I went across the dorm corridor and asked a boy named Mark for help. Mark was a year ahead of me and was reputed to be very bright, particularly in the areas of math and science. Mark was not only an excellent student, but was also a brilliant teacher. He started out by asking me what I didn't understand. I pointed to a problem at the end of a chapter. Mark then began a step-by-step explanation. Suddenly, in midstream he paused.

"What is *geometry*?" he asked.

I shrugged.

"I'm serious," he went on. "Tell me what geometry is."

"Something you study," I replied.

Mark had a profound insight. He understood that I didn't have a clue as to the big picture. I was trying unsuccessfully to learn a mass of unconnected details that made no sense to me whatsoever. In one hour, Mark presented the big concepts of geometry. He presented them simply and anchored them to concrete examples. Suddenly the pieces were falling into place. We didn't look at a single textbook problem. He helped me see connections and relationships that I had never grasped before.

Mark understood something that Mr. Park didn't. Most of us learn from whole to part. We need to see the big picture before we fit the details into place. When we are assembling the 100 plus pieces of a racing bicycle, most of us look first for the diagram of the finished product. We need to see the big picture. Mark understood this intuitively and I learned more geometry in that hour than in all the previous three months put together. I scored an "A" on the big test and earned A's in geometry for the rest of the year. I was very grateful to Mark and was saddened when our dorm master found a bottle of Chivas Regal in his steamer trunk and he was expelled.

A teacher I remember with some fondness was Dr. Dessireat, who taught history. Unlike any teacher I had had before, Dr. D. actually encouraged students to think. He would ask provocative questions, such as why your history text made no mention of the violence of the American labor movement in the latter half of the 19th century. Out of this discussion came a research project I undertook on Big Bill Haywood and the Industrial Workers of the World.

Dr. D. was a gifted storyteller and some of his most memorable lessons involved stories. I remember vividly how he introduced the topic of World War I. He started by setting the scene: It was late June, 1914 in a Bosnian town called Sarajevo. He then narrated how Gavrilo Princip and a small group of schoolboys had planned and carried out the assassination of Archduke Franz Ferdinand, the heir-apparent of the Austrian Empire. He described their tragic-comic mistakes and how their ultimate success happened virtually by accident. The class was enraptured.

I was so taken by the story that it stayed with me for years. I read more and more about the assassins, the Austrian royal family, and the origins of World War I. The characters and the period of history fascinated me. Fifteen years later, Dr. D's inspiration would find its way into print with my first historical novel, *The First Casualty*.

I only received one award at SKS and it is worthy of mention because it illustrates an interesting dimension of attribution theory: Success without challenge is devoid of any sense of achievement. Attribution theory suggests that we can attribute our success or failure to causes that are either within or outside our control. For example, if I have studied hard for an examination and I do well on the test, I may well attribute that success to effort. Hard work is something I have control over.

In order to feel pride of accomplishment, we must associate challenge with achievement. This was not the case for me in earth science.

In tenth grade I was assigned to an earth science class taught by Elmer Fud (the nickname I gave him). Like his cartoon counterpart, Elmer wore red-checkered hunting shirts, suspenders, and hiking boots. He was a cross between a lumberjack and frontiersman. He did not have a lisp, but he did speak very, very slowly in a southern drawl. There were only five students in earth science and I don't know how we were selected. The remainder of the grade was taking biology. Since my four classmates were very unlikely to win Mensa prizes any time soon, I guessed we had been put in earth science as a result of someone's perception of our academic ability. My classmates struggled with even the most basic ideas and Elmer dutifully slowed down the pace of the class. It was unbelievably slow, like a model T chugging up hill with an overheating radiator.

We spent weeks scratching rocks against white tiles to determine their color or hardness or whatever. We spent so long on the tilt of the earth's axis that autumn conveniently passed into winter thus demonstrating its usefulness, but nobody noticed. The rate of learning was even slower than Elmer's speech. The simplest ideas crept across the curricular landscape at a snail's pace. It was agony. A glacier would get a speeding ticket in that class. I still hate volcanoes, not because they're scary—which they are—but because in Elmer's class they went on forever. And so it was that I felt a degree of chagrin when I was recognized at the end of year awards ceremony as the outstanding earth science student. In the kingdom of the one-legged, no one is going to win a sack race.

During the summer of 1965, Ben, one of my SKS classmates and I went on a grand tour of Europe. It really was a grand tour, ten countries in five weeks. There were about twenty-five American high school students and one rather disinterested and disengaged adult tour leader. There was virtually no supervision, and so with Byronic fervor we gallivanted from city to city visiting museums and art galleries, castles, palaces, and cathedrals. We dipped into the Louvre and Westminster Abbey, climbed the Leaning Tower of Pisa, and watched the eagles circle over Delphi at twilight. We attended concerts and frequented cafes, bars, nightclubs, brothels, and more brothels. We embraced our European summer freedom with Zorba-like abandon. Excess was the key to success. Inhibitions were left in the airline's overhead storage bins and sobriety and virginity jettisoned mid-Atlantic. It was a red-letter summer.

I didn't make it through the 1965-1966 school year at SKS. I was expelled in January or February—I can't remember which, but it was one of the dark months when death and depression shoot craps on the doorstep. I will relate the events that led up to my expulsion from the point of view of the rest of the world, and then in the closing paragraphs of this chapter I will describe what actually occurred; a series of events that I have not previously shared.

Soon after we returned to school from our summer European frolic, Ben and I started to spend weekends on the Lower East Side of Manhattan with his brother, Steve Hancock. Steve was in his early twenties and had a small railroad-style apartment on St. Marks' Place in the East Village. The Lower East Side was still in a state of transition from a Jewish, Polish, Eastern European ghetto into a hippie tinsel town. There were still a few of the old Ukrainian restaurants and mom-and-pop Jewish deli's that sold smoked sturgeon and bialys. But the invasion of organic eateries, avant-garde bookshops, and stores selling drug paraphernalia and psychedelic posters had begun. These weekends were significant because they represented my introduction to the counterculture that would come to grip America and most of Western Europe. The East Village opened a door into a world that I had only faintly been aware of.

It was during these weekend forays into the East Village that I learned that I was not alone in my opposition to the war in Vietnam and there was a growing population of long-haired, gypsy-like young men and women who were as disillusioned with the Washington political establishment as I was. On St. Marks' Place I was introduced to the novels of Jack Kerouac and Ken Kesey; the poetry of Alan Ginsburg, Lawrence Ferlinghetti, and Charles Bukowski; and the music of Bob Dylan, Simon and Garfunkel, and the Stones. It was during these weekends on the Lower East Side that I first encountered the surrealist films of Luis Bunuel and Julian Beck's anarchic Living Theater. It was also during these weekends away from boarding school that I made my first acquaintance with marijuana, amphetamines, and LSD. Whether I was sitting stoned under the stars in Tompkins Square Park listening to the Blues Project's *Flute Thing* or reading protest articles by Howard Zinn in *Ramparts* magazine, the Lower East Side opened a door into a tremendously exciting, turbulent, and dangerous time to come of age. It was, in a sense, an Alice-in-Wonderland experience. Suddenly, nothing was as it seemed. Perspectives shifted the way images do in the warped mirrors of a carnival fun house. Illusion and reality vied for airtime. Values and beliefs that had previously seemed permanent and immutable, now seemed relative, old-fashioned, and as malleable as silly putty or Semtex.

Back at SKS, I auditioned for a part in a school theater production and, to my surprise, got the lead role in a one-act play by Bertolt Brecht. The more I learned about the German playwright, the more intrigued I became. Here was a writer with a political message who defied both Adolf Hitler and Senator Joe McCarthy. I saw parallels between Brecht's world and what I perceived to be the military adventurism of the United States in Vietnam—and of course the growing anti-government sentiments that were finding expression in demonstrations and peace marches.

The play went well and the school newspaper gave it very favorable reviews. The director, Mr. Bennett, who was also my English teacher and dorm master, was very pleased with my performance and almost immediately launched into the casting of Jean Anouihl's *Antigone*. Again, the political message captured my imagination—the defiant, idealistic heroine standing her ground against the brutal forces of opportunism and pragmatism. I auditioned for the part of Creon and got it.

During the rehearsals for *Antigone*, Mr. Bennett would also take select members of the cast to see theater productions off campus. We drove to the Long Wharf Theater in New Haven to see *Death of a Salesman* and into Manhattan to see an off-Broadway production of *A Streetcar Named Desire*.

During the latter trip, we had an hour before curtain time so Ben and I and two other cast members slipped away and drank a few beers. Mr. Bennett smelled the beer on our breath and reported us to the headmaster when we returned to campus. By rights, we should have been expelled. There was a no alcohol policy and the consequences were straightforward. I expected to be booted out.

We were not expelled. Later, I learned that Mr. Bennett had appealed on our behalf against expulsion. Instead, we were assigned 180 hours of work crew—overseen by none other than Elmer Fud. So the time we would normally spend engaged in sports, we spent cutting wood, raking leaves, and digging ditches. We were a chain gang without the chains. Elmer Fud looked right in his element.

Soon after our sentencing, I went to see Mr. Bennett and told him that I would not continue to rehearse the role of Creon. I told him that I had too much homework to cope with and couldn't manage the competing demands. He was predictably irritated and I received a lecture on meeting my obligations and personal responsibilities. Nevertheless, I was replaced as Creon.

On a particularly dark night in February, 1967, Ben and I shared several joints and belted back a third of a bottle of Absolut vodka. I then left the dormitory and found Mr. Bennett's car in the parking lot. Our dormitory was located on a slope that ran down to an ice hockey rink. I released the hand brake and pushed the car down the slope. I watched it roll down into a shallow ravine, twenty or thirty feet and crash into a tree. There wasn't a huge amount of damage, but there was a lot of noise. At first the scene struck me as immensely funny, but then I realized that it was a matter of time before Bennett and other teachers would arrive to investigate. I took off running through the woods and found my way to Route 9W and started hitchhiking south. I had a vague idea that if I could get to Manhattan I might be able to stay with Ben's brother, Steve, on St. Marks' Place. I knew my time at SKS was over. Even as zonked as I was, I understood that convicted beer drinkers who pushed cars into ravines, would not be welcome to stay on the mountain top.

After about a half an hour of hitching, a car stopped to give me a ride. It turned out to be the deputy headmaster. I was returned to campus and spent the night locked in the headmaster's cellar—actually it was a fairly comfortable recreation room and I found a copy of Walter Lord's *A Night to Remember* and spent the time of incarceration reading about the sinking of the Titanic.

By noon the next day, my parents had arrived and I was formally expelled from SKS.

Now some more information that the headmaster and my parents didn't have.

During the rehearsals for the Brecht one-act, Mr. Bennett invited me on several occasions to his apartment in the dorm to run lines. This was in the evening and after we had finished practicing my lines, Mr. Bennett offered me beer, which we drank together. I recognized at the time that this was unusual, but assumed that our work together in theater allowed for some bending of the rules. During those evenings, Mr. Bennett would often suggest authors that I might like to read. The one he focused on most often was Jean Genet's *The Thief's Journal.* He offered to loan me his copy. I read it only years later and, given what transpired later, the content didn't surprise me.

During the second such session, I became uncomfortable. It wasn't anything that Mr. Bennett did or said, it was just the strange intensity of the interaction. It was as though there was another agenda that I wasn't aware of. Despite the prospect of more beer, I declined both the third and fourth invitations claiming to be overwhelmed with homework.

It was soon thereafter that we went into Manhattan and Mr. Bennett reported us for drinking beer. I confronted him on the double standard giving me beer in his apartment and then reporting us for drinking on a school trip. He said something to the effect that they were completely different situations. One was private and the other was public. He then went on to say that he would argue my case with the headmaster. He would appeal for me not to be expelled.

I am not proud of the next part of the story. Like many boys' boarding schools, there was considerable bullying at SKS. It could take the form of verbal teasing but at times even involved physical violence. Unlike my time in Britain and White Plains, I was not often a victim of bullying at SKS, and yet the memory of being bullied was constantly with me. And so, I did what many insecure and anxious boys do, I passively accepted it and did nothing to interfere.

The target of the bullying was a boy by the name of Richard Breakfield-Hodges. He was a nerdy bookworm who never did anyone any harm. The hazing flavor of the week was to subdue the victim by tying his hands and legs to the bunk bed, removing his trousers and smearing BenGay on his testicles. Although I was on the periphery of the action, I was present and I did nothing to stop it.

Understandably, Richard was distraught and reported the incident to our dorm master, Mr. Bennett.

Oddly, I was the only one summoned to Mr. Bennett's apartment. It was after lights out and I was in my pajamas. Mr. Bennett asked a number of questions and I gave a reasonably accurate version of what had transpired. At this point, Mr. Bennett went into his bedroom and returned with a jock strap. He instructed me to go to the bathroom and put it on. I did so and returned to the living room wearing only the jock strap. He then ordered me to lay on the couch and rubbed BenGay on my stomach. After a few minutes, his other hand slipped into the jock strap and he began to fondle me.

"You like that, don't you?"

After a few minutes, I told him I had to go to the toilet. I put my pajamas on and slipped out of the apartment and retreated to my dorm room.

I never told anyone. Perhaps I thought that in some way I was responsible for the situation. I'm not sure, but the episode disturbed me. I wasn't hung up by the idea of homosexuality. What disturbed me was the sordid manipulation of the relationship. There had been a time when I had liked and even admired Bennett. Now, I simply felt used by him.

And so I answered his rhetorical question by pushing his second-hand Rambler into a ravine.

Part Two: My Life as an Anarchist

CHAPTER 4
Coming of Age in Turbulent Times

THE SPRING OF 1967 WAS WET and cold and it seemed that world events conspired to mirror the dismal mood of the meteorologists. There was a steady increase in American military activity in Vietnam. In January and February, 25,000 US and South Vietnamese forces launched Operation Junction City to smash the Viet Cong. A little later, Haiphong and Hanoi were bombed for the first time. The colonels mounted a military coup in Greece and Biafra declared independence from Nigeria, starting a three-year genocidal civil war and famine that claimed over a million lives. The US carried out numerous nuclear tests in Nevada and, surprise, surprise, in mid-June the Chinese touched a match to the fuse of their first ever hydrogen bomb.

Muhammed Ali refused induction into the US military and, in one of the weirdest non sequiturs of the 20th century was stripped of the World Heavyweight Title. Mick Jagger and Keith Richards were busted for drugs, and black students seized the finance building at Northwestern University.

Assuming that it was about to be attacked, Israel launched a so-called pre-emptive attack on Egypt, Syria, and Jordan and caught them so off guard that the war was over in six short days. Israel's rapid victory seemed to belie their propaganda that the Arabs themselves were days away from an attack. I was also struck by Israel's Orwellian logic. It claimed that even though it had beat the pants off its Arab neighbors, its pre-1967 war borders were indefensible. I remember relating this absurdity to a workmate on the 3rd Avenue uptown bus and being clobbered from behind by an elderly woman's umbrella. To add insult to injury, I was compelled to listen to her passionate Zionist harangue for the remainder of the journey.

I was seventeen and a high school dropout. My father and I had what he called "a serious talk." I wanted to be independent and autonomous. In short, I wanted to go to work and be financially free from parental ties. My dad desperately wanted me to finish high school. We compromised. We found a tutorial service in mid-town Manhattan that I could attend while I was working at the UN Bookstore (a job that he helped me find). If I behaved myself I could earn a certificate of high school attendance.

I went to visit Miss Smith's Tutoring Service with great trepidation and a chip on my shoulder the size of Gibraltar.

I remember my interview with Miss Smith vividly. She was a woman in her late thirties with flaming red hair, emerald eyes, a million freckles, and a rotund milk-fed figure. I took an instant liking to her. She exuded purpose, resolution, and gentleness. She was an excellent listener and had a keen, inquiring mind. Perhaps I started to fall in love with her then and there. She began the interview by asking me what I had disliked about the Storm King School. An easy question and she got an earful. The next question wasn't so easy. She asked what I liked about learning. At first I couldn't think of much and I shrugged. But as I began to talk, I heard myself making a distinction between learning and being taught. I realized that I had always liked, no . . . loved learning, but I hadn't always liked being taught. This is a distinction that has had a major influence on my career as an educator.

Miss Smith asked what books I had read recently. I had just finished Somerset Maugham's *The Moon and Sixpence*, a fictional biography of Gauguin (Ironically recommended by my dad). At thirty-four, the protagonist quits his job as a bank clerk in London, deserts his wife and children, and leaves for Paris in order to paint. I was enthralled by the character's independence and determination, the way he was able to thumb his nose at societal values and become the architect of his future. As I spoke about the book, I noticed Miss Smith was listening very intently. Occasionally she would offer a paraphrase or a question, but she never broke eye contact. She really seemed to be interested in what I was saying. At the end, she announced that she would like to be my English tutor, if I would accept her. I was surprised, but pleased.

Miss Smith's Tutorial Services was an amazing place. By all rights it shouldn't have been successful, but it was. It was a school that stayed under the official radar. It wasn't accredited and, to my knowledge, wasn't licensed by any government or municipal office. It was located in a series of tiny cubicle-like spaces in a mid-town office block. The venue moved fairly frequently and the name changed once or twice, I suspect because the rent was due or some bureaucrat was targeting a close down. None of the tutors were qualified teachers and if there was a curriculum, no one knew it or cared about it. The tutors were all out of work actors, musicians, and writers. Miss Smith had founded her tutorial services to provide a living for down-and-out beatniks. It was the perfect school for me.

Together, Miss Smith and I read *The Great Gatsby* and talked about Fitzgerald's disillusionment with modern America. We explored the Jazz Age and read Hemingway's *The Nick Adams* stories. I was fascinated by his theory of "iceberg storytelling." Every time we finished a book, Miss Smith would ask what I wanted to read next. I would rarely have a suggestion, so she took the lead. We read Camus' *The Stranger* and talked about existentialism and alienation. She took me to an Off-Broadway production of *Waiting for Godot,* and afterwards we sat in an Italian restaurant until nearly midnight trying to make meaning out of it. If Miss Smith had not been twice my age, I might have pursued a less platonic relationship.

We often selected books to read that she hadn't already read. This meant that our conversations about books were authentic. We were learning together. It was exhilarating. For example, we read Sartre's *No Exit* followed by a selection of short pieces by Andre Gide. She suggested a Gide quotation contest. My favorite quote was: "It is better to be hated for what you are than loved for what you are not." Miss Smith's favorite quote was: "Believe in those who are seeking truth. Doubt those who find it." In some respects, my life has been a movement from my favorite quote to hers, but of course I didn't recognize that at the time.

Miss Smith also encouraged me to write and explore connections between the literature we were reading together and my life. I started to keep a journal.

Other tutors introduced me to the poetry of Rimbaud and Verlaine. My sociology tutor was a graduate student at Columbia, so we read the texts he had been assigned by his professors. I can't say I appreciated all the nuances, but I was fascinated by our discussion of Riesman's *The Lonely Crowd* and Marcuse's *One Dimensional Man.*

And our conversations didn't end at the cubicle door, but followed us to various cafes and bars throughout Greenwich Village. We talked about drama, music, and politics; about the Vietnam War, civil rights, women's liberation, and the fragile environment. These conversations often went late into the evening, and were more energizing than a triple espresso. I would often find myself lying awake after such an evening with ideas tumbling through my mind like underwear in a Whirlpool dryer—totally unable to sleep.

One afternoon, Miss Smith asked me when I would know that I was finished.

"Finished?" I responded. "Finished what?"

"How will you know that you have finished high school?"

I couldn't wrap my head around the question. I shrugged, but she persisted. How was I supposed to know when I was finished with high school? Wasn't that someone else's job? Since I wasn't going to receive a recognized high school diploma, I couldn't call on the New York State Board of Regents or the College Board for help. What was the criteria for high school completion at Miss Smith's Tutorial Service? Students weren't normally asked when they were finished. But that was exactly what Miss Smith did. When I didn't respond, she said it was "a walkaway question"—one that I didn't need to answer immediately, but one that I should think about.

And I did. I thought a lot about high school and a lot about learning, but I thought even more about the implications of her question. It contained the gift of a lifetime. Her question implied that I was responsible for my own learning and I didn't need to rely on external sources, authorities, or evaluations. I could establish my own goals and celebrate my own milestones of achievement. It was a clue on the treasure hunt of self-directedness. For the first time, school was not interfering with my education.

I didn't answer her question for nearly three months. I procrastinated. I didn't want to be finished. I was enjoying school for the first time.

In a very small way I was part of the collateral damage of the Six Day War. As soon as the Israelis launched their surprise attack, the UN Security Council went into twenty-four hour emergency session. This meant the Secretariat Building was closed to tourists and visitors and I was laid off from my job at the UN bookstore. This represented a problem since I had moved into Steve Hancock's apartment on St. Mark's Place, and was now responsible for half the rent. Fortunately, Steve, who was a manager in the Bookmasters chain, knew of a vacancy for a bookstore clerk at Crossroads, a small paperback bookstore on 42nd street and 5th Avenue. I applied for the job and was appointed on the spot. Thus began a three-year stint that would see me working four different stores in the Bookmasters chain.

I could not have found more stimulating employment. I loved working around books and enjoyed coming to associate titles, authors, and publishers. I read voraciously. Bookmasters was a counterculture chain of bookstores that prided itself in being on the cutting edge of anything that was new, hip, and potentially controversial. We hosted book-signing events for Salvador Dali, Andy Warhol, and the crew from the Velvet Underground, Abbie Hoffman, and the photographer Richard Avedon. The owners of Bookmasters published the first edition of Tomi Ungerer's classic work on sex machines, entitled *Fornicon*, and the opening scenes of the anti-war film *Greetings* were shot in the 3rd Avenue Bookmasters. I especially enjoyed trying to predict reading and cultural trends.

I wasn't always very diplomatic. One afternoon in the late spring, a well-dressed couple came into the bookstore and asked for a copy of the season's runaway bestseller *The Valley of the Dolls*. I guessed the couple to be in their mid-fifties. The man wore an expensive suit and the woman was heavily made up. She looked like an aging department store mannequin. I went to the shelves and brought back a copy of the sensationalist novel they had asked for.

"Why is the book not displayed in the store's window?" the man demanded.

I didn't like his tone of voice.

"Why should it be?" I asked.

"It's the number one bestseller!" he shouted. "It's selling millions of copies."

"You want to buy it or promote it?" I asked. "I think its sensationalist trash."

The man's complexion turned a sickly shade of green, he gagged twice and then ran out of the bookstore and vomited on the pavement.

His name was Irving Mansfield and he was the husband of Jacqueline Susann, the author of the bestselling book. In retrospect, I was more diplomatic than Truman Capote who announced on a TV talk show that Jacqueline Susann looked like a "truck driver in drag." Threatened with a lawsuit, Capote apologized—to truck drivers across America.

A dismal spring turned into the proverbial long hot summer with race riots in Newark; Cairo, Illinois; Durham, North Carolina; Memphis, and Detroit. The long-standing Uncle Ben stereotype of the African American was being engulfed in flames or blown away in clouds of tear gas. Black was beautiful and increasingly violent. Ironically, or perhaps not, the racial rage that consumed the inner cities coincided with the Beatles release of "All You Need is Love." Just as consistency has never been my strong suit, nor was it a hallmark of the decade.

Summer turned into fall. In early October, Che Guevara was captured and executed in Bolivia. Pictures of his bullet-ridden body were featured in all the left-wing newspapers. We ordered extra copies of his books and put them in the store window. They shared pride of place with Lenny Bruce's iconoclastic autobiography *How to Talk Dirty and Influence People.*

In late October I took a Greyhound Bus to Washington DC with several of the teachers from Miss Smith's Tutorial Service. We were part of the crowd of 70,000 people who would gather in Washington for the first of many anti-war protests. Organized by MOBE, The National Mobilization Committee to End the War in Vietnam, a vast array of different groups were represented—from Quaker pacifists to young militant Viet Cong sympathizers. Dave Dellenger, the organizer of MOBE, had asked Jerry Rubin to be the project manager of the October 21st demonstration. It was Jerry Rubin who selected the Pentagon as the most appropriate venue to "Confront the War Makers."

During the afternoon, a huge crowd of people gathered in front of the Lincoln Memorial to listen to impassioned speeches. Dr. Benjamin Spock, bestselling author of *Baby and Child Care*, said that he felt personally betrayed by President Johnson, who had campaigned on the promise of not sending more American troops to Vietnam. Dellenger announced that the time had come to move from protest to resistance.

After the speeches most of the crowd moved off in the direction of the Pentagon. It took less than an hour or so to walk there. The building was ringed by 2,500 armed federal troops and a boundary line was set up beyond which the protestors were not allowed to go.

Although I was unaware of it at the time, Abbie Hoffman and a group of hippies (The Yippies weren't founded until the spring of 1968) had set themselves up at the south end of the parking lot. They were engaged in attempting to exorcize the Pentagon. Abbie's plan was for people to sing and chant "Out Demons Out" until the Pentagon building levitated, turned orange, and disgorged all its evil spirits—thus ending the Vietnam War. As history has dispassionately recorded, the Pentagon remained earthbound and the evil spirits firmly ensconced.

There were numerous incidents of civil disobedience and many arrests were made. Some of the troops used their rifle butts to control the crowd and some of the protestors tried to place flowers in the gun barrels. Lunacy always expands to fill the container provided for it whether it is a single cranium or the collective consciousness of the mob. And there was madness on both sides of the police cordon. In front of the Pentagon, I perceived *historic* lunacy. I understood something important, however irrational, was happening. Established authority was being openly challenged. It was invigorating and inspiring, and I suspect many who were present that day went home in some way changed. Rebellion against the scoundrels in power seemed to be the zeitgeist—*Up against the wall motherfucker*, was becoming the spirit of the age.

Susan Blackmore wrote a fascinating and disturbing book entitled *The Meme Machine*. She defines the word "meme" as an idea that seems to take on a life of its own. A meme has three characteristics: a high degree of fidelity replication (the copies closely resemble the original), fecundity (lots of copies), and longevity. The concept is disturbing because Blackmore suggests that memes may actually be driving human evolution and that these ideas may have an existence that is beyond the individual mind. In other words, our frontal lobes may be the host for parasitic ideas. This bruises my ego. I like to think that the mind is the creator of ideas, not the other way around.

Defiance, disobedience, and dissent were the meme trinity of the late 1960's.

Several weeks later, Steve and I decided to take a holiday. Steve had grown up in Texas and suggested a getaway weekend in Juarez. Accordingly, we flew to Laredo, rented a chrysanthemum-yellow Camaro convertible and drove across the Mexican border with The Doors' "Light My Fire" blaring from the radio. Like most of the border towns, Juarez was wide open in terms of alcohol, drugs, guns, and working girls, but it was not nearly as narco-violent as it is today. The greatest misfortune that we encountered was having Steve's shoes painted crimson by a playful shoeshine boy, and being so drunk that we didn't notice it until the following morning.

The reason I mention our trip to Juarez was because we purchased several thousand Dexedrine tablets (amphetamine-based, heart-shaped pills), which we stuffed into packages of Camel cigarettes and smuggled back into the United States. I soon developed a taste for these heart-shaped pills and spent many euphoric days working tirelessly in the bookstore while chewing most of the skin off the inside of my lower lip. At seventeen, the foreground completely camouflaged the background and the seduction of short-term pleasure painted over longer-term consequences. It would be many months before the psychological effects of my amphetamine habit became evident—at least to me.

Steve and I shared an apartment on 10th Street between 1st Avenue and Avenue A, close by Tompkins Square Park. It was a typical three-room, railroad-style tenement walk-up—cheap but drab. The walls were covered with posters that reflected our eclectic tastes: record covers, psychedelic mantras, political slogans from the Berkley Free Speech Movement, and several large sado-erotic drawings by Aubrey Beardsley. There were always people staying with us—long-haired hippies would arrive in a beat-up VW camper from the West Coast, girls dressed like gyspies would come in for the weekend from the suburbs, or organic farmers would hitchhike down from some commune in Vermont. Steve seemed to know a vast number of people. Every night was a party of sorts, marijuana was in ample supply and the kitchen was always littered with Ballantine Ale bottles. I was never sure who I would find in the morning crashed out on the mattresses that covered the floor. Bonnie and Joyce stayed longer than most— several months. Bonnie was waiting for her boyfriend, Billy, to be released from prison—he was serving a term for possession of cannabis. Joyce was shacking up with Steve. Given that none of the rooms had doors; there was no shower and that the bathtub was in the kitchen; the apartment engendered a communal intimacy that I had not previously known.

No one wished me happy returns of the day on December 6th, 1967, but my eighteenth birthday did not go unnoticed by those Kafkaesque file clerks at the Selective Service Office, whose job it is to notice such things. I had reached the age where it was legal to kill and be killed, but in someone else's country.

A week after I turned eighteen, I made my way to the post office just off Times Square to register for the Selective Service. I was now out of school and had no excuse for a draft deferment. I knew I would be considered cannon fodder par excellence. Like Yossarian, the main character in Heller's *Catch 22*, I had come to realize that there was a widespread and extremely well-financed conspiracy, involving very senior and powerful government figures, that was out to kill me.

This revelation made the possibility of patriotism even more remote.

Most Americans would now agree that the US intervention in what was essentially a civil war in Vietnam was one of the greatest foreign policy mistakes in American history. That was not the case in 1968. The nation was deeply polarized and emotions were running high. I considered not registering for the draft. There was a small likelihood that I could have slipped through a bureaucratic crack, but I decided against it. Better boiled for a crime of commission than steamed for one of omission. I filled out the requisite forms and went home to await my fate.

The spring of '68 played out like a Greek tragedy, except there was no Chorus to help us connect the dots and the pattern was too large and complex for many to recognize. A few Cassandra-like figures cried out in the wilderness, but were for the most part dismissed as crazies. The new year began with the Viet Cong Tet Offensive and followed soon after by the US massacre at My Lai. I remember vividly being mesmerized by Eddie Adams' Pulitzer Prize-winning photograph of a Viet Cong officer being summarily executed by a South Vietnamese Police Chief. For me, as I expect was the case for many Americans, the iconic photograph brought home the emotional realities of the war.

In March, militant activists took control of the administration building of Howard University, effectively shutting down the university over protests aimed at the ROTC program. Later that same month, General Lewis Hensley, the then head of the US Selective Service (draft) attempted to address the students at Howard, but was shouted down by chants of "America is the black man's battleground."

The day after General Hensley's abortive speech, Daniel Cohen-Bendit, better known then as "Danny the Red" (referring to both his politics and the color of his hair) lead a small group of students in occupying the administration offices at the University of Nanterre in France. This set in motion a string of events that would bring France to the brink of violent revolution in May. The political upheaval was worldwide.

Two weeks later, in Germany, Rudi Dutschke, a left-wing political activist and student protest leader was shot in the head by a right-wing extremist. The assassination attempt failed and Dutschke survived, but radical students all over Germany held the right-wing publishing empire of Axel Springer responsible for the attack. This resulted in street battles in many German cities and arson attacks that destroyed two department stores in Frankfurt. A young female journalist wrote about the attacks attempting to explain them to the German reading public: "Protest is when I say this does not please me. Resistance is when I ensure that what does not please me occurs no more." The writer was Ulrike Meinhof and her articles brought her into contact with Andreas Baader and

Gudrun Ensslin, the authors of the arson attack. Together, they would form the Red Army Faction, aka the Baader-Meinhof Gang that would wage urban guerrilla warfare in Germany for the next decade.

All was not quiet on the home front. One of the support players in this tragedy—an ordinary-looking, clean-shaven man from Alton, Illinois—would have been a chronic loser, unknown to history, had it not been for an event that occurred at a sleepy motel in Memphis, Tennessee. The man from Alton had a criminal rap sheet as long as your arm. At twenty-one, he was convicted of burglary in California and three years later served two years in prison for the armed robbery of a taxi driver in Illinois. In 1955, he was convicted of mail fraud and served three years in Leavenworth. Soon after his release from Leavenworth, he was caught stealing $120 in an armed robbery attempt in St. Louis. Because he was perceived by the court to be incorrigible, he was sentenced to twenty years behind bars. That should have been the end of the man from Alton. But it wasn't.

In 1967 he managed to escape from the Missouri State Penitentiary by hiding in a van transporting bread from the prison's bakery. The man from Alton was now on the run. Evidence that was later uncovered suggests that he hid out in Chicago, Montreal, Toronto, and Birmingham, before emerging in Acapulco, Mexico where he attempted to set himself up as a film mogul. At the time, he was using the alias Eric Starvo Galt. Using mail-ordered film equipment, Mr. Galt used local prostitutes to make hardcore porno films and then smuggled them across the border to the United States. His foray into filmmaking was short-lived and ended in an unpleasant dispute between the prostitutes and himself, presumably over compensation.

In early 1968, Galt returned to the United States, taking dance and bartending lessons in Los Angeles, and followed Governor George Wallace's presidential campaign with great interest. Galt had long-harbored racist beliefs and Wallace's segregationist platform was right up his alley. In fact, there is correspondence from Galt during the same period which suggests he was considering emigrating to Rhodesia because he was attracted by Ian Smith's white supremacy.

Eric Starvo Galt's birth name was James Earl Ray and he was convicted of the assassination of civil rights leader and anti-war activist Martin Luther King Junior at the Lorraine Motel in Memphis, Tennesee. He was arrested at London's Heathrow Airport where he was attempting to leave the UK on a forged Canadian passport. He was convicted of the killing and sentenced to 99 years imprisonment.

It was not credible then or now to believe that this minor miscreant acted alone—if indeed he was responsible for the assassination. Conspiracy theories were abundant—and the accusing finger was more often than not pointing at the white establishment.

Riots ripped apart over a hundred US cities. Washington, Chicago, and Baltimore were among the most devastated. The day after the assassination, Stokley Carmichael spoke at Howard University:

White America killed Dr. King last night. She made it a
whole lot easier for a whole lot of black people today.
There no longer needs to be intellectual discussions, black
people know that they have to get guns. White America
will live to cry that she killed Dr. King last night. It would
have been better if she had killed Rap Brown/or Stokley
Carmichael, but when she killed Dr. King, she lost.

By noon, a large crowd had gathered on Washington's 7th Street and Northeast Corridor, and a violent confrontation with the DC police ensued. As the news of the assassination spread, thousands of African Americans took to the streets of the nation's capital. Numerous buildings were set on fire and firefighters where prevented from trying to extinguish them by rock and bottle throwing mobs. It was not long before President Lyndon Johnson ordered more than ten thousand Federal Troops into Washington to restore order. Marines mounted machine guns on the steps of the Capital Building and soldiers from the 3rd Infantry guarded the White House. Washington was a city under siege.

Over a hundred other American cities followed suit.

One that did not erupt into violence was Indianapolis. And this may have been the result of a short, but heartfelt speech given by Robert Kennedy who was campaigning for the democratic presidential nomination. Earlier in the day, Kennedy had spoken at the University of Notre Dame and it was here that he had learned that King has been shot. However, Kennedy didn't learn that King had died until his arrival in Indianapolis on the evening of April 4th. He was scheduled to give a campaign speech in a predominantly black neighborhood. The Chief of Police attempted to dissuade Kennedy from giving the speech. The Chief of Police even went so far as to say he could not provide protection for the candidate and that riots were likely. Kennedy decided to go ahead with the speech and he spoke for less than five minutes from the back of a flatbed truck. The audience was aware that King had been shot, but did not know that he had died. Kennedy brought them that news. A stunned silence followed his announcement. Then there were the sounds of screaming and wailing. This was a defining moment. At that point, the audience could have easily become a violent mob.

Kennedy acknowledged the pain and anger of the crowd. "For those of you who are black and are tempted to be filled with hatred and mistrust of the injustice of such an act against all white people, I would only say that I can also feel in my own heart that same kind of feeling. I had a member of my family who was also killed, but he was killed by a white man."

This was the first time Bobby Kennedy had spoken publicly about his brother's assassination.

Kennedy went on to urge the country to go beyond "these difficult times" and quoted the great Greek Tragedian Aeschylus in saying that wisdom often "comes, against our will, from pain. . . ."

Bobby Kennedy's speech was credited in part with preventing post-assassination rioting in Indianapolis.

Two months later, Bobby Kennedy was himself gunned down in the lobby of the Ambassador Hotel in Los Angeles. The worst were indeed filled with passionate intensity.

It was a springtime to remember: Daniel Ellsberg leaked the Pentagon Papers to the *New York Times* and thousands of poor people marched on Washington and set up a protest shantytown called "Resurrection City," while the Soviets marched into Prague and crushed the pro-democracy movement. There was a general strike in France and the intensity of the street battles in Paris caused President de Gaulle to go into temporary exile in Germany. The entire world seemed to be poised on the edge of political upheaval.

However, the ridiculous never fails to nestle with the significant. London Bridge was sold to an American oil magnate, dismantled and reconstructed in Arizona, *The Night of the Living Dead* opened in movie theaters across the country, and Pope Paul VI, in a moment of Canute-like arrogance, attempted to hold back the sexual tide by barring Catholics from using the contraceptive pill.

Amid the chaos and carnage, like birdsong at dawn in the trenches of the Somme, Bill Graham opened the Fillmore East on 2nd Avenue. For four remarkable years, the Fillmore East served as a musical Mecca, the high church of rock and roll. The Allman Brothers Band was a staple and Crosby, Stills, Nash, and Young were frequent guests. I heard Jimi Hendrix, The Who, and The Doors. One very memorable night, Frank Zappa and the Mothers of Invention played until dawn. Between sets, the Joshua Light Show provided a stunning psychedelic backdrop.

In mid-May, a rather eccentric woman came to the bookstore and asked me to take a slim, self-published volume on consignment. I remember the incident well because of the subject of the book.

It was entitled *The S.C.U.M. Manifesto.* SCUM stood for the Society to Cut Up Men. I was intrigued and took fifteen copies and even placed a couple in the store window. It was the kind of weird stuff that might just sell. I had no idea at the time that I had just met Valerie Solanas, the author, who would in a week's time be arrested for attempting to assassinate Andy Warhol.

Some time towards the end of the summer, I received a phone call at Crossroads Bookstore from my flatmate, Steve Hancock. Steve was the manager of the Times Square Bookmasters, and he warned that they had just had a visit from the police. I needed to remove certain magazines from sale because the cops were almost certainly on their way to Crossroads. This is interesting because Times Square and 42nd Street at the time was full of adult, X-rated bookshops that sold truly graphic and raunchy porn. Bookmasters carried erotica, but it was soft porn by comparison. None of the adult bookstores had been bothered by the police, just Bookmasters. And the cops were looking for specific titles: *Fuck You—A Magazine of the Arts,* the brain child of Ed ("I'll publish anything") Sanders of Peace Eye Bookstore and Yippie fame. This mimeographed magazine had a remarkable masthead of contributors including: Tuli Kupferberg, Allen Ginsberg, Gary Snyder, Norman Mailer, William Burroughs, Leroi Jones, and Robert Creeley. Nevertheless, it was now on the cops' hit list.

The other magazine that they came looking for was Robert Crumb's infamous *Zap Comix #4,* that in addition to being an ode to cannabis, contained a script about an incestuous middle American family with the caption: "A family that lays together, stays together." I managed to get both magazines off the counter before the police arrived. We continued to sell *Zap Comix* under the counter even after they were officially banned in New York.

The message was clear. The Establishment wasn't interested in obscenity that merely evoked prurient interest. It was the political, counterculture stuff they were keen to suppress.

In early September, I received the letter I had been dreading. It was headed "Greetings" and every young American male in 1968 knew what that meant. My draft board had summoned me to a pre-induction physical at Fort Hamilton, New Jersey. I was classified 1A at the time and the only thing that stood between me and a C-130 flight to the Mei Kong Delta was a urine test in New Jersey.

Actually, the pre-induction physical was much more than just a urine test, but I'm getting ahead of myself.

One of the most popular subjects of conversation in the East Village at the time was the strategies that had been successful in helping young men avoid the draft. I had listened to stories of young men smearing their underpants with peanut butter (it didn't work); announcing that they were gay (unreliable—in one, possibly apocryphal, case the drill sergeant pulled down his zipper and ordered the draftee to "prove it"); and, tattooing the words "fuck off" onto the knife edge of the right hand so that the sentiment appeared just in time for each and every salute.

There was also the conscientious objector route. I wrestled with this. It was a possible way forward. I certainly wasn't, under any circumstances, going to fight in Vietnam. There were two problems with declaring myself a conscientious objector. First, I wasn't a pacifist. I could imagine situations when I would fight and perhaps even kill. The second reason was more complicated. A conscientious objector refuses to kill, but recognizes his obligation to perform alternative non-combatant service in support of the war effort. I did not accept any such obligation and didn't want anything to do with America's vicious adventure in Southeast Asia.

I didn't want to go to Canada or Sweden. Both had interminably dark winters. The other alternative was even less attractive: four years in a federal penitentiary.

I was confused right up until the bus pick-up at 5 a.m. on the corner of 1st Avenue and 10ᵗʰ Street. The night before, I had thought that a couple of heart-shaped pills would help my thinking. At midnight, I realized that the Dexedrine might be picked up in the urine test, so I attempted to "cover it up" by drinking four or five quarts of Ballantine Ale. Ah youth!

I was picked up on the corner of 1st Avenue and 10ᵗʰ street and found myself riding in a bus with about thirty other young men from the Lower East Side. Not surprisingly, a good number of them appeared stoned.

Once at Fort Hamilton, we were ordered into a locker room and told to strip naked, but keep our shoes on. I had worn cowboy boots. We were given plastic Ziploc bags for our valuables. It was a surreal experience wandering the corridors with a flock of naked men with nothing on but shoes, or in my case cowboy boots; all of us clutching little plastic bags of valuables.

The message of the day was *hurry up to wait*. And we did just that. We scurried from one room to another only to find ourselves at the end of a long queue. We waited in line to have our height and weight checked, to pee in small bottles, and to have blood taken. We waited for a medical orderly to listen to our chests, squeeze our balls while we coughed, peer into our ears, test our eyesight, and examine our teeth. All the time a sergeant kept reminding us, at the top of his voice, to keep our fucking shoes on.

"Why are they so worried about our shoes?" the guy ahead of me asked.

"It's not your shoes they care about," another fellow answered. "It's your feet. And they ain't yours anymore, anyway!"

That remark set me thinking. I had sensed a subtle shift in physiological proprietorship. It was an odd feeling, like a second-rate science fiction film in which aliens from outer space take ownership of your body. The army was staking a claim on our bodies. Some years later, when researching *Alia,* a historical novel I was writing, I read descriptions of the physical examination given to slaves at the Zanzibar auction block in the 19th century. They were remarkably similar to what we were undergoing at Fort Hamilton.

My body might be up for grabs, but they didn't have my mind yet.

After we had finished the physical examination, we were ordered to get dressed and re-assemble on the second floor in what appeared to be a classroom. We were told that we would now take an intelligence test. There were three parts: verbal, mathematical, and mechanical. A dull normal fourth grader could have aced the verbal and math sections. But the mechanical portion was another matter altogether. The test consisted of picture analogies. I was presented with pictures of two parts of a machine and, I was supposed to recognize the relationship between the parts and then identify the same relationship in a multiple-choice question.

If I was blindfolded and gagged at the bottom of a deep well, I couldn't have done worse. I had not a clue what any of the machine parts were. So I simply guessed.

At the end of the test, we were told to wait outside for the results. They gave us warm Coke and we were allowed to smoke. About forty minutes later the drill sergeant reappeared and called out three names: two others and mine. The two other fellows had presumably failed the intelligence test and were being scheduled for a re-test. I watched with bemusement as these bovine louts expressed appreciation at having been given a second chance to prove themselves intellectually worthy of becoming cannon fodder.

When my turn came, the sergeant ordered me into a small office, threw his large rear end into a chair behind a desk and flung a sheaf of papers across the surface. He was clearly pissed off.

"So, what have we got here, a fucking mechanical genius?" he demanded.

I remained silent not so much out of respect as out of confusion.

"You know what your results are, lover boy?"

I shook my head.

"You scored in the 99th percentile on both the verbal and math and the 27th percentile on the mechanical."

"I didn't recognize any of the pictures. . . ."

"Shut up. If I want your opinion, I'll beat it out of you." The sergeant thrust a page of the mechanical aptitude test across the desk at me. "What's this?" he demanded, pointing at the picture of a machine.

"A lawn mower?" I guessed.

"It's an eggbeater, asshole! Haven't you ever seen an eggbeater?"

"Not an eggbeater that looked like that."

"Shut up. What's that?" he shouted, pointing at yet another picture.

I didn't have the faintest idea, I was crashing from the amphetamines I had taken the night before and the sergeant's interpersonal skills were grating on my nerves like a fingernail drawn across a blackboard.

"I don't fucking know!" I shouted back at him.

He sat back in his chair and folded his arms.

"You're a wise guy. You're a regular wise guy. But Mr. Wise Guy, you've made a mistake. You can't score in the 99th percentile in the verbal and math and in the 27th percentile in mechanical. It's . . ." He struggled to get his tongue around the polysyllabic word. "It's stat-tis-tic-ally impossible. You're a clever bastard. You know machines inside out. You're a regular mechanical genius. But you're not clever enough to get out of this man's army, Mr. Fucking Wise Guy!"

The sergeant scooped up all the papers from the desk, threw them into a sickly green file folder.

"Room 78."

"Can't I go home like the rest of them?" I might have been whining.

"Room 78, wise guy."

There was a bench in front of Room 78 and I sat there holding the puke-green file and feeling generally disconsolate. I didn't know it at the time, but the bench I was sitting on would become immortalized in Arlo Guthrie's *Alice's Restaurant* as the Group W Bench, where sat those who were possibly not moral or sane enough to napalm women and bayonet children in Indochina.

I learned that I was waiting to see the army psychiatrist.

I didn't have to wait long before a rather bored-looking officer ushered me into an office. Lt. Fielding (not his real name) had narrow deep-set eyes; a flat-top, no-hair-out-of-place, crew cut; blotchy skin; and, a sharp nose that turned up slightly at the tip, making him look rather like a sleepy puff adder.

"Now, what do we have here?" he asked rhetorically, but pleasantly, taking the file of papers from my hands. The shrink was distant and professional, but in contrast to Sergeant Genghis Khan, he appeared positively huggable. However, by this point, I was in a thoroughly bad mood.

"You're an army psychiatrist?" I demanded.

"I am. Lt. Fielding." He extended his hand but I didn't take it.

"How do you live with your conflict of interest?"

"Conflict of interest?"

"As a doctor, you've pledged to do no harm. As a military officer you're part of a machine that kills people."

Lt. Fielding snorted softly, ignored my remark and buried his long nose in my file. After a few minutes, he closed the file and looked me in the eye.

"Did you deliberately fail the mechanical portion of the test?"

"No."

"It's hard to understand how someone as obviously intelligent as yourself could score so low." Fielding smiled benevolently like the spider to the fly. "For example, what is this?" He pointed to a picture from the test.

"An eggbeater," I ventured.

He looked puzzled.

"That's not an eggbeater. It's an electric hair dryer."

"I don't care what it is, I want to go home."

"You don't want to join the army?" he asked.

"Hell, no."

He gave me a broad smile and patted my shoulder, taking on an awkward, homespun chumminess—a goofy cross between Andy Griffiths and Svengali. With exaggerated sincerity, he asked, "Are you a pacifist?

If I answered in the affirmative, I could guess the next question: *If your sister was being raped by a drug-crazed maniac, would you fight to protect her?* For nearly a century, it had been the standard hypothetical situation that had been thrown at would-be conscientious objectors. In the early days of World War I, Lytton Strachey faced the same question at a military tribunal that was to decide on his conscientious objector status. "Tell me, Mr. Strachey," the chairman asked, "what you would do if you saw a German soldier trying to violate your sister." Strachey is reported to have responded without any air of noble virtue: "I would try to wiggle my way in between them."

Fielding repeated the question.

I shook my head.

"I don't understand. You're not a pacifist, but you don't want to join the army?"

"What makes you think that its only pacifists that would want nothing to do with your army?"

He smiled patiently. "Do you object to all wars or just the present conflict in Vietnam?"

I was tired and the shrink's supercilious charm was irritating.

"I have mixed feelings about the Punic Wars. The sacking of Carthage was totally unnecessary. The city had already surrendered. . . . "

Fielding held up his hand: "Why don't you want to join the army?"

I wanted to say something flip like "I never have enjoyed blood sports" or "because you could get killed in the army," but I didn't. I remained silent for a long time. An idea was forming. I tried to match his faux sincerity.

"You know, Lt. Fielding, there are two decisions that a person has to make on his own. These are probably the most important decisions of his life. One is to create life and one is to destroy it. I don't think it's morally right to delegate either of those decisions."

Fielding was quiet for several moments.

"What do you mean delegating?"

"I mean that if I'm going to destroy life, I will make that decision. Not someone else."

"You wouldn't be delegating anything. You would be serving your country."

"I would be passing the moral buck. I'm not a pacifist. I am not opposed to killing people. I just don't take it lightly. It's one of the most serious decisions a person can take. Accordingly, I would need to think long and hard about when and where and why I would kill."

"You mean you might refuse to obey an order."

"It depends on the order."

Fielding sighed and pushed my file aside.

"I am going to order a psychological re-appraisal of your readiness for the military in six months."

I actually sang in the subway on the way home. I had a six months reprieve. It turned into a red-letter day.

CHAPTER 5
The East Village

I PROBABLY SHOULD SAY A WORD or two about my relationship with Stephen Hancock, the man who got me a job at Bookmasters, whom I shared an apartment with, who rescued me from the "Tombs," kept me off heroin and first introduced me to the idea of *The Anarchist Cookbook.* For several years, Steve was my closest friend, and yet "friend" is not really the right word to describe our relationship. Steve was seven or eight years older than me and I viewed him more as an older brother than a friend, as a sort of trail guide or mentor as we navigated some very turbulent times together. There's no question that he led the way. He was older, had vastly more experience and perhaps most importantly, a great deal more self-confidence.

Steve was a short, slender man in his mid-twenties at the time we shared an apartment on Manhattan's Lower East Side. He had grown up in Texas, but found the South intellectually, socially, and politically claustrophobic. Steve had had a rebellious adolescence and was estranged from his parents. He had married and separated and had two infant daughters.

Intelligent, articulate, charming, and rebellious as hell, Steve had come to New York's East Village on the tail of the beat generation. He wanted and needed to be part of the romance and the rebellion of it, and he never accepted or forgave himself for missing it by a decade. His heroes were Jack Kerouac, Ken Kesey, and Neal Cassidy. He hitched across the country several times in the footsteps of Kerouac. Steve wanted Bookmasters, the bookstore chain that both of us worked for, to be the East Coast equivalent to San Francisco's City Lights Bookstore—a center of counterculture literature, pop culture, and political activism. Steve's bookshelves were crammed with the poetry of Ferlinghetti, Snyder, and Corso, and his eyes would light up with enthusiasm and passion when he spoke of events like the Berkeley Free Speech Movement or his early work with the Congress of Racial Equality (C.O.R.E.). Steve had also done a short stint in the US Army. He didn't speak much about it, but I learned much later from his first wife, Eugenia, that he had left with a psychiatric (not dishonorable) discharge. He was full of unorthodox opinions and very conversant about books, but I very rarely saw him actually reading.

Steve was a self-professed anarchist who lurked in the twilight around the perimeter of radical political camps—Resurgence Youth Movement, Students for a Democratic Society, the Yippies, and the Weather Underground—but could never bring himself to actually join them. He needed a degree of alienation even from those whose ideology was closest to his own.

He had an uncanny genius for predicting counterculture trends and he became the chief wholesale book buyer for the entire Bookmaster's chain. He instantly knew what tomorrow's hip flavor of the month would be. Publishers would actually call him to ask his advice. He promoted eccentric authors like Edward Gorey, and for many months kept a copy of John Cage's *Silence* in the bookstore window. Under Steve's management, Bookmaster's wasn't just a repository of the counterculture, it was a showcase. I recall a terrific argument between Steve and the owners of Bookmasters. Steve had discovered a new magazine-type publication and was in the process of ordering thousands of copies for the chain. The owners agreed that the new publication would probably sell, but thought that ordering thousands of copies was way over the top. Why not start with a hundred and see how it goes? The publication was Steward Brand's *Whole Earth Catalogue* and the two thousand copies that Steve insisted on buying were sold within a month. In fact, virtually every other bookstore in New York had sold out, while Bookmasters still had copies available.

Steve was zealous and passionate about almost everything he did. I watched him start scores of projects, although he rarely finished any. He was charismatic, wedded to the moment, cavalierly dismissive of the future, and provocatively playful. Women found him handsome and charming and I can't remember a time when he didn't have an attractive woman living with him. Some he married, some he didn't. But those relationships, married and unmarried, tended to be intensely sexual, emotionally tempestuous, and, in most cases, short-lived.

His second marriage was to a young rock and roll groupie who went by the name of "Gypsie." They met at a Cat Steven's concert at the Fillmore East. On their wedding night, Steve filled the kitchen bathtub with food coloring and dyed himself jade green from the waist down. Their marriage lasted less than a month and when she filed for alimony, Steve appeared in court wearing a barrel.

Steve Hancock worked so hard at being a rebel that sometimes he got himself in a tangle. He despised Marxist rhetoric, and yet was a card-carrying member of the IWW. He gave money to support LeMar (Allen Ginsburg's organization to legalize marijuana) but didn't smoke grass himself—claimed it made him withdrawn and paranoid. He hated big business and commercial capitalism, and yet was an absolute sucker for the newest and most expensive gadgets. He could manage a huge book and record store, but not his own personal finances.

There is no question that during this time I admired Steve. I put him on a pedestal and listened eagerly to his stories, teasing out his ideas, values, and beliefs, hungrily absorbing them in order to make them my own. It was probably during this time that Steve mentioned the idea of an anarchist cookbook—a collection of recipes for the revolution. The idea wasn't original with Steve. He had been party to a conversation with other political radicals and the idea had emerged. I thought it was nothing short of brilliant. When you revere someone the way that I did Steve, curious and potentially dangerous things begin to occur. First, the other person's obvious flaws and hubris disappear. Second, you fail to see or understand your own vulnerability.

If I believed in talisman, mine at this point in my life would have been an IBM Selectric Typewriter. A talisman is an object that is thought to have supernatural powers. It may protect the owner or it may guide the hero on his mythic journey. I doubt that IBM Selectric Typewriters imbued me with supernatural power; nor did they protect me, but they certainly did influence the events of my life.

In the long hot summer of 1968, during the police riot that is historically referred to as the Chicago Democratic National Convention, Steve rented an IBM Selectric Typewriter. It was top of the line at that point in time—the most expensive typewriter that you could buy or rent. Steve never started a project without the very best equipment. I cannot recall what the project was. Like so many of Steve's projects, this one was never finished, but this time it wasn't his fault.

One morning, there was a knock on the door of the apartment on 10th Street and Avenue A. Steve had already left for work so I answered the door. Two down-and-out-looking men stood in the doorway. The short one was pale and sallow, his features pinched and drawn. The tall one had bad facial skin, a scrubby beard, and looked exhausted. Despite the summer heat, both were wearing well-worn coats. They asked for Steve.

At the time, I didn't think this was particularly strange. Most of the inhabitants of the Lower East Side looked disreputable. Many worked hard at it. They said they were friends of Steve who had just arrived on a Greyhound bus from the West Coast. I invited them in and made coffee.

About a half hour later, I announced that I had to get to work and asked if they wanted to wait in the apartment for Steve. We were always having people arrive at the apartment asking for a place to stay. This was nothing out of the ordinary.

When I arrived at work, I called Steve to let him know that two of his friends had arrived. Needless to say, Steve knew nothing about his supposed friends, and when we hurriedly arrived back at the apartment we found the front door open, the bedroom chest of drawers rifled, and, of course the IBM Selectric Typewriter missing. Steve was furious. I was mortified.

"The coats were a dead giveaway," Steve raged. "Even in the middle of summer, junkies are always cold."

"But they seemed to know you."

"I'm known by a lot of bad fucking people."

I spent the next six months paying off the typewriter rental company.

It would be almost a year later before the second IBM Selectric Typewriter entered my life and helped to steer my destiny.

I worked very hard and long hours at Crossroads, the bookstore on 42nd Street and 5th Avenue, and with a lot of help from my heart-shaped amphetamine friends got the store into tiptop shape. I was rewarded by being appointed store manager. I was very pleased and proud.

It was at this time that Steve told me that he was going to give his marriage another try. He had invited his wife Eugenia and their two daughters to return to New York. Steve was, as ever, charming and persuasive and it was not long before Eugenia agreed to the move. Like everything Steve did, he approached the prospect of domesticity with zeal and enthusiasm. The return of the family and his role in it was not just something he was going to do, it was something he was to become—it became part of his newly forged identity. Everything had to be arranged perfectly. He took a large advance on salary and rented a spacious and expensive apartment on Henry Street in Brooklyn Heights, had it completely redecorated and furnished it lavishly. He maxed out one or two of his credit cards at FAO Schwarz on toys for Anna and baby equipment for Monja. Steve wanted, perhaps more than anything else, to be part of a family. I know that he felt hatred towards his biological father, and had been rejected by his stepfather. This had caused distance between himself and his mother. On several drunken occasions Steve told me that he really loved his mother and her attitude towards him hurt.

Eugenia and the girls arrived in New York and they all moved into the large apartment Steve had rented. I visited them frequently and enjoyed playing with Anna, the elder of the girls.

At first, the domestic scene played out well. Both Eugenia and Steve genuinely wanted the relationship to work. There were family trips to Central Park, to the Natural History Museum, China Town, the Bronx Zoo, and ringside seats at the circus. But foremost, there was a sense of family, and I remember after spending a Sunday afternoon with them, actually envying the safety and warmth of the familial hearth.

But that was fairly short-lived. I don't know whether one or the other of them was more to blame, but after six weeks of being together it was clear that the relationship was not going in the direction they had hoped. Eugenia said that Steve could only manage to be himself for three weeks; after that he would change into a different person. To my discomfort, both Eugenia and

Steve began to confide in me their misgivings about the situation. Although most of what I did was simply listen, I felt my allegiances were dreadfully divided.

I admired Steve enormously and felt a very strong bond of loyalty to him, but I also liked Eugenia a great deal. She was an attractive, intelligent, sensitive woman, probably six years older than I was, with a wonderful sense of humor and a lightening wit. She was a talker par excellence and was amazingly and refreshingly open and honest.

Seven weeks into the second marriage attempt, Steve announced he was moving back to the East Village to the apartment he and I had shared. Eugenia phoned me. She was devastated and said she was desperate to have someone to talk to.

At first, I thought I could balance their continued friendships, but as Eugenia's emotional needs became more and more apparent, I knew that I was being called upon to make a choice—a choice I didn't want to make. I was attracted to Eugenia. She needed support and friendship, but whenever I was with her I felt anxious and guilty.

Betrayal can be a slippery slope. The first clue I should have had was when I returned one evening to the apartment in the East Village and told Steve I had been working late. I hadn't been at the bookstore. I had been having coffee with Eugenia in the West Village. I had never lied to him before. There was no logical need to be dishonest. At the time, there was nothing between Eugenia and me other than friendship, and yet I had felt the need to lie.

Something I have learned over the years is that temptation is an invitation to the implausible. Morality aside, temptation just doesn't work. What I mean by this is that often the behavior that we are tempted to engage in produces the exact opposite results than those we had originally desired. The unfulfilled businessman, who equates the accumulation of wealth with achieving meaning in life, often finds that his overflowing coffers leave him even more unfulfilled. The lonely man who spends the sordid hour in a brothel, may find himself feeling even more alone.

The temptation to deceive is like a creeping mold, it spreads and grows, feeding on fear and guilt.

I don't know which came first—the deceit or the betrayal, but fairly soon my relationship with Eugenia ceased to be platonic. Perhaps when I first lied to Steve, I knew subconsciously that was the direction the relationship was headed. Or perhaps the initial deceit, the harmless white lie, simply opened the door to greater and greater deception. Rarely have I felt so miserable. On the one hand I was deceiving my closest friend, on the other I was trying to support a very emotionally needy woman whom I cared for.

Within a few days, Eugenia announced that she was leaving New York and taking the girls to Florida. She wanted me to come with her. At first I told her I had a job and an apartment in New York. I couldn't just pick up and leave. It was impossible.

Eugenia stared at me in disbelief. Her eyes were wide with astonishment and that innocent confusion that tears at the heartstrings. She obviously had taken it for granted that I would go with her. She shook her head and covered her face with the palms of her hands. She started to sob. Her body heaved and she became frantic, crying and clutching me. She told me she was frightened of the move. Couldn't I see that? She couldn't make the move on her own. But she couldn't stay in New York. I was the only person she could turn to. She was all alone with two small children. Couldn't I see that? Didn't I care for her? Didn't I care for the girls? She got hysterical and threw herself face down on the bed. I actually wondered if she might be suicidal. I went to the kitchen and made her a cup of lemon tea. I then put both the girls to bed. When I returned to her room, I told her I would go with her to Florida.

Eugenia and the girls flew to Florida at the end of the next week. I was to follow shortly by Greyhound bus.

I felt cornered. If I went to Florida, I would be betraying my best friend. If I didn't go, I would be breaking my promise to Eugenia. I knew I had compromised myself.

Feeling even more alone, I took the subway downtown and took a long walk through Battery Park. It was September and there was hint of autumn in the early evening air, but the leaves had not yet begun to change. It was cloudy and the harbor water was steel gray. There weren't many people in the park, so I had time and space to think. But my thoughts were overwhelmed by emotions. I felt pressured to make a decision. But then I would tell myself that I had already made a decision. I had made a promise to Eugenia. After all, Steve had left her. She was a free agent. I repeated that several times inside my head, but the words rang hollow. Something far more primeval told me that, whatever the circumstances, you don't sleep with your best friend's wife. I sat for a long time on a park bench staring out over the oily water of New York harbor to the Statue of Liberty. I was ashamed of myself and slowly became resigned to the disgrace of not just betrayal, but also cowardice.

The following day, I put some clothes and a bottle of my heart-shaped friends into a backpack and emptied my bank account. I told Steve that I had just learned that my parents were concerned about my mental health and were considering to have me institutionalized. As a result, I needed to leave town in a hurry. I have no idea how credible I was. The story was the best I could do under the circumstances.

In the late afternoon, I boarded a Greyhound bus with a ticket to Fort Walton Beach, Florida.

I may hold the record for being the shortest resident in Fort Walton Beach, Florida's history. I arrived in the morning and made my way to the house that Eugenia had rented. In the afternoon, I opened a bank account and went through the classified ads in the local newspaper looking for work. I spent the late afternoon playing with the children, and then helped Eugenia cook dinner. After dinner, Eugenia excused herself, saying that she needed to visit a neighbor. I put the children to bed and waited up for her. It was a long wait. She returned at three o'clock in the morning drunk, her hair in disarray and her clothes disheveled.

The next morning I went to the Greyhound Bus station and bought a ticket on the next bus leaving. It happened to be going to San Francisco.

I spent the next three weeks in San Francisco. I knew no one in the city and my stay there was a little like self-imposed solitary confinement. I can't remember ever being so depressed and feeling so insecure. I don't think I spoke to more than three people during my time there. I had thoroughly screwed up my life. I stayed at a dollar a night flophouse on Mission Street and spent a dollar a day on one meal. The food was distributed in a charitable cafeteria and I lined up with the homeless. I was chronically hungry and lost a lot of weight. My clothes hung on me like a guilty conscience. I knew that money was running low, but my search for work was half-hearted.

But outside forces would intervene. Change agents, what in an earlier age might have been called "angels of mercy" or "fairy godmothers" come in all different sizes and colors.

Mine was short and black.

It was midday and I was walking towards Golden Gate Park. It had become my favorite place to kill time. There was free admission to the Asian Art Museum and I had spent many hours wandering amongst the exhibits. When I turned from Stanyan Street on to Fulton, I was confronted by a group of five young African American boys. The oldest could not have been more than eleven. The leader confronted me.

"Lemme hold a quarter, brother."

I shook my head. "You're barking up the wrong tree. I'm broke."

The boy opened his jacket and withdrew a handgun and thrust it into my gut.

"Gimme your fucking wallet, honkey!"

I opened my wallet and he snatched the last four dollars I owned.

"If you tell the cops, we'll come back and kill you."

And they disappeared as quickly as they had appeared.

In less than a minute, the young thief had magically succeeded in jerking me out of a slough of self-pity and recrimination. He thoroughly pissed me off. Anger replaced depression. Why me? Why take my last four dollars? It probably wasn't even a real gun. I should have grabbed it away from him and slapped him around the side of the head. What the hell was I going to do now? I didn't have a place to stay and there was no money to buy food.

As I sat on the grass overlooking Stow Lake and Strawberry Hill, I realized that my encounter with the young thief was an apt and fitting climax to my stay in San Francisco. Having no pride left to choke on, I phoned home collect and asked my father to send me bus fare to New York. As always, Mom and Dad were there to support me.

My meeting with Steve took place on a Sunday afternoon at McSorley's Old Ale House on East 7th Street. In the past, we had frequented it fairly regularly. I phoned him after I arrived in New York and asked for time to get together. After the mugs of ale and the plate of cheese and raw onions had arrived at our table, I told him about my relationship with Eugenia and about the lies I had told him. I said I was sorry.

When I was finished, he was quiet for several minutes. Finally, he said something that surprised me.

"You know, *I'm* really sorry. I'm really sorry that your relationship with Eugenia didn't work out. If someone was to be a father to my children, I would have wanted it to be you."

I didn't cry in front of Steve, but I did later in private. It was one of the most beautiful statements of forgiveness that anyone has ever received.

My admiration for Steve took a quantum leap. He combined a passionate vision and deep humanity and I found myself feeling more and more in his debt. And so the old order reasserted itself with a vengeance. I moved back into the apartment with Steve on 10th Street and Avenue A and was re-employed by Bookmasters at the Times Square bookstore. Long-haired travelers continued to suddenly appear at the apartment, crash for a few days and then suddenly disappear. Those who stayed longer, such as Bonnie and Joyce, fought a valiant battle to free the sink of filthy dishes and to keep the cockroach population to a manageable size. Having said that, the kitchen was constantly littered with old issues of *The Village Voice*, *Ramparts*, and *The Realist* amid a forest of empty Ballantine Ale bottles.

Beyond the bohemian squalor of the apartment, the world was all too much with us. The US Government continued the war of aggression in Vietnam. In October, Operation Sealord was launched, an offensive against the National Liberation Front in the Mekong Delta. Later that fall, although we didn't know it at the time, the "secret war" in Laos began. In total, more than three million tons of bombs would be dropped on that tiny country in a largely ineffectual attempt to disrupt the movement of North Vietnamese troops and supplies along the Ho Chi Minh trail. In mid-October, Tommie Smith and John Carlos won gold and silver medals respectively at the Mexico City Olympic Games and were photographed on the honor stand giving the black power salute. We sold hundreds of that poster at Bookmasters.

Perhaps one of the most significant developments of 1968, from a personal point of view, was the advent of the Youth

International Party. The Yippie Movement was formed at the East Village apartment of Abbie and Anita Hoffman on New Year's Eve 1967. Paul Krasner, editor of *The Realist*, claims to have named it. In addition to Hoffman, Rubin, and Krasner, Ed Sanders, Phil Ochs, Judy Collins, Willian Kunstler (who defended the Chicago Seven), and Tuli Kupferberg were guiding forces. The Yippies, under the leadership of Abbie Hoffman and Jerry Rubin, stood for rebellion via street theater with huge doses of iconoclastic, and often hilarious, humor. During the 1968 Democratic Convention, the Yippies put forward a pig ("Pigasus the Immortal") as a presidential candidate, only to find Pigasus' caregivers arrested in Chicago for livestock law violation. Eight years later, the Yippies ran "Nobody" for president with the slogan "Nobody's Perfect."

In addition to attempting to levitate the Pentagon in order to purge its evil spirits, Yippies led by Abbie Hoffman joined a tour of the New York Stock Exchange in mid-1967, and threw handfuls of dollar bills from the visitors' balcony to the traders on the floor below. A few of the traders booed, but many scrambled to seize the greenbacks. The balcony was closed to the public until a glass wall could be installed.

The Yippies staged fairly regular public events. In early March 1968, *The Village Voice* announced that the Yippies were calling for a "Yip In" at midnight on March 22nd at Grand Central Station. This was to be a Festival of Life scheduled to coincide with the Spring Equinox. *The Voice* predicted the event would attract a thousand "flowered, belled, bearded, and body-painted people." Participants were urged to bring blankets and pillows and to come in costume. "If you want to come in costume, but don't own one, you can get one free at the Free School, 20 East 14th Street." The announcement went on to suggest that participants in the "Festival of Life" would leave Grand Central just before dawn and "Yip Up" the sun on Sheep's Meadow in Central Park.

Very little of that Yip In event went according to plan.

Steve and I arrived at Grand central Station just after 11 p.m., sans costumes, to find the Grand Concourse completely full of people. The crowd had overflowed out onto 42nd street and was threatening to block traffic. *The Village Voice* had seriously underestimated the draw of the event. Even before midnight, there were between 3,000 and 5,000 people present, and more and more were arriving. A large black banner hung of the wall of the Grand Concourse. It read *Up Against the Wall Motherfucker.* The huge crowd of young people smoked dope, threw hot cross buns, let off firecrackers, and floated multi-colored helium balloons towards the station's iconic celestial ceiling. Some joined a massive snake dance to the tune of "Have a Marijuana."

There was a significant police presence around the perimeter, but there had been no attempt to set up crowd-control barricades. The balcony that led to the Pan Am Building had been cordoned off and seemed to be reserved for the police brass. The journalist Don McNeill, who would have his head broken in the police riot that followed, wrote: "A dozen privileged persons lined the balcony . . . observing the melee below like Romans digging the arena."

Just before midnight, a couple of young male Yippies climbed up the clock above the central information booth and ripped off its hands. It was as if this was a signal for the police to attack. And attack they did. Alan Levine, staff counsel for the New York Civil

Liberties Union, said at a press conference the following day: "It was the most extraordinary display of unprovoked police brutality I've seen outside of Mississippi." The Tactical Patrol Force (TPF) waded into the crowd swinging their batons. I saw several people forced to run a gauntlet of club-wielding cops while trying to flee from what was later characterized as a police riot. Instantly, the mood changed from celebration to confrontation. Some of the young people struggled to get away from the violence, some struggled to get closer to it. Steve was one of the latter. Twice, I grabbed his arm and told him to be careful. Suddenly, just in front of the 42nd street main entrance there was an opening in the crowd. A group of plainclothes policemen had identified Abbie Hoffman and went after him. They grabbed him, swirled him around, and threw him to the floor. Uniformed cops broke through the crowd and proceeded to beat Hoffman with their batons. Again, Steve attempted to move towards the fracas.

Some days later, Don McNeil wrote in the *Village Voice*: "Spitting invective through clenched teeth, cops hit women and kicked demonstrators who had fallen while trying to escape the flailing nightsticks. It was like a fire in a theater."

And Howard Smith added in the same issue of the *Voice*: "I was a witness to the entire Grand Central Riot. As a reporter I've been at many events that generated violence between the police and mobs. Faced with certain kinds of demonstrations, such as those by peace, youth, and minority groups, the police seemed to become violent easily. In Grand Central Station last Friday night, the police seemed to have no plan about what to do, so all that was left was pure brutality. . . ."

Scores of people were hospitalized and dozens arrested.

Steve and I returned to the 10th Street apartment in silence. We shared a sense of outrage; anger and, I suspect, the thundering adrenaline that witnessing such unprovoked violence can produce.

"I'm sick and tired of not doing anything!" Steve announced. "I'm fed up with being a fucking spectator. You're either part of the problem or part of the solution. You can't be both."

He was quoting Eldridge Cleaver. Nevertheless, his words were prophetic.

The following day, Steve went out and purchased two motorcycle helmets; one for him and one for me. The days of placing flowers in the barrels of soldiers' guns were over. It was the dawn of the Days of Rage.

About two weeks later, there was a rumor that there would be a Friday evening anti-war demonstration along 2nd Avenue just up from the Fillmore East.

Steve and I dropped acid early in the evening.

I had taken LSD a number of times before. LSD had been legal in the United States until about a year earlier. It had arrived almost twenty-five years before from Switzerland where in 1938, Albert Hoffman (no relation to Abbie) had managed to synthesize it. "Acid," as it was commonly known, was readily available in the East Village, usually sold as small squares of blotting paper, sugar cubes, or Saccharine pills. Until the mid-1960's, it had been produced by the Sandoz Laboratories and had been available legally to medical doctors and psychiatrists. Ironically, the move to make it illegal dramatically *increased* its black-market availability. LSD is an odorless, colorless, and extremely potent drug that is relatively easy to produce in a modest lab with readily available chemicals.

For me, the effects of LSD were fascinating; all the senses were heightened, colors were more vivid, details and textures were richer and more intricate, and music more poignant. It was almost as if you were seeing and exploring, like a child, for the first time. The mundane experiences of everyday life took on much deeper significance. New and unusual connections became evident and even the most trivial aspect of the world around me seemed brimming and burning with unexplored meaning.

When I was high on acid, I was highly introspective and reflective. It was as though I was on a journey of discovery into myself, but I was also aware of relationships with other people—the gentle interaction and the playful humor. Bonds of friendships seemed stronger and more trusting. Peter Fusco, our poet and philosopher friend, would read Walt Whitman aloud and his words would resonate at the deepest levels. On one occasion, we roared with uncontrolled laughter as we painted vines and flowers all over Joyce who posed nude in the kitchen. On another occasion, five of us went moon-bathing on the footpath on top of the Brooklyn Bridge. When I was on acid, there was a sense of decreased vulnerability.

That was until the 2nd Avenue riot.

Steve and I arrived on 2nd Avenue, probably between 6th and 7th Street somewhere after eight o'clock. A small crowd of demonstrators had gathered, probably no more than two hundred. Among them were the usual suspects—the organizers, the instigators, the publicists, the agent provocateurs, and, of course, the naïve cannon fodder. But unlike the Grand Central Station Yip In, the mood was anything but a celebration. There were no painted faces, no snake dancing, or multi-colored balloons. There was a chill in the air and the demonstrators appeared angry, grim, and determined, and many, like Steve and myself, wore motorcycle helmets. Others wore army surplus coats and camouflage flak jackets. A few even carried sawed-off baseball bats.

Within minutes, three or four police squad cars careened down 2nd Avenue with sirens screaming and their reds and blues flashing. They screeched to a stop at 8th Street and parked, so as to block traffic and demonstrators. At the same time, a phalanx of uniformed cops started to move up 2nd Avenue towards the demonstrators. It was a classic pincer move with the demonstrators caught squarely in the middle. But, unlike the Grand Central fracas, the demonstrators didn't wait to be attacked. Somewhere across the street a demonstrator hurled a rock through a shop window. As the police approached, cherry bombs and bottles were flung at them. The Yip In had taught the protesters to come prepared. More shop windows were broken and a handful of protestors attempted to overturn a parked car. Someone shouted "Burn Baby Burn." Someone else screamed: "Up against the wall motherfucker." A canister of tear gas exploded about a block behind us.

Suddenly, without warning Steve started running up the sidewalk towards the four police cars that were blocking the avenue. At first I was confused, I didn't know whether he was running away or towards something. I followed him up the sidewalk. About fifty feet in front of the police cars he veered off the pavement and ran out into the street. I had no idea what he was doing. Two cops flung open their car doors and stepped into the street. Steve saw them and dashed back to the sidewalk where he stopped dead in his tracks—as though he was momentarily confused or had lost his train of thought. Then he suddenly appeared to regain his sense of purpose. He ran toward a municipal litter basket—one of those heavy ones that are constructed out of woven steel, hoisted it above his head with both arms outstretched, paused, and then brought the litter basket crashing through the rear window of the nearest police car.

It was a magnificent gesture of monumental stupidity. From the expression on their faces, I'm not sure who was more surprised—the cop in the car or Steve. The cop in the car leapt from his seat and removed his gun from its holster. Oh shit, I thought to myself. He's going to shoot Steve.

Two cops got to Steve before the one with the drawn gun. They caught him from either side, knocked his legs from beneath him, and threw him to the street face down. One kicked him in the ribs and the other brought his baton crashing down across the small of his back. And then the two of them picked him up and tossed him as gracefully as one might a ballerina on the hood of the police car. There, any gracefulness ceased. His arms were jerked behind him and handcuffs were snapped shut around his wrists. The cop with the gun punched him in the kidney while the other two hustled him into the back seat of a squad car, which moments later disappeared into a blur.

I took refuge by ducking into a side street and then slipping into an overheated, greasy spoon diner that appeared to be blithely unaware of the violence on the street. The server behind the counter was a large, bald-headed man in a dirty T shirt with a vast beer belly.

"What's your hog?" he greeted me.

I stared at him in complete confusion.

"Huh?"

"Your bike? What're ya riding?"

I remembered I was wearing a motorcycle helmet. I quickly removed it and asked if he had a public phone. He nodded towards the rear of the diner.

I called Peter Fusco and told him Steve had been busted. He must have also been stoned because he thought the whole thing was tremendously funny. He waffled on about how we would make Steve into an irresistible martyr for young groupies. We'd build a shrine to him in Tompkins Square Park all decked out with black anarchist flags. He would be the East Village's equivalent to Che Guevara. For Peter, it seemed that Steve's arrest was all a marvelous lark. I tried to interrupt, but he went on to describe how when Jean Genet had been arrested in France he had asked the policemen if he could stroke their bellies. He wanted to see if they would purr. Peter was gay and loved to flaunt it to the point where Steve called him a closet heterosexual.

Peter finally settled down and we arranged to meet the following day at the Tombs, the colloquial name for the New York Halls of Justice and House of Detention, where Steve was most likely to be held and charged.

Steve was charged with malicious mischief and vandalism and released on five hundred dollars bail. After his release, Peter, Steve, and I walked across Centre Street to a small Chinese bar and restaurant. Steve desperately wanted a cold Ballantine Ale and a cigarette.

The middle-aged bartender, who turned out to also be the owner, greeted us by asking which of us had just been bailed out. Steve raised his hand.

"It's like that everyday. Somebody gets out bailed of the Tombs and he's hungry for Chinese food! That why I make a restaurant here. Good business. Good dough. Lotta dollar. What'd they charge you with?"

Steve explained that he had thrown a litter basket through a police car window. The Chinese bartender looked like he could have hugged him.

"No shit? Through a fucking window?" the bartender was as excited as a kid on Christmas morning. "That's fabulous! That's fucking fabulous! Hey, Mei Ling," he called towards the kitchen area. "Hey, Mei Ling come out and meet a guy that's thrown a garbage can through a police car window! Can you figure that?"

The other diners were turning to stare in our direction.

Nobody thought to ask Steve why he threw the litterbin through the cop car window.

Mei Ling appeared in the doorway to the kitchen and gaped at the trash can thrower.

"I'd give a hundred bucks to have seen the expression on that cop's face!" the Chinese bartender roared as he extended his hand to Steve who shook it vigorously.

"Beers on the house, boys, and so's the food. Mei Ling, get these guys a menu!"

During lunch, Steve regaled us with a description of his night in the Tombs. Apparently, he had been placed in the same holding cell with Abbie Hoffman, who, when the police demanded to know what he did for a living, responded: "I'm a chemical engineer. I blow up police stations!"

My reaction to Steve's arrest was complicated, and I'm not sure to this day that I completely understand it. Initially, I was concerned about finding out where he was being held and getting him out on bail. Navigating the intricacies of lower Manhattan's bail bond offices was an education in itself.

Once Steve was released, I had a chance to digest what had happened and reflect on it. When Steve had impulsively thrown the litter basket, I had been stunned. Surprise, however, rapidly became fear. I remember the cop jumping out of the car and taking his gun from the holster. I was frightened both for Steve and for myself. And fear caused me to freeze like a deer in headlights. I watched helplessly as Steve was thrown to the ground and pummeled by the cops. The events replayed themselves in slow motion. I didn't ask myself what I should or even might have done. There was just a vague underlying feeling of guilt and inadequacy. I wondered if I had let Steve down, yet again.

Over the days and nights that followed Steve's release from the Tombs, I slowly came to realize what I needed to do to redeem myself.

I needed to get myself arrested. Most of the people I admired had spent some time in jail. I didn't put it in so many words, but it was in a sense a rite of passage, like a red badge of courage.

But before I could organize my arrest, I received a letter from my draft board ordering me to Fort Hamilton for a second interview with the army psychiatrist. It was blessedly brief; Lt. Fielding seemed to remember me from our last encounter.

"Ready for this man's army?" he greeted me with a smile.

"Is the army ready for me?" I countered.

"You know that the Army doesn't recognize selective conscientious objectors. You can't just object to the Vietnam War. You have to object to war in principle." He had what I assumed was my file open on his desk. He did not invite me to sit down.

"I told you before, I'm not a conscientious objector."

"Under what conditions would you voluntarily join the military?"

"Make me a colonel," I replied.

Lt. Fielding ignored my facetiousness.

"Other than your attitude towards authority, what else is wrong with you?"

"Wrong with me?"

"Any physical disabilities?"

"Althete's foot and a trick shoulder."

"Trick shoulder?"

"Sometimes I throw it out of joint."

"When was the last time you threw it out of joint?"

"Six years ago when I was playing basketball."

"Look, you're not making this any easier on me."

"Easier on you!" I almost shouted back at him. "I didn't ask to be here, and frankly, the last thing I want to do is make your job easier."

Lt. Fielding was silent for a moment. I had clearly pissed him off.

"The last thing I want to do is to put a jerk like you in the military. The second to the last thing I want to do is NOT put you in the military!"

I won another six-month reprieve.

My opportunity to be busted occurred a couple of weeks later.

Forty years later, when I was writing *Becoming an Emotionally Intelligent Teacher* (the irony of which is not lost on me), I stumbled across some fascinating research undertaken by Professors Richard Nisbett and Dov Cohen from the University of Michigan. Their research culminated in a book entitled *Culture of Honor: The Psychology of Violence in the South*. Nisbett and Cohen became interested in why the homicide rate in the South was consistently higher than in the North—most notably amongst White Southerners. Nisbett and Cohen do not attribute the greater prevalence of violence in the southern states to socio-economic factors, poverty, population density, the legacy of slavery or even to climate, but rather to a "culture of honor" brought to the south with English cavaliers and later the Scott Irish settlers for whom personal reputation was central to economic survival. This obsession with reputation (predominantly among white males) resulted in a hypersensitivity to insult that often led to argument and violence. In order to test their theory, Nisbett and Cohen collected a team of graduate students who would serve as research assistants. The research assistants were divided into teams with each team assigned to a different geographical location—some in the South, some in the North. The task assigned to the research assistant was to publically offend total strangers and to observe their propensity to violence. This was later then correlated to geographical locations. In order to achieve suitable offensiveness, the graduate students were told to come close to the stranger, to invade their personal space in a public location, such as a drug store or supermarket, and say under their breath: "asshole."

I thought this was one of the most hilarious research designs that I had ever encountered.

Nisbett and Cohen's results show a far greater proclivity towards violence among white southerners than any other group that was tested.

Although I didn't know about this research at the time, let the record show that this offensive little two-syllable expletive also provokes New York City cops.

It was early November and the leaves from the trees in Washington Square Park were mottled red and brown and crunched underfoot like Animal Crackers. Light was failing and the ubiquitous chess players, bundled in greatcoats and down vests, were packing away their knights and pawns. Steve and I and several other friends, were headed towards the West Village. I can't remember whether our destination was Café Wha? or The Bitter End or some other café cum watering hole. Whatever it was, I never reached it.

At the corner of Bleeker and McDougal Streets there was a crowd of Friday evening tourists. A police squad car was parked and two or three cops were attempting to keep the flow of pedestrian traffic moving. I stopped on the pavement and waited for the cops' instructions.

"Keep it moving."

I remained motionless.

"Keep it moving!" the officer said with greater vehemence. I didn't move. The cop walked over to me and planted himself directly in front of me: "What're you deaf or something? Move it!"

Still, I didn't move.

The cop took two steps closer and the pointy tip of his tongue caressed his upper lip.

"Asshole," I said.

"What did you say?" The cop's initial surprise quickly turned to anger.

"I said," I continued in a whisper, " you're an asshole."

He caught me by the front of the shirt and half pushed and half dragged me to the squad car. His buddies joined him. My arms were spread eagled against the side of the car, my legs kicked apart, and one of the cops frisked me while the other put handcuffs on my wrists.

I was taken to a nearby police station and ordered to sit on a bench. I sat there for several boring hours. Before too long, I needed to pee. I explained this to the officer in charge. He shrugged and pointed to a door that led into a communal toilet. The problem was that I couldn't unzip myself while my wrists were handcuffed behind my back. I also explained this to the officer. He feigned surprised.

"Really? I don't think you're trying hard enough."

"I need you to take the handcuffs off."

"Against regulations."

"Then I need you help me get my dick out!"

"Hey, guys," the cop called to his uniformed buddies. "This fellow needs help getting his dick out. Any of you guys want to volunteer?"

"Another long-haired, hippie queer," one of them announced.

His buddies joined him as they watched me struggle to open my pants. This was a challenge that would have stretched Harry Houdini. You had to be a circus contortionist. I struggled and struggled and finally managed to get my pants open and took one of the most satisfying pees of my life to the accompaniment of a round of applause by the three cops.

I was taken by paddy wagon to the Tombs. It was at about this time that I started to have second thoughts about my present situation. Some of the people I shared the paddy wagon with were downright scary. These guys weren't university students arrested at an anti-war demonstration. These were dregs of society, petty crooks, muggers, gang members, junkies, and possibly rapists and murderers. There were eight or nine of us. I guessed some were picked up for drugs. One guy was already getting sick from going cold turkey. He sat on the steel bench in almost a fetal position with arms wrapped around his knees and his eyes closed. He rocked back and forth and emitted guttural noises that sounded like he was drowning in his own saliva. Across from me sat three guys who I assume were from the same gang. Two of them had jackets with the same insignia and they all sported tattoos of daggers and snakes. These three were clearly bad guys, who worked hard at being tough. They were talking in a mixture of Spanish and English and from what I could make out, the guy in the middle was pissed off with someone named Siggy who had stolen his stash or messed with his old lady—or both. Siggy was in Bellevue, and if he survived, there were other bloods to finish what these three guys had started.

Suddenly the guy who had been doing most of the talking stopped, turned to me and said: "Whachado?"

"Huh?"

"Whachado?" he repeated.

"I don't speak Spanish," I said.

"I'm not speaking Spanish. So whachado?"

"I called a cop an asshole."

The three guys all started to laugh.

"Why you do that?"

"He pissed me off," I said and was relieved when they fell back in the reverie about what the other bloods would do to Siggy if he was stupid enough to survive Bellevue.

When we arrived at the Tombs, we were ushered into a processing hall and told to strip naked and shower. My valuables were placed into a plastic Ziploc bag—just as they had been at Fort Hamilton during my pre-induction physical. I was asked at least four times if I was going to get sick—meaning was I a junkie? I was placed into a cell overnight with a massive African American whose only comment to me was that I was going to occupy the top bunk. The cell was lit with a naked ceiling light that was never shut off. I didn't sleep well.

The following morning, we were all called out of our cells and marched to a large cafeteria where we stood in line to collect a tray of breakfast food. The prisoners occupied one half of the cafeteria—the other half was empty except for two of the most alluring and provocatively dressed women I have ever seen. The contrast was stark. I found my eyes glued to them.

"Drag queens," the guy behind me in line muttered when he saw me staring at them. "Gotta keep'm separate. Otherwise, the guys'll go ape shit."

After breakfast, I was taken to a small office where an officer of the court interviewed me.

It was then that I realized my dilemma. New York State had an assessment system for determining whether people accused of misdemeanors could be released on their own recognizance. It was a point system. If you had a home address, you got so many points. If you had regular employment, you got more points. If you had a wife and kids, you got even more points. Once you reached a threshold number, you could be released without bail. That was the good news, but it was also the bad news. The questions involved the name, address, and telephone number of my parents. The last thing I wanted was for Mom and Dad to rescue me yet again. That would have defeated the purpose of being arrested in the first place.

I gave my name but refused to provide any further information. The court officer was clearly confused by this.

"Don't you want to get out of here?" he asked.

Later that morning, I appeared in court and was duly charged with disorderly conduct and bail was set at $500 because I was unemployed and had no fixed residence. I was then bundled into another paddy wagon and taken to the Brooklyn House of Detention for Men at 275 Atlantic Avenue where I remained for two days until Steve managed to find me and post bond. A month later, I came to court and was fined twenty-five dollars for disturbing the peace.

What did I take away from the experience? First, there was nothing romantic or glamorous about being locked up. I don't know who was scarier: the inmates or the guards. There was a raw culture of intimidation and violence that made their behavior virtually identical. Inside those holding pens, the human condition was reduced to a predatory pecking order—in which I perceived myself as close to the bottom.

Second, as a rite of passage, being "busted" was a chimera—a foolish fantasy. I felt no greater clarity in terms of my beliefs and values, and no clearer vision of who I was. I didn't sense that I had redeemed myself in Steve's eyes. I probably had an increased sense of confusion.

Third, I recognized that I desperately needed an amphetamine holiday.

CHAPTER 6
Your Mother's Worst Nightmare

THE WINTER OF 1969 WAS MEMORABLY brutal. December and January were meteorological appetizers for the February main course. A nor'easter tore into the mid-Atlantic and New England area in early February, dropping more than twenty inches of snow in New York City and effectively paralyzing the entire Northeast. But the brutality of the winter of 1969 wasn't limited to the weather.

The Washington warlords were also working on a food metaphor. In late winter, Nixon authorized Operation Breakfast, named after the early morning meeting at the Pentagon that had planned it. Operation Breakfast started on March 18th with 48 B-52 Stratofortress bombers flying from bases in Guam to drop ordnance on Cambodia. It was the first time that the United States had officially violated Cambodian neutrality. During the next fourteen months, Cambodia would see Operations Lunch, Snack, Supper, and Dessert. This was the so-called "carpet bombing" of Cambodia with almost three million tons of explosives dropped on that country. Each of these operations, President Nixon and the Joint Chiefs of Staff kept as a secret from Congress and the American people.

When one looks back at the comparatively petty violence of the New Left during the same period, it is glaringly apparent that the greatest danger to the United States of America and, in fact, the world, resided in the White House and Pentagon.

The harsh weather seemed to parallel the hardening attitudes of the radical left. While there was some continuing humor and playfulness in the trial of the Chicago Seven, there was also the emergence of a much more extreme and violent faction. In early April, 300 Students for a Democratic Society (SDS) took over the administration building at Harvard University and before the occupation ended, 45 would be injured and 184 arrested. It was a mirror image of the protests and violence that had beset the campus of Columbia University a year earlier, and a harbinger of the autumn Days of Rage in Chicago.

Weatherman John Jacobs attempted to sum up the position of the more radical faction of SDS: "We are against everything that is 'good and decent' in honky America. . . . We will burn and loot and destroy. We are the incubation of your mother's worst nightmare."

The love child of yesteryear was throwing a temper tantrum. Beads and bells, paisley shirts, and hip-hugging bell-bottoms were traded in for Army surplus garb—khaki fatigues, flak jackets, and boots. The stench of tear gas was replacing the aroma of sandalwood.

I never joined SDS, the Progressive Labor Party, and had nothing to do with the emerging extremist wing: The Weather Underground Organization (WUO), although I followed their developments with great interest. The WUO was named after a line in Bob Dylan's song, *Subterranean Homesick Blues*: "You don't need a weatherman to know which way the wind is blowing." To which a radical wit would later add: "You don't need to be a proctologist to know who the assholes are."

I was certainly sympathetic to a number of the Weather Underground's political positions: their anti-war passion, their support of the Black Power movement, their radical feminism, and their socialist policies. However, there emerging amongst the radical fringes of SDS was a dictatorial arrogance and intolerance that was not dissimilar to the warmongers in Washington that they railed against.

The country was widely polarized and everyone seemed to be embracing extreme, and in many cases, false dichotomies. Anyone who tells you that the sixties were a time of individualism doesn't know what they are talking about. It was a time of extreme conformity that manifested itself in warring factions. Bumper stickers mushroomed across the country: "America: Love it or Leave it" and "My Country Right or Wrong." Or on the other side of the divide: "Bring Our Boys Home" or more provocatively: "Nixon— Pull Out Like Your Father Should Have."

At one point several years later, the Weather Underground announced that when the revolution in America was complete there would be a "dictatorship of the proletariat." The Marxist-Leninist rhetoric was a caricature of the original, but no less frightening.

Both political extremes were demanding emotional allegiance to brutal ideologies that subordinated the individual to the mass mind.

I decided to take the advice of the bumper sticker, and failing to be infatuated with the United States, left for a short stay in Europe. In fact, my trip to Europe was absolutely apolitical and had nothing whatsoever to do with my draft status or my conflicted feelings about the state of the union—something my parents found very hard to believe. My dad wanted to put me in touch with a Quaker organization that helped draft dodgers escape to Sweden. Several months later, my father would phone me to let me know that the Canadian government had specifically barred immigration officials from asking about the military status of young Americans seeking permanent residence.

Actually, my trip to Europe had to do with leaving my heart-shaped amphetamine friends behind.

For a number of months I had been concerned about my regular, read—daily, consumption of Dexedrine. The high was mildly euphoric and I felt a pleasant sense of alertness, increased confidence and a storehouse of energy. I was compulsively talkative, restless, and was able to concentrate for long periods of time without a break. When I wasn't working, I read voraciously. But there was an unpleasant side to amphetamines and that was coming down from them. I found myself experiencing mood swings, depression, irritability, and increasing paranoia. It was time for a mental health break.

I told Steve that I was going on holiday and took a cheap Icelandic Air flight via Reykjavik to London. A customs inspector went through my backpack and found my hash pipe.

"So what do you smoke in here?" he asked, pointing to the pipe.

"Tobacco."

"It's awfully small for tobacco."

"I'm trying to quit."

The weather in London was milder than New York so I spent the best part of the night engaged in nocturnal sightseeing. I walked from Tower Bridge down through Fleet Street out to Westminster and then up through Hyde Park to Nottinghill Gate. I'm not sure I understood it then, but perhaps one of the reasons for coming back to Britain was to see if I fit in. I didn't feel very American, and perhaps I wondered if Britain was where I belonged. I had lived most of my childhood in Britain. Perhaps I would feel more at home here.

But I didn't. If I felt a lack of belonging in the United States, I felt it even more intensely in Britain. For me, it was a sham of a natural habitat like the artificial enclosures for bears at the Bronx Zoo. I spent several hours in an all night laundromat off Earl's Court reading Maugham's *The Razor's Edge* before making my way to St Pancras Station to catch the boat train to France.

At least in France there would be no pretense of belonging.

Like my stay in San Francisco, my brief sojourn in Europe was a self-imposed solitary confinement. Other than the last few days in Spain, I spoke to no one socially. I didn't come to Europe looking for companionship and the lack of social contact didn't perturb me at the time. In fact, the opposite was the case. I felt that I needed to be alone and I actually avoided situations that might have brought me into social interaction. Once when I was sitting in a café in Saint-Germain-des-Pres, an American couple came over to my table and asked if I spoke English. He was holding a map of Paris and I suspect they were looking for directions. I pretended that I didn't understand and they left.

I occupied some of my time looking for inexpensive places to stay and even less expensive places to eat. My budget was very limited, so I frequented venues that didn't charge admission. When the weather was decent, I read in the Tuileries and the Luxembourg Gardens. I spent hours perusing the second-hand book stalls that lined the Seine. I read non-stop and kept a journal. In Paris, I found a cheap hotel in a side street off the Boulevard Haussman, an easy walk to both the Left Bank and Montmartre.

My arrival in Paris was the fulfillment of an adolescent pilgrimage of sorts. For some time, I had been reading the works of Henry Miller and had become enamored with his descriptions of Paris in the 1930's. I had devoured *Tropic of Cancer* and had the first volume of *The Rosy Crucifixion* in my backpack. While Miller had returned to the United States at the start of World War II, his masterpiece, *Tropic of Cancer*, had been banned in the US until 1964 when the US Supreme Court, in its literary wisdom, declared the book "non-obscene."

For me, Miller represented the exact opposite of what I had left behind in the United States. He was a vital and irrepressible life force, what the Greeks had termed Eros—a passionate, rebellious individual, unfettered by convention or public opinion.

I was fascinated with Henry Miller's Paris, his relationship with Anais Nin, and the literary circle they moved in. I had read Lawrence Durrell and was familiar with the works of James Agee and Gore Vidal. I hadn't yet encountered Antonin Artaud, but would come under his influence after I became involved with the Inner Theater later that year.

Accordingly, one of the first places I visited was 18, Villa Seurat (which Miller would rename Villa Borghese in *Tropic of Cancer*). I took the Metro to the Place Denfert district and from there to Villa Seurat via Rue St. Jacque. Miller lived at Villa Seurat off and on throughout the thirties. His rent was paid by Anais Nin who for some of that time was also his lover. Alfred Perles describes Miller's apartment at Villa Seurat as "host to cranks, nuts, drunks, writers, artists, bums, Montparnasse derelicts, vagabonds, psychopaths . . ."

Perhaps, although I didn't think this explicitly at the time, Villa Seurat was a place where I might have found a sense of belonging.

I was also taken by the honesty and independent rebelliousness of Anais Nin. I visited the famous bookstore, Shakespeare and Company, on Rue de la Bucherie near Place Saint-Michel and purchased an English translation of her collection of short erotica, Little Birds. In the preface, Nin asks rhetorically "what happens to a group of writers who need money so badly that they devote themselves entirely to the erotic?" She then answers her own question: "I became what I shall call the Madame of an unusual house of literary prostitution. . . . Most of the erotica was written on empty stomachs. . . ."

An anonymous patron had offered Miller a dollar a page to write pornography. The literary crowd that surrounded Miller and Nin were desperately poor and the offer was soon translated into a literary sweatshop that produced twenty plus pages of erotica a day against the refrain of "less poetry and philosophy and more sex."

I spent about three weeks in Paris before taking a train to Lausanne in Switzerland. It was a whim. Switzerland must be lovely in the summer, but it was still winter in the Alps and it wasn't long before I was back at the train station looking for warmer climes.

On an overnight train to Barcelona I shared a compartment with a young American man from Oklahoma, who called himself Fox Walker. I'm not sure whether Fox was his real name or not. He was a SPC 4 in the US Army, stationed in Germany, on leave for a week's holiday in Spain. He was dressed in civilian clothes: blue jeans, hightop sneakers, and a New York Knicks sweatshirt. He was clean-shaven with short-cropped hair. I was reading and trying to give the impression that I didn't want to talk, but Fox ignored all my nonverbal cues. We were alone in the compartment, so there was no one else to fob him off on. Fox initiated the conversation.

"You . . . speak . . . English?" he spoke slowly to assist my comprehension.

I nodded.

"OK!" he responded eagerly. "Can you imagine that? What a coincidence! I thought you might be French or Dutch or something. You're American or British?"

"American."

"No shit! Me too. How about that for a coincidence! You and me in the same train compartment. And both of us being American. Where're you from?"

"New York."

"No shit? I'm from outside Tulsa. You know in Oklahoma. I'm in the Army. Stationed in Germany. But you're not in the military."

The length of my hair was a dead giveaway.

"Are you dodging the draft?" he asked. There was no accusation in his voice, just curiosity. It wasn't the first time I had been asked the question. At the time, draft dodgers evoked some strong emotional reactions. They were either heroes or cowards. There wasn't much in between. In a working class bar in Clichy a crowd of road workers had bought me three rounds of drinks believing, mistakenly, that I was escaping the US draft. I did nothing to disabuse them.

"I'm just here for a vacation," I said. "I'm not dodging the draft. But I'm sure as hell not going to Vietnam."

"Nam's a bad scene," Fox agreed somberly.

"Have you been?"

"One tour then I was transferred to Germany. Germany's OK."

"Did you kill people?" I asked. There's something about the anonymity of strangers meeting on a train that permits intimate questions.

Fox looked up sharply as though expecting a pacifist sermon.

"I dunno." Fox shrugged.

It wasn't the response I had expected. How could you not know if you killed someone?

"What do you mean you don't know?"

"I mean I was in some fire fights. Sure. We all were. I used a brush cutter."

"A brush cutter?"

"A shotgun with a sawed off barrel. It was good in the jungle. You know there's like dense brush. It's the jungle and you don't know where the VC is hiding."

"How could you tell if the person in the jungle was Viet Cong and not some innocent peasant?"

"You can tell. I take one look at them and I can tell."

"But how could you tell?" I persisted. I had heard that the Viet Cong didn't wear uniforms and came in all shapes, sizes, ages, and genders.

"The brass would designate free fire zones. Everyone in those zones were VC. It was as simple as that. We found them. We killed them. And once they were dead, they were definitely VC."

"The dead were definitely VC?"

"Yeah, otherwise they wouldn't be dead."

"But you don't know if you killed anyone?" I asked.

"After the fight was over there would be some dead gooks. But who knows who killed them? One bullet hole looks much the same as the next."

I hadn't thought about this before. There was anonymity to the slaughter. I wondered if that was comforting.

"Does it bother you?"

"What?"

"Does it bother you that you might have killed someone?"

Fox seemed to warm to the subject. He shook his head.

"Nay. Not really. I mean it was just something you did. The VC was there to be killed. That was our job. I mean that was the reason we was there. I didn't think about it much. You just get on and do what you have to do. I didn't enjoy it. I just got on and did my duty. Some of the guys took real pride in the body counts. They claimed each and every dead gook as their own. They'd keep a tally and would brag about their kills. For some of them it was like a competition. Who gets the most kills? I wasn't into that shit."

"You just did as you were told," I replied. Perhaps Fox sensed the sarcasm in my voice. He got testy.

"I served my country and I'm fucking proud of it. I didn't go running off to Canada or Sweden. No sirree Bob, I signed up as soon as I was of age."

"And you love your country?"

Fox looked at me as though I had dropped from another planet.

"Sure I love my country. What kind of question is that?"

"Are you in favor of the war?" I asked.

That gave him a moment's pause.

"It's bad news, but we gotta win it."

"Why?"

"Cause them North Vietnamese are communists."

I wasn't actually baiting Fox. I was genuinely interested in his perspective. He was the voice of what Richard Nixon was increasingly calling the silent majority.

"What's a communist?" I asked.

Fox looked at me, again, like I was born yesterday.

"A communist is a North Vietnamese. They want to take over the country."

"Isn't it their country?"

"We can't let communists take over." Fox spoke slowly as though he was explaining something complex to a retarded child. "If they get a foothold in Vietnam, there'll be no stopping them. It's called falling dominos. You know how you line up dominos in a row and then knock one over and the whole rows goes down. Well, it's just like that with communists. If they win in Vietnam, they'll be in Boston and New York next week."

"You believe that?"

"Yes, sirree."

And he did.

Fox Walker probably wasn't a bad man, nor I suspect was he a particularly brave or noble citizen. No one was going to build a statue to Fox Walker or haul him in front of a tribunal at Nuremburg. He was a simple, honest man who in another age would have been plowing a cornfield. Over the next few days I would learn that he had two sisters who he loved dearly and that he had got his girlfriend pregnant in their last year of high school. His passion was Mexican food and trout fishing, and once he left the military he would join his father's air conditioning repair business. He wrote weekly letters to his parents and was frightened of heights. Fox Walker was a modern day Everyman, the unknown citizen—a slab of animated flesh moving inexorably through a historical meat grinder.

Compassion tempered condescension. I say compassion, because pity is contempt masquerading as benevolence.

I changed the subject. "Have you been to Barcelona before?"

Fox shook his head. Neither had I, but I had read parts of Jean Genet's *The Thief's Journal* that were set in Barcelona.

"You think there's whores in Barcelona?" he asked.

"Sure. Male or female?"

"Huh? What do you mean male or female?"

"Male or female whores?"

"There are men whores?" he asked incredulously.

"Sure. In Barcelona there are male and female whores."

"How d'ou know? You said you'd never been to Barcelona."

"I read it in a book," I replied, and that seemed to satisfy Fox's need for reliable sources.

"No shit? That's far out!" This was a new idea for Fox and he was trying to get his head around it. "And like women would pay the guy for sex?"

I was beginning to enjoy myself.

"No, most of them are homosexuals."

"Homos?" Fox eyes grew even wider.

"And some of those guys dress and look like women."

"Wow. We gotta be careful."

Fox's words were prescient. Barcelona is a rough city that doesn't suffer the ignorant, the innocent, or the foolish gently. But, in fairness, Fox wasn't a fool, he was simply naïve. Neither his experience in Vietnam nor Germany had made him any more worldly than an average fourteen-year-old farm boy from Tulsa, Oklahoma. He had virtually no street sense and couldn't spot a scam even when it slapped him in the face. I spent three days with

Fox in Barcelona and his innocence and simplicity continued to surprise me throughout.

From the train station we made our way to the Barrio Chino, or as it was called on the tourist maps, El Ravel. Just off the Ramblas, Barrio Chino was a warren of narrow streets and dark alleys, lined with cheap pensions, graffiti-covered walls, and seedy tapas bars. Overhead, balconies were encrusted with flowerpots, toothless old women, and rusting birdcages. Barrio Chino has a century-old reputation for vice, poverty, drugs, and petty crime of all descriptions. Genet immortalized its decadence in *The Thief's Journal*—a moral no man's land beyond the grasping reach of the fingers of respectability. Henri Cartier Bresson's black and white images captured both the dissipation and despair. Every third or fourth doorway sported a bored and unhappy looking prostitute. It was a labyrinth of barefoot children, worn out old men, painted ladies, and dangerous looking young North African men. The Barrio Chino had a century-old reputation for being ragingly raucous and unrepentant.

We found a cheap pension and Fox went out immediately looking to score some Moroccan *kif*. He returned a couple of hours later with a couple of bottles of wine, a small piece of hashish, and a large Brazilian fellow in tow. I didn't know what to make of Thiago—that was the Brazilian fellow's name—but his presence made me anxious. We smoked some hash and then went out for something to eat.

At the end of the meal, Fox announced that he needed to change some money.

"Don't go to the bank," Thiago advised. "And the cambios are worse. The government sets the exchange rate and they charge a commission. I can get you a better deal."

"How much more?" Fox asked.

Thiago mentioned an exchange rate about fifty percent above the bank rate.

Fox withdrew a wad of US dollars.

"I wanna change a hundred bucks."

"Fox, I don't think this is a good idea," I interjected.

"You don't know," Thiago snapped. "Hey, I'm only trying to help. You want to throw money away, that's up to you."

Fox was already counting out a pile of bills.

"Fox," I said, and then shook my head knowingly.

And then there was a metallic click close by. I looked down into Thiago's lap and there was an open pocket knife—out of Fox's sight, but clearly visible to me. Thiago gave me a thin smile. I shrugged and fell silent.

Thiago took the money and disappeared into the street.

I ordered coffee.

Twenty minutes later, Fox was still mumbling about how he didn't understand why it was taking so long to change money. At the thirty minute mark, I told him about the knife. He still didn't believe he had been taken. At forty minutes, Fox went out to the street to look for Thiago. After an hour had passed, Fox was just coming to realize that he had been conned.

We walked back to the pension to find our bags had been emptied on the floor, and Fox's watch and my jeans had been stolen. Thiago and his confederate had been good enough not to take the piece of Moroccan *kif*—so Fox and I extinguished our sorrows in a cloud of cannabis smoke.

The next afternoon we went to Plaza de Toros Monumental.

"You can't go to Spain without seeing a bull fight!" Fox countered when I expressed reluctance. Given the state of the world, I thought of blood sports as gilding the lily.

The regular season of bull fighting had not yet begun, but the afternoon presented the *novillada*—the student bullfighters who had not yet become professional. The average age of the *toreros* was about twelve or thirteen, the bulls were smaller, usually three or four years old and, most importantly, the bull was not killed at the end of the performance. On these terms, I agreed to buy a ticket on the cheaper "sol" side of the arena.

Frankly, the bullfight with all its glittering arrogance and exaggerated pomposity, bored me. I even found myself secretly hoping that the bull would gore one of its tormentors.

My boredom lasted until the third of the *toreros* entered the arena. He was the youngest of the afternoon, just twelve years old, but his manner was as haughty and disdainful as the rest. He strutted like bantam cock, waited for the honorific bugle blast, and bowed to the presiding dignitary. Then, of course the bull came bounding into the arena.

A pretty little girl with a basket of flowers sat down next to Fox. She was probably about eight years old.

The first two *toreros* were clearly young and nervous. They made mistakes and had to be rescued by the *banderillos*. A couple of times they actually ran and jumped over the arena wall to avoid being gored or trampled by the bull. Nevertheless the crowd loved them. The whistling and cheering provided continuous encouragement.

But the third *torero* was different. There seemed to be a single-minded determination that resided beneath the bravado façade. He didn't flinch as the bull charged. His concentration was intense, but like his predecessors he made mistakes.

Within the first four minutes, the bull had out-maneuvered him and had thrown the boy in all his glittering finery ten feet in the air. He performed an awkward spiral and landed with a dull thud in the sand.

"The bull got him!" Fox screamed with excitement. "Holy shit, the bull's got him!"

The *banderillos* immediately arrested the bull's attention away from the semi-conscious *torero*. Two men in white ran out into the arena and half carried the young matador off.

"I didn't think that happened," Fox called out "I mean that kid could get seriously hurt."

Moments later the same young matador, the dust brushed off his glistening outfit, was strutting out into the arena again. The crowd went wild with applause, whistling and cheering. Fox threw a flower from the young girl's basket into the arena.

"The kid's got balls!"

After three passes, the kid—as Fox called him—got his *capote* hooked on the bulls horns and having nothing with which to guide the bull away from him, made a dash to the arena wall and attempted to scale it. But the bull was too fast for him and pinned him to the wall.

"Jesus Christ, you think the kid has any ribs left after that?" Fox shouted above the roar of the crowd.

Again the *banderillos* distracted the bull and again the men in white rushed out and carried the young lad out of the arena.

Three or four minutes passed. The bull was walking around the arena and the crowd was waiting to see how the event would end. Suddenly, the bugle blew and the same young matador again strutted out into the arena.

The crowd was beyond control. The entire audience was on its feet, cheering, whistling, shouting tributes to the young man's courage.

"Can you beat that! The kid's got brass balls!"

A blizzard of flowers fell in front of the young matador. He strode over to the far side of the arena and stood facing the chief dignitary in the stands. The crowd was hushed. The dignitary called out something and the crowd went beserk with cheering and shouting.

"The girl says they're gonna let the kid kill the bull. Because of his courage, he gets to kill the bull. This is far-fucking out!" Fox was now pelting flowers into the arena.

The bugle again sounded and picadors on horseback rode into the ring to torment the poor bull with their lances. I had read somewhere that until 1930 the horses were not provided with any protective padding and it was usual for a horse or two to get disemboweled. In fact, the number of horses killed during a fight was greater than bulls.

Next, the *banderillos* reappeared with sharp barbed sticks that they attempt to plant into the bull's shoulders.

And then, the bugler sounded the third and final stage of the bullfight (or so the little flower girl told Fox) the *tercido de muerte*. The young matador entered the ring alone with a small red cape and a sword. He planted himself about ten feet from the bull and held the sword straight in front of him, casting his eyes down the blade as if sighting a rifle. The crowd was absolutely silent, waiting for the bull to make its move.

The matador flicked the cape at the bull. The bull pawed at the ground and made its charge. The matador moved his body to the side and guided the sword into the mound of muscle behind the bull's neck. The momentum of the bull's charge drove the sword to its hilt. The bull stopped in its tracks, as though confused. It took several steps backward and swung its head violently back and forth. It then opened its mouth and a geyser of blood broke forth. It staggered sideways and attempted a short run, but collapsed near the arena wall. A man dressed all in blue ran forward with a knife to cut its jugular.

The crowd was now entirely on its feet, cheering and waving white handkerchiefs.

"She says the kid is going to get the bull's ear!" Fox shouted over the crowd. "It's like an honor."

The whole miserable spectacle seemed to me to be a remarkably apt metaphor for the screwed-up world I found myself inhabiting.

As the crowd then began to disperse, a heavily made-up woman in a scarlet flamenco dress appeared. She had so many ruffles that when she walked she rustled like a deck of playing cards being shuffled. She claimed to be the little flower girl's mother and presented Fox with a bill in pesetas for the equivalent of a hundred and twenty seven dollars for all the flowers he had thrown.

The last time I saw Fox was on the morning of my departure from Barcelona. He had been out most of the previous night visiting the fleshpots of the Barrio Chino. I had remained at the pension. I had just enough money to buy train and ferry tickets to London from where I'd catch the cheap Icelandic flight back to New York. I had packed my backpack and was waiting to say goodbye.

Fox returned to the room we were sharing from the communal toilet at the end of the corridor.

"What does it mean," he asked, "when you're pissing and your dick feels like it's on fire?"

I didn't have the heart to tell him.

CHAPTER 7
The Anarchist Cookbook

I RETURNED TO NEW YORK ON the day that John Lennon and Yoko Ono started their Bed-In for Peace at the Amsterdam Hilton. I remember it because it coincided with the release of the *White Album*—with the photograph of the two of them naked. The album was impounded by the police at Newark Airport and we, at Bookmasters had to paste strips of paper over their genitals in order to sell the record.

I returned to the 10th Street apartment with a promotion. I was invited to become the assistant manager of the Bookmasters on 59th Street and 3rd Avenue. It was a position I accepted with relish. The store was located between two movie theaters and the potential for sales was huge. Steve Hancock was the manager.

I should probably mention something about Steve's financial situation since it would influence future events. Steve lived financially in the present. Money was there to be spent, which is a healthy attitude as long as you have it to spend. Steve often didn't have it, but this never stopped him from spending. When he was shopping, he would never settle for anything but the best quality—cost was no object. The year before, we had cooked a Thanksgiving dinner at the 10th Street apartment for a group of friends. As part of the preparations, Steve had bought a cast iron roasting pot and a set of copper-bottomed saucepans that ran close to five hundred dollars. When his salary was insufficient to meet his expenses, Steve used credit cards. He would charge the card to the maximum of his credit limit and then pay the minimum monthly payments. When he had maxed out the cards, he simply applied for more and given that he already had a wallet full, the new credit card companies were more than happy to oblige. When the credit cards were maxed out, Steve took loans from the bookstore. He would take cash from the cash register and put in an I.O.U. There was an honor system of sorts at the bookstore and this was not an unusual practice; although neither the owners nor the accountants were informed. What made Steve's use of it unusual was that he never had money to repay the loans. Accordingly, the balance of his debt increased steadily until it was more than one day's income for the bookstore. At this point, Steve started to delay the bank deposit of the daily receipts. So, in essence, today's cash would appear as yesterday's takings.

I watched this with great misgivings. It was a time bomb that was sure to explode in Steve's face. Perhaps it made me more conservative and careful with my own money.

There was one area where I did start spending money. Soon after my return from Europe I met Rafael Bunuel and Otto Schimpf at the Frog Pond, a small, friendly neighborhood bar and grill on 9th Street.

Rafael Bunuel, the son of the surrealist filmmaker Luis, was an avant-garde playwright and artist, and Otto Schimpf was an out-of-work actor. We met over some of the Frog Pond's delicious *cevapcici*. Rafael, Otto, and I hit it off immediately. We shared a common interest in literature, film, art, and theater and it wasn't long before Raphael announced that he and Otto were part owners of an off-off Broadway theater.

The Inner Theater was indeed off-off Broadway. At 356 the Bowery, it was a derelict storefront that Raphael and Otto had converted, on the proverbial shoestring, into a hundred and twenty-seat theater. I was intrigued. They invited me to become involved, and within a week I had auditioned for a part in a medley of short plays by Bertolt Brecht. Thus began a rich and fulfilling portion of my New York experience.

The Inner Theater was devoted for the most part to new and previously unpublished playwrights. Everyone was a volunteer and we never made ends meet financially. In fact, there was not a month that went by that we didn't lose money. But the experience and the company were without equal—the people I worked with reminded me of the teachers I had had at Miss Smith's Tutorial School. Everyone—the actors, the directors, costume constructors, and stagehands—all had full-time day jobs. Some were waiters or taxi drivers, some taught school and others worked travel agencies. But all shared an abiding passion for the theater. After acting in a couple of productions, Rafael and Otto invited me to join them as a part owner in the theater. I jumped at the opportunity.

We tried to produce one play a month, but it was extremely hard work. It meant that we had one play in rehearsal while we had another in production. This would be an exhausting schedule for professionals who didn't have full-time day jobs—for us it would prove to be unsustainable.

In addition, we were always looking for ways to raise money to support the theater. One of the more original ideas came to me while I was browsing in the Peace Eye Bookstore on Avenue A. I came across a long out-of-print book of wildlife photography. In the midst of the photos was a large image of two rhinos mating. I bought the book, made sure the copyright had expired, and then had a thousand posters printed with the caption "The Inner Theater Reopens." No one, including me, had a clue what the caption had to do with the two fucking rhinos, but we sold the entire thousand at Bookmasters within a month. Famous Faces, the largest poster company in the country, approached me and asked to buy the rights to the rhino poster, but when they discovered that the image wasn't covered by copyright, they simply took it (as I had done). They printed it with the caption "Make Love Not War" and it sold millions of copies across the country.

We produced a number of original plays that were well reviewed in *The Village Voice* and elsewhere. In May, we produced a version of Machiavelli's *The Mandrake Root* and in June, I directed an original play written by Raphael entitled *The Seventeen Boxes.* Under the influence of *Oh! Calcutta* that was playing less than a block away, we produced in the fall *A Dirty Evening*—a collection of short dramatized sketches from Chaucer, Boccaccio, Shakespeare, Edward Gorey, and others. *The Village Voice* heralded the production as refreshing in that it used "talent in lieu of nudity."

For Christmas, we decided to do a children's production of *The Little Prince,* specifically designed so that we could present it in the city parks, free of charge, for inner-city kids. We wrote the script, rehearsed, built the set, and advertised our production dates only to receive a rather intemperate letter from Paramount Pictures threatening legal action if we proceeded with the play. They claimed to own the dramatic rights.

Rafael and I had a long discussion about how to respond to the threatening letter. In the end, we decided to proceed with our rehearsal in the hopes that Paramount Pictures would consider us too small and insignificant to bother with.

Wrong assumption. Two days later we received a court injunction prohibiting the presentation of *The Little Prince* and ordering Rafael and me to appear in the Supreme Court of the State of New York. We rapidly put our defense together.

A week later we were standing in front of an incredibly old and deaf judge who presided over the Supreme Court of the State of New York.

"Well," he shouted, "what do you have to say for yourselves?"

"*Por favor*, your excellency, *no habla inglés*," said Rafael.

So I, a modern day David, was left with the job of defending the poor little Inner Theater against the capitalist Goliath—Paramount Pictures. My argument followed these lines:

On a close reading of the text of *The Little Prince*, it will be obvious that the author, Antoine de Saint-Exupéry, never intended his little book to be subject to copyright conventions. Perhaps the most important theme in the story is that creativity is open-source. The content defies private intellectual property. . . .

I didn't get any further.

The old judge had a sense of humor and burst out laughing. I didn't think this boded well for our case.

The court ordered the show closed, but didn't award damages since we hadn't actually performed before an audience. Rafael and I went out for an Italian lunch.

Spring slipped into summer as the newspapers and television stations filled our consciousness with descriptions and images of the so-called Battle of Hamburger Hill. The Battle took place at Dong Ap Bia, referred to by the US military as Hill 937, in the jungle-covered mountainous region of South Vietnam close to the Laotian border. Hill 937 had virtually no strategic value and was heavily fortified by North Vietnamese troops. Despite this, the US Command ordered a direct frontal assault, which resulted in the capture of the hill at the cost of 74 American lives and 630 North Vietnamese lives. The US abandoned the hill soon after it was taken. The senselessness of the debacle was described in detail in the press, and the controversy even reached the halls of Congress. It seemed symptomatic of the tragic absurdity of the entire war.

Closer to home, on Christopher Street in the West Village, another battle began. On the evening of June 28th, the New York Police raided a small "private club" called the Stonewall Inn. The Stonewall was owned by the Mafia Genovese family who a few years earlier had invested $3,500 to turn a rundown restaurant into an even more rundown gay bar. The Stonewall had no liquor license, no running water behind the bar (glasses were "washed" in a plastic tub), no fire exits, and the toilets ran constantly. It was not the first such police raid. Regulars at the Stonewall were familiar with the routine. The bouncer at the door with the peep hole would signal the presence of police by turning on a white light—this was a warning for the dancing to stop and for the more flamboyant patrons to escape via the bathroom windows. The cops would then have the clientele line up and produce identification. Generally, only the bar's employees and the transgendered crowd would be arrested, and in the past, the patrons had been passive and compliant. All that changed on June 28, 1969.

There are conflicting reports as to how the Stonewall Riots began. One report has four undercover police from the Public Morals Squad entering the bar early in the evening, and then calling on the bar's public phone for reinforcements for a large scale raid. The raid did not go as planned. The standard procedure was to have the patrons line up, with female police officers taking the transgendered people to the toilet to verify their sex. On June 28th, they refused to go with the policewomen and the male patrons refused to produce identification. There was a standoff and a crowd grew on Christopher Street. A scuffle broke out when the police tried to hustle a woman in handcuffs out of the bar into a police wagon. The woman didn't go quietly; she struggled and called upon the crowd to help her. The mob began throwing pennies, rocks, and beer cans at the police. Bystanders started shouting "kill the pigs" and "gay power." A few began singing "We Shall Overcome."

The following morning, *The New York Times* and *The New York Post* carried the story of the riots on their respective front pages. That night, Christopher Street was thronged with thousands of demonstrators, graffiti blossomed on the buildings—"They invaded our rights" and "Drag Power" and "Support Gay Power." The Stonewall Riots continued with the arrival of hundreds of members of the Tactical Patrol Force (TPF). Rocks and bricks were thrown and scores of trash cans were set on fire.

Within a week, the Gay Liberation Front was founded.

Again, another tipping point had been reached. Questions were suddenly formulated—what had previously been rhetorical questions became those with an urgent need to be answered: *What's wrong with this picture? Why do we tolerate this harassment? Where does power come from?*

The questions may not have been articulated in as many words, but they were contagious and ripped through the mob faster than any police phalanx. The process of answering rhetorical questions often leads to revelations and sometimes revolutions. The answers to the Stonewall questions were an epiphany—the emergence of Gay Pride.

But emerging pride wasn't limited to the gay community. The nation also took enormous pride in the July 20th Apollo 11 landing on the moon. That evening, Steve and I took the Lexington Avenue IRT up to Sheep's Meadow in Central Park to join the thousand other New Yorkers who were watching Neil Armstrong and 'Buzz' Aldrin stroll on the moon. It was an awe-inspiring spectacle, made even more so by the hush and breath-holding excitement of the enormous crowd.

Some time later, Buzz Aldrin would describe the view from the moon as "magnificent desolation." I wondered if he was speaking of the physical landscape or perhaps more metaphorically. I also wondered if you needed to travel as far as the moon to reach that conclusion.

In the first week in August, all employees at the 59th Street Bookmasters entered a lottery. The prize was time off from work on August 15-17 and tickets to attend a rock concert that was scheduled to be held on a pig farm in upstate New York. The Bookmasters stores were selling advance Woodstock Festival tickets like there was no tomorrow. Even before the event, we guessed that the promoters' estimates of 150,000 in the audience were gross under-estimates. Both Steve and I drew the short straws and so had to work instead of attending the concert. But we followed the concert closely from a distance.

The Woodstock Festival was far more than just another rock concert, but very few would understand that until it was all over. Among those musicians who were invited but declined to attend were Jethro Tull, Procol Harem, The Moody Blues, Bob Dylan (who lived a stone's throw from the concert site), Led Zeppelin, and The Beatles (an unconfirmed report suggests that the Beatles did not play because Richard Nixon had blocked John Lennon's entry to the US from Canada). The Doors declined the invitation to play assuming that Woodstock would be a "second-class repeat" of the Monterey Pop Festival. Tommy James and the Shondells also declined the invitation. Later, Tommy James would write: "We could have kicked ourselves. We were in Hawaii and my secretary called and said 'Yeah, listen there's this pig farmer in upstate New York that wants you to play in his field. That's how it was put to me. So we passed, and we realized what we'd missed a couple of days later." The Byrds also passed on Woodstock. After the fact, bass player John York wrote: "No, we wanted a rest and missed the best festival of all."

And it was the best festival of them all with over half a million young people listening to the likes of Santana, the Grateful Dead, Janis Joplin, The Who, Jefferson Airplane, Jimi Hendrix and a very pregnant Joan Baez. Hundreds of thousands of young people joined Country Joe in the "Fish Cheer:"

> And it's one, two, three,
> what are we fighting for?
> Don't ask me, I don't give a damn,
> next stop is Vietnam.
> And it's five, six, seven,
> open up the pearly gates.
> Well there ain't no time to wonder why.
> Whoopee! We're all gonna die.

But Woodstock was more than just a music festival. For many, it was a political watershed as well, an Alice-in-Wonderland-like glimpse of the secret garden that we can never really enter, that counterculture utopian mélange of music, drugs, sex, and peace.

It was very early in the morning on the closing day of the Woodstock Festival that a pale white man with long, matted hair and a jean jacket entered the bookstore with a huge cardboard box on his shoulder. Even at that early hour, he was sweating profusely. I had just opened the shop and was alone behind the cash register.

"You wanna buy a typewriter?" he asked, without any other form of introduction. It was an odd question for early Sunday morning, but many odd things happened in the bookstore.

He placed the cardboard box on the counter and opened it. Inside was what appeared to be a brand new, shiny IBM Selectric Typewriter—the top of the line—an exact replica of the one Steve had rented and I had inadvertently caused to be stolen.

If my life were an ancient myth, I might have seen the IBM Selectric Typewriter as some sort of archetypical prize: the fabled golden apple or the giant pearl guarded by the undersea dragon.

"How much?"

"Gimme twenty-five bucks."

I did and he disappeared.

I had harbored a secret desire to be a writer for some time, now I had the tool to make that happen.

Towards the end of September, the trial of the Chicago Eight (soon to become seven) began. Abbie Hoffman, Jerry Rubin, Dave Dellinger, Tom Hayden, Rennie Davis, John Froines, Lee Weiner, and Bobby Seale were charged with conspiracy and crossing state lines in order to incite a riot. All the charges were in connection with the civil disturbances that had occurred a year earlier at the Democratic National Convention. Bobby Seale asked that the trial be postponed until his lawyer could be present. Judge Julius Hoffman (no relation to Abbie) denied the request and Seale responded with a barrage of expletives. He called the Judge a "honkey," "a racist," and "a fascist pig." When Bobby Seale refused to be silenced, Judge Hoffman ordered him bound and gagged. Within days drawings of Bobby Seale, bound and gagged in the Chicago courtroom, emerged as protest posters. Seale was ultimately sentenced to four years for contempt of court and his trial was separated from that of the other seven.

The trial of the Chicago Seven was theater of the absurd. I recall not knowing which was more surreal, the antics of the defendants, or the reactions of the judge. It was as though Ionesco and Kafka had conspired to write the script. On one occasion, Abbie Hoffman and Jerry Rubin appeared in court wearing judicial robes. When the Judge ordered them to remove them, they did so only to reveal that they wore Chicago police uniforms beneath. As the trial got underway, the US National Guard was called in to help control the crowds of demonstrators outside the courthouse. The list of witnesses for the defense were singers Phil Ochs, Judy Collins, and Arlo Guthrie, writer Norman Mailer, LSD enthusiast Timothy Leary, and civil rights activist Rev. Jesse Jackson.

About ten days later in early October, three things occurred almost simultaneously. First, the statue commemorating the police killed in the 1886 Chicago Haymarket Bombing was itself dynamited; a harbinger of the "Days of Rage" that would soon be released by the Weather Underground. In the second week of October, Weathermen converged on Chicago to protest the trial of the Chicago Seven and "to bring the war home." There was nothing about the planning or attitudes of the Weathermen that suggested that this would be a peaceful demonstration. The protestors came in motorcycle helmets, some of them armed with pipes, chains, and makeshift batons. And hundreds of them soon broke out of the police cordon surrounding Lincoln Park, streaming north and south on Clarke Street smashing windows and vandalizing parked cars. For four days, the Weathermen unleashed their nihilistic fury on Chicago's Loop. Even the Black Panthers wanted to distance themselves from the rampage. Fred Hampton called it "opportunistic, individualistic, chauvinistic, and Custeristic—it's nothing but child's play—it's folly." Within two months Fred Hampton would be dead—murdered in his sleep by the FBI and Chicago police.

The second thing that occurred in early October was a late-night conversation with Steve in which he expressed his frustration with living in the city. He said he was thinking about leaving and getting back to nature. Cities were polluted, ecological wastelands. The crime of the Lower East Side was getting to him. (A Puerto Rican kid had been shot dead in front of our apartment a few days before. He had attempted to run away from a cop who stopped him for drugs.) Steve waxed lyrical about how the future resided in wilderness areas. He would build a cabin by a stream and grow organic vegetables. Northern California, Montana, or Idaho were possibilities. He had wanderlust.

At about two o'clock in the morning the real picture emerged Steve was in debt to the bookstore to the tune of about fifteen thousand dollars—almost a year's salary in those days. The daily receipts from the bookstore were now being delayed by four or five days, and Steve knew it was a matter of time before his financial house of cards came tumbling down.

The next day, Steve wrote a letter to the owners of the bookstore explaining his debt and promising to pay them back. Then, with nothing more than a backpack, he left New York City for points unknown.

The third event that occurred in early October was my receipt of another order from my Draft Board to report to Fort Hamilton for a psychiatric review. I had had two such interviews under my belt and felt that I should be able to handle a third. What I didn't know at the time was that Lt. Fielding had been transferred somewhere and that Dr. Joseph Mengele had taken his place. Of course, that wasn't his real name, but that's how I thought of him—the medical doctor who sent young men to their death.

I was kept waiting for more than an hour after the scheduled appointment time. This should have been a clue that everything was not going to go well.

A pinched-faced man with thick, round steel-rimmed glasses sat behind a metal desk that was piled high with manila files. The expression on his face was of irritated boredom. He barely looked up when I entered his office and continued to peruse files for several minutes before recognizing my presence.

"Sit down," he ordered.

I remained standing.

"Where's Lt. Fielding?" I asked.

"He was transferred to Colorado."

After another few minutes, he finally looked up at me.

"I said 'sit down'! If you remain standing I will call this interview to a close, classify you 1-A and recommend your immediate induction."

I sat down on a straight-backed wooden chair facing his desk.

"Now, I have read your file and can see nothing that should preclude your induction." He paused, perhaps waiting for an argument. I remained silent.

"Well, what have you to say for yourself?"

"It's already been said and you've made up your mind. This interview is a waste of time."

"You think it is a waste of time?"

"You should be ashamed of yourself."

"What did you say?"

"I said you should be ashamed of yourself. I want to know how a medical doctor who has sworn to do no harm can be working for the US Military?"

"You're a smart-ass."

"It's a real question."

Dr. Mengele was quiet for a few moments.

"It says here that you claim not to be a conscientious objector?"

"I'm not a pacifist."

"So its not war that bothers you, its this particular war in Vietnam that you don't want any part of?"

"It not war or violence that bothers me. It is the decision-making process," I replied. "On something as important as killing people, I prefer to make my own decisions about who and when."

"You might not follow orders?"

"I have a bad track record for following orders."

"Three weeks in boot camp and we'd have you begging for orders."

"What you're saying is possibly true," I said. He hadn't expected me to agree with him and Mengele looked momentarily confused. "I've always been impressed with the effectiveness of the army's brainwashing. Parents, teachers, and priests spend eighteen years teaching their sons not to kill and the army undoes all that training in thirteen weeks. That's pretty far out. In thirteen short weeks, the army produces killers. Are you proud to be part of that process?"

I had succeeded in angering Dr. Mengele. This may not have been the wisest course of action.

"One last question, would you refuse an order to shoot a Vietnamese enemy?"

"I'm opposed to gratuitous killing. I'll hunt and fish. But I'll eat what I kill. You expect me to eat Viet Cong?"

Not surprisingly, Mengele didn't see the humor in my question.

"I'll ask the question again. Would you refuse an order to shoot a Vietnamese enemy?"

"The Vietnamese aren't my enemy. They've never done anything to harm me or my family. Why should I want to kill them?"

Dr. Mengele sneered.

"You're a smart-ass coward and all this crap about decision-making is bullshit. You simply want to avoid serving your country. You make me sick! You're classified as 1-A and I'm not changing that. Get your ass prepared for Vietnam."

"I told you this interview was a fucking waste of time." I said and stormed out of his office.

On the bus on the way back to Manhattan, I wondered how long I had before Mengele's threat became a reality, and how I would respond when the induction order finally did arrive.

At about this time a young woman came to work as a cashier at Bookmasters. Her name was Celia Armstrong and she had recently been a shop assistant at a fairly upmarket delicatessen on the

Upper West Side. She had dropped out of university and was living up on Morningside Heights near Columbia University. We shared a leftwing political perspective, an anti-war stance, and an interest in history. Celia had been a history and political science major before she dropped out. We also shared a sense of loneliness. We started to see quite a bit of each other. We both liked European art films and went to a number of screenings of films by Fellini, Truffaut, and Bergman. Celia also got involved with the theatrical productions at the Inner Theater. I don't think she ever acted, but could always be relied upon to help with props or costumes. We also attended a number of anti-war demonstrations together, the two largest were the Marches Against Death on October 15th and November 15th in Washington DC.

On October 15th we took a Trailways bus to Washington and participated in a candlelight vigil on the Capitol steps. Benjamin Spock, the author of the bestselling *Baby and Child Care*, addressed the crowd calling the war in Vietnam a "total abomination that was crippling America." We spent the night in the Washington National Cathedral, which had generously opened its doors and housed hundreds of protestors. There were similar demonstrations across the United States. The BBC called the October Moratorium to End the War in Vietnam "the largest demonstration in US history with an estimated two million people involved." For the first time, America's middle class and middle-aged had joined the youthful protestors.

By the end of 1969, almost 45,000 American soldiers had been killed in Vietnam, and each day when I emptied my mailbox at the

10th Street apartment I looked with dread for the invitation to join them.

On November 15th, Celia and I again returned to Washington for the Peace Moratorium. This was an even larger demonstration of anti-war sentiment. There were over half a million demonstrators in Washington alone. Celia and I had planned on spending the night again at the National Cathedral, however, as we were walking in that direction, a car stopped. In the front seat were an elderly man and woman. They asked if we were anti-war demonstrators. We acknowledged that we were and they invited us to stay at their house. They had been out all evening picking up student protestors, taking them home and feeding them. The couple turned out to be Quakers and the man had been a conscientious objector in World War II. I listened until the small hours of the morning to his experiences being a CO at a time when that was not a popular or well-understood option. I deeply admired his courage and conviction. In total, this couple must have housed and fed at least a dozen protestors.

Later, I would come to understand that this was not an isolated gesture of hospitality. All over Washington, churches, schools, and private homes opened their doors to anti-war demonstrators. It was a marvelous and moving gesture of solidarity.

The following day, Pete Seeger led a quarter of a million demonstrators in singing John Lennon's new song "Give Peace A Chance."

But not everyone was sympathetic to the demonstrators. General Earle "Bus" Wheeler, Chairman of the Joint Chiefs of Staff, called the protestors "interminably vocal youngsters, strangers alike to soap and reason."

This General Wheeler, the self-proclaimed paragon of reasonableness, common sense, and personal hygiene, was the most senior US officer overseeing the mindless debacle of Hamburger Hill.

More disturbing still was President Richard Nixon's post-Moratorium comments. During the demonstration, Nixon had remained secluded in the White House (he was rumored to be watching a football game on television). The White House had been barricaded behind buses that were parked bumper to bumper. In a moment of truly imperial arrogance, Nixon announced: "Now I understand that there has been, and continues to be, opposition to the war in Vietnam on campuses and also in the nation. As far as this kind of activity is concerned, we expect it, however under no circumstances will I be affected whatever by it."

Retrospect makes fools of all of us, including monumentally arrogant presidents.

It was on the bus coming back from the Washington Peace Moratorium that I turned to Celia and told her that I was going to write a book—and I was going to entitle it *The Anarchist Cookbook*.

I had been thinking about *The Cookbook* for some time. The idea had come out of a conversation with Steve, but it wasn't original with him. It had been born out of prior conversations with political radicals in the East Village, but it had never been written.

Why did I decide to act upon it? Like most life-changing decisions, there wasn't a single cause. There is no question that I wanted to write. Most of my heroes were rebellious or avant-garde writers.

And now I had a spanking new IBM Selectric Typewriter that was chomping at the bit!

I was also frightened and angry. I wasn't going to war in Vietnam. About that I was sure. But I also didn't want to go to prison or Canada. Dr. Mengele had made it clear that I would indeed need to make such choices in the very near future. I was angry and frightened by my own indecision. I really didn't know what I would do when the inevitable induction order arrived.

Dr. Mengele had effectively reduced my life expectancy, or at least I thought so at the time.

Celia listened to my description of the book that I would write. I don't think she ever commented on it, even after it was published and there was a storm of controversy.

I didn't tell anyone else about the project. Perhaps I didn't want to be talked out of it, or perhaps I didn't want anyone else to write it before I had a chance to do so. Or maybe I just wanted to avoid criticism. I might have spoken to Steve about it, but he was on the run—homesteading in Idaho or Montana.

One of the defining features of *The Cookbook* was that it was written in solitude. I completed the manuscript without discussing it or sharing it with anyone. Much later, when the FBI released the file they had accumulated on *The Cookbook*, it became apparent that for some time they wondered who had actually written the book. There was even a suggestion that it might have been an underground collaborative venture. Nothing could have been further from the truth. I had absolutely no help writing the book, and that is glaringly apparent. No one read chapters and provided feedback. No one looked at the outline. No one even corrected my dreadful spelling.

In late November, I asked for a leave of absence from the bookstore, without explaining the reason, and then proceeded to write flat out, eight to ten hours a day for three months, but always in solitude. Without a foil or sounding board, my ideas snowballed within me. They reinforced and confirmed themselves. Without anyone to challenge them, they became a web of personally-skewed meaning—an insular cognitive process that my colleague, Bruce Wellman, would later identify as "self-sealing logic." I wrote what I believed, and I came to believe in what I wrote—at least for a time. On many occasions, passion and pithy phrases drowned reason and common sense.

I suspect that this is not an uncommon process in individuals who become radicalized.

In the 1970's, Yale psychologist Irving Janson researched a phenomenon that he called Groupthink. He recognized it as a pre-mature striving for group cohesiveness. It is a desire for harmony in group decision-making processes that overrides realistic appraisal of alternatives. Group members try to minimize conflict and reach consensus without rigorous critical thinking or evaluation.

Because *The Cookbook* was written in isolation, Groupthink obviously played no part in it. However, there may be a similar dangerous process at work when individuals work alone. Call it "Isolation-Think." I suspect some of the symptoms that are akin to Groupthink may have come into play while I was working on *The Cookbook.* By isolating myself during the writing, I may have come to create for myself the illusion of invulnerability and morality (two hallmarks of Groupthink). I can remember the emotional snowball effect of lashing out at what I considered to be a vicious, immoral, and war-mongering government in Washington. Once the immorality of the White House and Pentagon had been established, it followed that anyone opposed to US foreign policy was, ipso facto, moral—irrespective of what they might be advocating. There was a seductive simplicity to it. I recall feeling great excitement and energy as this naively dualistic thinking fell neatly into place. One false dichotomy scaffolded upon another, creating in my closed system of thinking, a greater and greater sense of certainty. There was an unexamined emotional momentum to writing *The Cookbook* that actually served at times to intoxicate the author.

Years later, I would attend an educational conference in California and listen to Stanford Professor Elliot Eisner, an educational thinker and practitioner that I greatly admire, argue that one of the most profound flaws in American education is its obsessive pursuit of certainty. The Holy Grail of American education is the idea that there is a simple, surefire formula to teach Johnny to read or Josephine to write; that objectivity is next to godliness, and that cause and effect must be the same for every child. We just need to find the formula. Bill Gates has thrown millions at this chimera. Time and time again we have seen the political establishment fall—hook, line, and sinker—for this panacea. The popular imagination hates the idea that genuine learning is complex, messy, and at times, chaotic.

I suspect that the writing of *The Cookbook* was, for me, a similar kind of fool's errand—a search for certainty.

In retrospect, I realize that I may also have subjected myself to other symptoms of Isolation-Think: self-censorship, stereotyping, and rationalization.

I practiced self-censorship when I only read magazines, newspapers, and books that served to confirm my existing political and social biases. I stereotyped people who didn't agree with my point of view, dismissing their arguments and ideas as either mindless or the products of vested self-interest. Clichés were not examined and were used in place of critical thought. In addition, I also engaged in a considerable degree of rationalization.

Looking back on the AC, the bibliography at the end of the book is a remarkable hodge-podge of works that occupy the entire spectrum from right-wing reactionary (*Minuteman Manual*) to libertarian (Robert Heinlein's T*he Moon is a Harsh Mistress*) to the extreme left (works by Che and Ho Chi Minh). Thrown into this heady brew are also books by Henry Miller and Antonin Artaud. With the exception of the Explorer Manual for Boy Scouts, they all seem to share a profound spirit of rebelliousness.

Reading sections of *The Cookbook* now, forty plus years after it was published, makes me cringe. My discomfort is not just with the ideas that are expressed, but most essentially that political violence can bring about constructive change, including the manner that they are presented. *The Cookbook* is an immature, pretentious, and simplistic work that often substitutes individualistic jingoism and anger for considered thought.

The actual research in preparing the book was not difficult. I had been collecting for some time broadsides and underground magazines that offered instructions for growing marijuana and brewing LSD in the kitchen. What I hadn't already collected was available in a dozen counterculture bookshops.

The instructions for bomb-making, sabotage, weapons, and self-defense came, for the most part, from US Army and Marine Corps publications that I found freely available at the New York Public Library. Others were reprinted by the publisher, US Combat Bookshelf, and were readily available by mail order. In addition, I used publications on guerrilla warfare by Che Guevara, General Võ Nguyên Giáp and Ho Chi Minh. The irony of using both US and North Vietnamese sources was not lost on me.

What struck me at the time was the incredible amount of serious thought that the US military had put into killing people. This was a real eye-opener. Reading field manual after field manual brought this fact home dramatically. What many of the critics found appalling when printed in *The Cookbook* had in fact been standard operating procedure in the US military and Special Forces manuals for decades. Apparently, the context made all the difference.

At the time I asked myself: Why shouldn't everyone have this information? Why shouldn't it be open source? The warmongers in the Pentagon and the Weathermen in Chicago already had this expertise. Why shouldn't it be available to everyone? Ann Larabee calls this the "Prometheus Premise."

After *The Cookbook* was published, some radical groups accused me of being motivated to make money from it—that I was exploiting the "revolution." I will not deny that the money was welcome. It most certainly was. Lyle Stuart provided an advance of two thousand dollars, more money than I had ever had together in one place before. However, my motivation was less for money than it was to become a published writer.

I wrote straight through Christmas and into the New Year. The domestic political situation remained tense. In mid-February a jury found the Chicago Seven not guilty of conspiracy (the most serious charge against them), but five were found guilty of crossing state lines in order to incite a riot. All of the convictions would later be overturned on appeal. The government commissioned report on the Chicago Democratic Convention violence, the so-called Walker Report, reviewed of over 20,000 pages of statements from 3,437 eyewitnesses and participants, 180 hours of film, and over 12,000 still photographs. The Walker Report coined the phrase "police riot" to describe the events of Chicago 1968, and concluded that the spontaneous acts of individual policemen were ultimately responsible for the violence on the streets and in the parks of Chicago.

During lunch on March 6th, the New York radio station WBAI broadcast a report of an explosion in the West Village. Shortly before noon, a large explosion had taken place in the sub-basement of a town house at 18 West 11th Street. At first, the police believed it was a gas main leak. However, as the reports filtered in throughout the day, it became clear that the house had served as a "bomb-making factory" for the Weather Underground and the explosion was the pre-mature detonation of a bomb. Three of the bomb-makers were killed instantly, two others escaped. The war was being brought home.

Each day I opened my mailbox with trepidation, wondering if my induction order would be waiting for me.

About a week later, a small article in the *New York Post* caught my attention. Apparently, a group of "gun-slinging hippie pacifists" had hijacked a merchant marine ship, the SS Columbia Eagle, that was carrying napalm, bombs, and arms to Vietnam. Since the gun-slinging pacifists were crewmembers, the hijacking was declared a mutiny—the first in the US Merchant Marine in 150 years.

You don't need a degree in logic to appreciate that genuine pacifists rarely pack guns. The article piqued my interest.

According to the available sources, Clyde McKay, a twenty-six-year-old fireman, and his twenty-one-year-old buddy, Alvin Glatkowski, had pulled pistols on Captain Swann and had informed him that they had planted a bomb on the ship. Given their cargo of ammunition and napalm, Captain Swann wisely complied with the mutineers' orders that he redirect the ship to Cambodia. McKay and Glatkowski ordered most of the crew into the lifeboats. Then, with a skeleton crew, the SS Columbia-Eagle was redirected to an anchorage about fifteen miles off the Cambodian port of Sihanoukville. After a brief, but tense, impasse with the US military, the two men turned the ship and its cargo over to Prince Sihanouk's government, declared themselves anti-war revolutionaries, and were granted political asylum in Cambodia.

My curiosity was further aroused when two days later, Prince Sihanouk, the Cambodian head of state, was ousted in a right-wing, pro-US coup that placed Lon Nol, the then prime minister, as head of government. Sihanouk, who was in Paris at the time of his ouster, soon became vocal about the connection he saw between the hijacking of the munitions ship and the coup. The CIA, he claimed, had orchestrated the mutiny of the SS Columbia-

Eagle in order to bring weapons to the coup plotters. The timing and anti-North Vietnamese stance of the coup leaders made CIA involvement likely.

Although CIA involvement in the coup that removed Prince Sihanouk has long been suggested (within a month of the coup President Nixon would order the land invasion of Cambodia by US forces), it has never been proved. Henry Kissinger, at the time National Security Advisor to Nixon, claimed to be completely surprised by Sihanouk's overthrow. However, it is doubtful that anything much ever surprised this cunning proponent of *Realpolitik.*

The coup was bad news for Mckay and Glatkowski, who were promptly arrested and thrown into prison. Glatkowski was extradited to the United States and tried for mutiny. He served a prison sentence. McKay escaped from the custody of the Cambodian government together with a US solider deserter, Larry Humphrey. Their self-professed objective was to disappear into the jungle and join the Khmer Rouge. A number of years later, the remains of a man thought to be McKay were brought home to his family. They were found in a shallow grave—the trademark of Khmer Rouge executions.

I finished writing *The Cookbook* at the end of March about the same time that Celia moved into the 10th Street apartment. It was the era before personal computers and I had used several reams of paper and scores of sheets of carbon paper. I then prepared an outline of the book and a query letter that I sent out to almost forty publishers. I don't remember receiving a single form letter ("Dear Author") in response. Perhaps a few publishers didn't respond, but most did with personal letters—some were mercifully brief. An editor at Dutton wrote: "No thanks, we'd be sued blue." Some were almost humorously understated; Viking wrote that the manuscript "doesn't quite match what we are looking for at this time." I received thirty-four rejection letters, which I pinned up on the wall of the 10th Street apartment.

And then Lyle Stuart's even briefer response arrived: "Let's see the manuscript. . . ."

Lyle was not your average New York publisher. His friends saw him as a brilliant marketer of books, a good, warm and generous family man, and an intrepid fighter for social justice. His detractors saw him as having rampaging affairs, Swiss bank accounts, a compulsive gambling habit, very dubious communist connections, and chronically poor taste in publishing. The truth probably lies somewhere in between.

Born Lionel Simon, he was the son of a secretary and a shoemaker. When Lionel was six, his father committed suicide. At twelve he got himself a job as a fur scrubber and at seventeen a song plugger. Soon thereafter, Lionel dropped out of James Madison High School in Brooklyn and joined the Merchant Marine. He would later change his name to Lyle Stuart because he was tired of the shipboard anti-semiticism. Specifically, he was fed up with being called the "ship's Jew."

After the war, Stuart went to work as a Hearst reporter in Columbus, Ohio. Over the next decade, he worked as a reporter for *Variety;* he produced a Chinese disc jockey show and wrote a couple of novels. As a reporter in the 1950's, Stuart found that some of his articles were being censored, so he started a magazine called *Expose* (later changed to *The Independent*). He collected articles and stories that other magazines and newspapers refused to publish because they were worried about the negative influence on advertising. Contributors included John Steinbeck, Upton Sinclair, and Norman Mailer.

At about this same time, Lyle was a regular contributor to Walter Winchell's syndicated column. In the 1940's and 50's, Winchell was arguably the single most powerful columnist in America. Lyle became incensed when Winchell had used a tasteless racial joke directed at Josephine Baker. An immensely popular African American singer, dancer, and actress, Baker would take on French citizenship. During World War II, she served as an allied spy and heroine of the French Resistance receiving both the *Croix de Guerre* and *Médaille de la Résistance*. She was also made a Chevalier d'honneur by General Charles de Gaulle. In the 1950's and 60's, Baker returned to the United States and became a well-known civil rights activist.

Stuart was outraged at Winchell's treatment of Josephine Baker and devoted an entire issue of Expose to muckracking about Winchell's private life. War between Winchell and Stuart was declared and the public exchanges grew more and more furious, until Stuart published a collection of pieces in book form entitled T*he Private Life of Walter Winchell*. Winchell retaliated and finally Stuart sued for libel. He won $8,000 in damages from Winchell, which he used to start the Lyle Stuart, Inc. publishing company.

Lyle not only didn't shy away from controversy; he sought it out. Paul Krassner, the editor of *The Realist*, wrote: "When I originally met Lyle Stuart in 1953, he had published an article in *The Independent* about how the Anti-Defamation League was secretly subsidizing anti-semitic publications and then using them to scare contributions out of wealthy Jews."

Lyle was an admirer of the Cuban revolution and the American publisher of Castro's *History Will Absolve Me*. Later, after *The Cookbook* was published, Lyle and I appeared on a late night WOR radio talk show together. Just before we went on the air, Lyle opened his sports jacket and showed me that he was wearing a shoulder holster with a pistol. He related that following the American publication of Castro's book, he had been a guest on a similar radio talk show. On his way out of the studio, he had been set upon by Cuban exiles and badly beaten. Needless to say, this did little to ease my nerves.

Lyle probably published the most controversial books of his era. These included a number that focused on sexually graphic material. *Naked Came the Stranger*, an X-rated memoir supposedly written by a demure Long Island housewife, became an overnight sensation. It was actually authored by twenty-five Newsday journalists in an attempt to show that the American reading public would buy anything. The book continued on the bestseller list months and months after it had been exposed as a hoax. Lyle also published *The Sensuous Woman* and *The Sensuous Man*. In an interview, Lyle would comment: "I did sex books for the same reason I did books about Cuba. Sex was controversial and controversy is what excites me."

Later, Lyle would say, "You can best describe me as a First Amendment fanatic because this is something I very deeply believe in. The strength of this nation is its First Amendment, its freedom to express all kinds of ideas . . . (about which) the public has to make their own determination."

I have no doubt that Lyle did believe passionately in the First Amendment. However, I also have a hunch that he was an adrenaline junkie and he loved the thrill of controversy, conflict, and confrontation. It was Lyle's proclivity for thrill seeking that kept him seeking out more and more controversial titles to publish. He printed exposés of the CIA, an unauthorized biography of J. Edgar Hoover, a book that suggested that the Nazi Martin Bormann was alive and well in Germany, an exposé of Jackie Kennedy, as well as The Turner Diaries, the right-wing novel of white supremacy that allegedly inspired Timothy McVeigh to carry out the Oklahoma City bombing.

It was certainly thrill seeking that made Lyle a regular at the casinos in Las Vegas. He was recognized in gambling circles as an expert at baccarat and craps, having authored several books on the games and earning himself a widespread reputation as a successful high roller. Brad Darrach, writer from *Life Magazine* who wrote a feature article on Lyle, accompanied him to Las Vegas for a gambling spree. About twenty minutes into playing craps, Darrach reported: "Stuart started to glow like a filament charged with a current. He was going to have a streak. The pit boss appeared quickly from nowhere. 'A Lyle Stuart streak,' he told me later, 'is one of the spectacles of gambling. In five minutes, counting the side bets, he can take the house for a hundred grand.' Stuart can't explain how it happens. All he knows is that for four or five minutes he knows exactly what the dice or cards are going to do." (p.68)

Lyle told me that in ten consecutive visits to Las Vegas he had won more than $150,000. He was also a regular in Atlantic City. He once entered two baccarat tournaments, winning first place at both Balley's Grand and the Taj Mahal for a total of $245,000.

I first met Lyle early in 1970, less than a year after his wife of twenty-three years, Mary Louise, had died of cancer. There was an aura of depression and apathy about him. An employee at the publishing house told me that he had been devoted to Mary Louise and her death had devastated him. They had spent a great deal of time together in Jamaica and Lyle was building an orphanage and school on the island in her memory. Brad Darrach also reports on Lyle's dark side. The morning after his huge winning streak in Vegas, Lyle confided to him: "I feel a thousand years old—I'm bored with so much—even with money. I could bet everything I have on one card and lose and not turn a hair. The same in business. I love the game, the battle of wits, the winning. But not what I've won."

About a month after sending Lyle the manuscript of *The Cookbook*, I received an invitation to meet with him in his office. I'm not sure what I expected a New York publisher's office to look like, but Stuart's didn't resemble anything close to what I imagined. His office was at 225 Lafayette Street near Union Square. You entered a dark hallway that led into an even darker warehouse and walked to a freight elevator. Stuart's office was on the third or fourth floor of this dingy loft. His desk was cluttered with books, pamphlets, and unopened mail. The wall behind was plastered news clippings and photographs, the largest of which was of his late wife. The poster on the back of the door was of Che.

After a brief conversation, Lyle offered a contract for the book. I accepted. It was the first of five or six face-to-face meetings we would have.

I remember returning to the 10th Street apartment and finding Celia sitting in the kitchen. Excitedly, I told her the good news. Her facial expression didn't change. She showed no reaction. It was as if her features were frozen.

"What's wrong?" I asked.

She handed me an envelope. Even before I opened it, I knew what it was. The return address was my Selective Service Center. The much dreaded induction order had arrived.

It was time for Bill to fish or cut bait.

CHAPTER 8
Time for Transition

I HAVE NEVER BEEN GOOD at opening things—parcels, Christmas presents, cans of soup, packets of nuts, CD's, or letters from government offices. In later years, three different secretaries would virtually forbid me from opening my own mail as more often than not I would end up shredding the contents.

The contents of the letter from my draft board did survive; the envelope did not.

The Selective Service had an established system for evaluating the status of registrants for military service. Classification 1-A meant the registrant was available for unrestricted military service. 1-A-0 was conscientious objector status and 2-S were student deferments.

I recall staring speechless at my new draft card. My classification was 4-F. After several moments of cognitive digestion, I let out a whoop of triumph. The 4-F status meant the registrant (me) was not acceptable for military service. I had been found by a Military Entrance Processing Board (MEPS) to be not qualified for any military service under the established physical, mental, or moral standards.

I never asked which standards I had failed to meet. That would have been pushing the damaged envelope too far. It could be that my trick shoulder was a sufficient disability. It did slip out of joint fairly regularly. However, I like to think that the MEPS determined that either I wasn't moral enough to be entrusted to go on search and destroy missions, or that I wasn't sane enough to participate in the meaningless carnage. I still retain my draft card in my wallet—a certificate of insanity issued by a lunatic state.

As Krishnamurti wrote: "It is no measure of health to be well-adjusted to a sick society."

Celia and I splurged and went to Little Italy for a celebration dinner. I say we splurged because I hadn't been working for three months and we had been living frugally on Celia's single salary. But now the status quo had shifted. I had an advance from Lyle Stuart and I didn't have the US Army's Sword of Damocles hanging over my head. Accordingly, I turned my attention to the future.

The first thing I did was ask for re-employment at Bookmasters. To my delight, I was immediately appointed the manager of the newly-opened book and record store on 8th Street and University Place in the West Village.

Celia and I spent the Easter Sunday with my parents in White Plains. For the previous three years, I had promoted a self-estrangement from my dad and mom. I'm not at all sure why. My parents had been consistently loving and supportive, although not always agreeing with or condoning my behavior. I know I had caused them considerable grief and probably more than a dozen sleepless nights. My dad was an open-minded, independent thinker who was very much opposed to the war in Vietnam, and sympathetic to the

New Left and counterculture movement. At his funeral in 1986, the officiating priest, Dick Barnet, called my father: "A man who lived in a world of rich ideas, but who never let an idea diminish another person." I wish I had more fully appreciated my father earlier than I did.

My dad and I should have had a lot in common, so I'm unsure why I felt it necessary to distance myself from him.

So it may have been with some surprise that my mom took my phone call and listened to my suggestion that Celia and I visit on Easter Sunday.

Mom cooked a traditional English Sunday lunch—a leg of lamb surrounded by roast potatoes, green peas, and fresh mint sauce. It was a sunny spring day, so following lunch we decided to take the dog for a walk on Rye Beach. And now I will quote very briefly from my father's memoirs, *A Letter to My Grandchildren*:

"I well recall the spring Sunday in 1970 when Bill came out from New York for the day and suggested we go for a walk. We took the dog for a stroll on Rye Beach. 'Dad,' he said. 'I've got something to tell you. I've written a book and found a publisher. It will be out later this year. . . . Also, I've decided to get married and both Celia and I want to go to college.' I could only pause in my tracks to say, 'Bill, any one of those announcements would have been sufficient for one afternoon!'"

The stroll on Rye beach was a breakthrough of sorts. For me it was the beginning of a different kind of relationship with my father—one that would not vacillate between control and rebellion, but rather by shared interests and common concerns. I don't know how my father viewed that walk on the beach, but we would come to see a great deal more of each other in the years to come.

At the beginning of April, Steve Hancock reappeared in New York. He hadn't been in Idaho or Montana. He had ended up in Taos, New Mexico—where Eugenia may have been living. Steve made an appointment to meet with the owners of Bookmasters at a West Side tavern and they managed reconciliation. Steve promised to repay the money he owed and was re-hired as the manager of one of the stores. Steve moved back into the 10th Street apartment, but his stay was temporary. Within a couple of weeks he had met a young flower child, a Cat Stevens' groupie who called herself "Gypsy" and fell head over heels for her. Their raucous and rasping sexual antics kept Celia and me awake at night. Very soon thereafter, Steve and Gypsy were married at a civil ceremony and Steve rented a large storefront apartment on 10th Street, but closer to Tompkins Square Park. He completely refurbished the interior, had two sleeping lofts built, and installed an antique dentist chair as the central feature of the living room. The marriage lasted less than a month and my last memory of the storefront apartment was Steve nailing his cut-up credit cards to a ceiling beam—they made a fairly large display.

T.S. Eliot begins his poem "The Waste Land" with the line "April is the cruellest month." As an undergraduate student of literature I learned that this might be an allusion to the opening line of Chaucer's *The Canterbury Tales;* heralding the beginning of Western poetry, "The Waste Land" the end. Many years later, living in the rural French countryside, I would come to understand the line more viscerally. In April, the countryside is awash with spring flowers, but the winter store of food is finished and the new harvest is still months away. New life blossoms provocatively with a casual, nonchalance that mocks the still gnawing winter hunger.

However, in 1970 I doubt that anyone appreciated the cruelty of April as deeply as the people of Cambodia.

On the evening of April 25, 1970, President Richard Nixon dined with his friends Bebe Rebozo, (a shadowy character who was investigated a number of times for money laundering and campaign contribution misappropriation and would become a lead player in the Watergate Investigation) and Henry Kissinger. After dinner, the three of them watched Nixon's favorite movie, George C. Scott's rendition of *Patton.* Nixon had already seen the film five times. Kissinger later commented that "when he [Nixon] was pressed to the wall, a romantic streak surfaced and he would see himself as a beleaguered military commander in the tradition of Patton."

The following evening, Nixon decided that he would "go for broke" and gave his authorization for the land invasion of Cambodia.

Not everyone in Nixon's inner circle was in favor of this extension of the Vietnam war. Secretary of State William Rogers and Secretary of Defense Melvin Laird both warned Nixon that the invasion of Cambodia would ferment further domestic political unrest. And it did. On May 4th, the unrest escalated into violence when the Ohio National Guardsmen shot and killed four unarmed students at Kent State University (two who weren't even protestors) and wounded nine others. Two days later, police wounded four more unarmed demonstrators of the University of Buffalo. On May 8th, a hundred thousand protestors descended on Washington DC and another hundred and fifty thousand gathered in San Francisco. Nationwide, over twenty-five ROTC centers went up in flames or were bombed, while twenty-six schools saw violent clashes between students and police. National Guard units were mobilized on twenty-one campuses in sixteen states. Student strikes spread nationwide, involving more than four million students and over four hundred and fifty universities, colleges, and schools.

Paradoxically, during the time when many, perhaps even most, American students were trying to shut down universities, I was applying to get in.

Celia and I were married in a private ceremony at an Anglican church in the Greenwich Village. Why did I decide at this point that marriage would be a good idea?

Looking back, marriage represented for me the start of a new and stable life. The previous few years had been chaotic and tumultuous—politically, socially, and emotionally. From day to day, I had not known whether I would be drafted, sent to Vietnam, or prison. Or whether I would need to escape to Canada or Sweden. Writing *The Cookbook* had also been an emotional experience. We were still trying to produce a play a month at the Inner Theater and this was also taking a toll on both my energy and bank account. Socially, life in the 10th Street apartment had been erratic and episodic. Prior to Celia, I had had several girlfriends, but the relationships were shallow, volatile, and ephemeral. While I had managed to stop gobbling Dexedrine, I had become a fairly regular smoker of marijuana and an occasional user of acid. Marriage, enrollment in a university, and a move away from the East Village all represented a reestablishment of order and stability in my life.

In many respects, my life has been an oscillating system that has moved me relentlessly back and forth between chaos and order. Until recently, I perceived those two alternatives as opposing forces, opposites that were at war with each other. Your life was either orderly or chaotic. I now question that simple dialectic. Now I think of order and chaos as rambunctious friends that tease each other into a sense of meaningfulness that neither could achieve on its own.

In June, Celia and I visited several New England colleges. We took campus tours, met with professors, and were interviewed by admission's directors. After some discussion, we decided to enroll at Windham College in Putney, Vermont. I used the advance from Lyle Stuart to pay some of the first semester's tuition and with what Celia and I had managed to save, we rented a house some five or six miles outside of the town. The house was actually a small, single-story, tar-paper-and-pine board shack without heating (other than a potbellied stove) or any form of insulation. If we had dumped the chassis of the 1930's Buick and some rusting farm equipment in front of it, it could have served brilliantly as the set for *Tobacco Road*.

I was still in the ever-present present and didn't anticipate how the house would be during a Vermont winter.

But it was still summer and there was an enormous sense of novelty in moving to the countryside. I bought a fishing rod and an ordinance survey map of Southern Vermont. I got a copy of the latest Burpee Seed Catalogue at the General Store and looked forward to putting it in a vegetable garden. I spent hours in the fields adjacent to the Connecticut River with Euell Gibbon's marvelous book *Stalking the Wild Asparagu*s in hand-searching for edible plants, roots, and mushrooms.

In many respects, this was the calm before the storm.

Classes at Windham College started in early September and I registered for six classes, one more than the normal compliment of five. I was paying my own way and wanted to make the most of the experience.

I came to the college with a chip on my shoulder. I had not had a good experience in the formal high school setting, and while I wanted the education that a university could provide, I was not prepared to accept stupid rules and regulations. I was twenty-one years old and had been working and supporting myself for the past five years. I was married and living off-campus. I was also paying my own tuition.

In fairness, I need to add that my dad and mom had offered repeatedly to help pay for the college tuition. I refused the offer because I wanted to be financially self-sufficient and independent. My refusal hurt my parents, particularly my father.

The chip on my shoulder also reflected the belligerence and arrogance that can mask a profound sense of insecurity. School had never been easy for me and I had never been a particularly good student. I was especially concerned about how I might perform in mathematics, foreign language, and science. I told myself I had come to the college in order to become a writer. I would focus on literature, history, psychology, and philosophy. I told myself that math and foreign language courses didn't matter—and yet I knew they formed part of the graduation requirement.

My experience in high school had resulted in a sense of learned helplessness. I simply didn't believe I had the intelligence to master math or foreign languages. This sense of learned helplessness is very common and I suspect it is one of the primary causes of school failure. Professor Carol Dweck suggests that we can develop two kinds of mindsets: a fixed mindset and a growth mindset. A fixed mindset is when we attribute our success or failure to causes outside of our control: native intelligence, natural talent, luck, or task difficulty. The belief is that I am a finished product. When we attribute our failures to causes outside of our control, we develop fixed mindsets. We hear those fixed mindsets when students say "I'm just no good at math" or "I don't have an aptitude for languages" or "Physics is just too hard." When we attribute our success to causes outside of our control (native intelligence or natural talent) we run the risk of becoming fragile and risk-adverse learners. If I fail or falter at something I should be good at, my image of myself is damaged so I may try to avoid new and demanding challenges.

A "growth mindset," on the other hand, is when we attribute our success or failure to causes over which we have control (effort, using feedback, seeking external support, or persistence). When we develop growth mindsets, we see challenges not as obstacles, but as learning opportunities.

I definitely went into Windham College with a fixed mindset in so far as math and foreign languages were concerned, and I managed to avoid these courses for all four years.

I can trace my fixed mindset in foreign languages to a well-meaning French teacher I had in grade seven. In the White Plains Public School system the study of a second language was introduced in grade seven, and I was given a choice of French or Spanish. After some consultation with my mom and dad, I selected French. I struggled in the class. Correct pronunciation was very difficult; I couldn't seem to reproduce the sounds that I heard and match them to their respective spellings.

By the end of the school year, I had managed to scrape by with a "D." I was not displeased, the alternative was worse.

The teacher, a gentle and sympathetic woman, called me in for a private conference.

"Bill," she said. "I know that you don't find French easy and that you have really struggled this year. It may be that you just don't have an aptitude for learning languages. Some people don't. You might want to think about transferring to Spanish next year. It is more phonetic than French. You might find it easier."

Time bombs can be gift-wrapped.

I took her advice and transferred to Spanish. I struggled throughout the year and ended up with a "D" in Spanish and the belief that I just couldn't learn a second language. This was a fixed mindset par excellence.

Had I grown up in Belgium or the Netherlands, I doubt I would have developed such an attitude. Second language acquisition in those countries is thought of as a necessity. You get on with it and do it. I probably would have struggled and I might not have ever been a fluent or eloquent speaker, but I would have learned a second language.

Now, I have lived in France for a portion of each year for over twenty years and I am still struggling with my fixed mindset.

Many parents and teachers help to develop fixed mindsets in their children with the best of intentions—my French teacher certainly did. As parents and teachers, we need to be especially aware of the pernicious effect of praising a child's native intelligence or natural talents. Such praise doesn't serve to encourage or build healthy self-esteem. It does exactly the opposite. If we must praise something, we should laud effort and persistence.

I went into Windham College with fixed mindsets, but also with an enormous determination to succeed. The first six courses I registered for were all within the English department; two were writing courses and four were literature courses. I was dreadfully worried that I wouldn't be able to keep up with the reading. In two of the courses, we were reading a novel a week. I have always been a very slow reader. My comprehension and critical reading are pretty good, but it takes me a long time. I remember during that first semester carrying my reading assignments everywhere with me. Even when I was stopped in traffic at a red light, I would read a page or two in order to try to keep up with the rest of the class.

During the autumn of 1970 I didn't think very much about *The Cookbook,* nor did I tell very many people about its imminent publication. I did reflect gratefully on my decision to leave the East Village drug scene. This was brought poignantly home when, in September and October—less than a month apart—both Jimi Hendrix and Janis Joplin died of drug-related overdoses.

There was a strong counterculture presence at Windham as there was at many colleges back then. Left-wing radicals had forcibly closed the college following the invasion of Cambodia. They had chained and padlocked the doors. There were also several hippie-type communal farms in the area, and there had been tension between the so-called "free farmers" and the rednecks from town that culminated in locals driving their pick-up trucks into the commune's vegetable garden and destroying it.

I didn't give much thought to *The Cookbook* because I was, as usual, living in the present. For a time, I actually forgot that it was in preparation. I was consumed with schoolwork and had little time for anything else. I didn't follow current events and our tar-paper shack had neither a television nor a radio. I had no subscription to newspapers, but would occasionally read a copy of *Time* or *Newsweek* that someone had left lying around in the Student Union. In some respects, the fall of 1970 represented a welcome sense of isolation. Having said that, I was starting to develop personal relationships with some of the professors. I took a freshman writing course with Daniel Schneider and found his critiques of my writing very useful. I appreciated the time he took to generate critical feedback. I also took a seminar on Mark Twain with Bruce Dobler, who, at the time, was also an aspiring writer. Later, I would take courses with John Irving who would become the bestselling author of *The World According to Garp* and *Cider House Rules*.

By November, I could honestly say that I was enjoying the Windham College experience. The professors were, for the most part, interested in and enthusiastic about their subjects, and responded extremely well to students who were eager to learn. My social life was nonexistent, but this was fine. I hadn't enrolled in college to make friends. And so, Celia and I would remain in rustic isolation in our increasingly frigid shack.

All this would come to an end in early January when a package arrived from Lyle Stuart. It contained advance copies of the *AC*.

In mid-January, I made an appointment to speak with the President of Windham College, Eugene Winslow. President Winslow wasn't everyone's cup of tea. It is fair to say that he was disliked and even despised by many of the faculty. He did, however, manage to keep the college open during difficult financial times— something his successor failed to do.

I actually liked Gene Winslow. I found him to be a frank, hard-nosed individual with a keen intelligence and, on occasion, a delightfully cynical sense of humor. He reminded me of an urbane *Mafioso* godfather.

I went to see President Winslow in early January 1971 because I guessed that it was better to try to take the bull by the horns. The book had been released the week before and there had already been a flurry of news reports that had included the fact that the author was a freshman at Windham College.

I sat opposite President Winslow across a large and imposing mahogany desk. I explained that I had written a controversial book that had just been released.

Winslow indicated that he had read the news reports. I went directly to the point of my visit.

"I have worked for five years in order to save up enough money to pay my own college tuition," I said. "I have not yet paid the second semester's tuition fee for my wife and I. If I am going to be expelled, I want to know now before I pay the fees."

I spoke with more resolution than I actually felt. I wanted to continue at Windham and had no idea how the college president would respond.

"I'm not bothered by your book," Winslow responded. "Pay your fees. You are welcome to continue here at the college."

I nodded and thanked him for his time.

"But there are people who are bothered by your book," he continued. "The FBI has contacted the college. They have spoken to some of your professors and they want to know if the college bookstore will carry your book."

I suppose I should have assumed that there would be an FBI investigation, but I hadn't and the news caught me somewhat by surprise.

Several years later, Windham County Sherriff Billy Graham would stop by my house on River Road and tell me that he had just come back from an FBI Conference in which they used the *AC* in a police workshop. He then asked, a little sheepishly, if I would sign his copy. It was one of the very few copies that I did sign.

As I rose to leave President Winslow's office, he reached out and picked up a newspaper from his desk.

"Take a look at this," he said, pushing the paper across the desk.

I assumed I was going to read another article about *The Cookbook*. Instead, the glaring two-inch headline read: THE MYTH OF THE VAGINAL ORGASM.

I looked up at Winslow in confusion.

"This is the most recent issue of the college's student newspaper," he announced. "Hot off the press. As a writer, what is your opinion?"

"I assume," I said, gesturing to the headlines, "that it is a local interest story."

Winslow collapsed into laughter. I waited him out.

"It doesn't do the image of the college much good," he remarked.

Neither, I thought, did *The Cookbook*. But I remained silent.

"You pay your own tuition fees and you need a scholarship," Winslow announced. "I run a college and I need a student newspaper I can be proud of. I want to be able to send copies to my mother. . . ."

Now here was a surprise: President Eugene Winslow had a mother!

"Think about it. With your background as a writer, you wouldn't find the editing of the paper that onerous. Let me know what you think."

And I thought—no one would suspect that the author of *The Anarchist Cookbook* was in the pay of the College President!

The debate about whether Lyle Stuart was a charlatan or maverick goes on even after his death, but no one will argue that he was not a genius promoter of the books he published. He managed to get the wire services—AP and UPI to carry the publication story. Between January 14th and March 5th, 1970, I would estimate that over a hundred newspapers in the United States and overseas carried stories on the publication of *The Anarchist Cookbook*. Short pieces popped up in newspapers as diverse as the *Arkansas Gazette, Cleveland Plain Dealer, Columbus Citizen*, and L*os Angeles Time*s. *Saturday Review* produced a damning review and *Newsweek* published a vignette on the author. Overseas there were articles in *Der Spiegal* and London's *Daily Telegraph*. A number of the articles were clipped and sent with letters of complaint to J. Edgar Hoover at the headquarters of the FBI in Washington DC.

Forty years later, the FBI released their files on *The Cookbook*. Let's sample a few.

On January 14th, Mrs. Charlotte Carson wrote to J. Edgar Hoover, enclosing a clipping from *The Miami Herald*. After complimenting the FBI director on his recent good health— which she had read about in the newspaper—she asked if the AC should be allowed on the market. George Kellog from Glendale, California was more direct and passionate in his letter to the FBI Director: "Mr. Hoover, this is not a cookbook! It's a bomber's book. It describes in detail how to make every kind of bomb from all kinds of materials available to anyone. I noted in *The New York Times* the US had something like 3,500 bombings. If this book gets wide distribution, your department had better get a bigger adding machine. . . ."

Mrs. Richard Madden of New York City won the prize for the best typographical error. She wrote to Mr. Hoover: "It's all communist oriented, but in the hands of dope fiends and revolutionaries (*The Cookbook*) can keep us in constant error (sic)."

It wasn't just private citizens that were writing to J. Edgar Hoover. There was a flurry of correspondence, all of which was marked "urgent," between senior members of the White House, the Department of Justice, and the FBI. In late January, Representative George Mahon (Democrat from the 19th district in Texas) wrote to the FBI Director asking the bureau to launch an investigation, and, on February 5th, John N. Dean III, White House Counsel and lawyer to President Nixon, requested a copy from J. Edgar Hoover. The conclusion of all these letters, memos, and telex messages was somewhat hyperbolic: "This is a manual for revolutionary extremists" and "the effects on a civilized society could be devastating."

There are several assumptions in the last phrase that warrant questioning. First, that the United States, a country that was waging a brutal war of aggression in South East Asia, was in fact a civilized society. And second, that individuals would be less responsible with the information contained in the book than the government. These remain real questions for me.

The prize for the most terse letter to J. Edgar Hoover goes to Joseph Singleton of Titusville, Florida who simply scrawled in the margin of newspaper clipping the words: "Danger! What are you doing about this?"

A good question: What was the FBI doing about the publication of *The Cookbook*?

From a review of the hundred and sixty odd pages of the confidential files that were released in February 2011 under the Freedom of Information Act, the FBI certainly was doing a lot of memo writing. Initially, the focus was on the publisher, Lyle Stuart, and an odd character named Peter Bergman who wrote the forward.

I need to make a brief admission: I have never been able to read Peter Bergman's forward to *The Cookbook.* I've tried several times. But the prose is unbelievably turgid and the content convoluted. In the end, I just gave up trying to make sense out of it.

At the start of the FBI investigation, there was very little attention paid to the author. This was because the memo writers had concluded that either William Powell didn't exist or he wasn't the real author of *The Cookbook.* A memorandum to J. Edgar Hoover includes the sentence: "Considering that the author, William R. Powell, is but twenty one years old, it appears doubtful that he could have had the extensive experiences to which he refers in his book. . . . His youth and lack of formal education raise questions and doubts. Did William R. Powell write this book?" The memorandum goes on to speculate that *The Cookbook* could have been authored by a collection of professional writers in the same way Lyle Stuart's bestselling hoax *Naked Came the Stranger* was.

It is not surprising that the FBI focused their attention on Lyle Stuart and Peter Bergman. Both already had FBI files as long as your arm. Lyle was known to have published Castro's *History Will Absolve Me* and to have been involved in the "Fair Play For Cuba" (FPFC) Committee. The FBI files suggest that Lyle was a financial contributor to the FPFC and may have even served at an officer holder. The files describe him as a "subversive."

Peter Bergman was a complex character, but the notes contained in the FBI files make it easy to see how he might fit near perfectly the 1950's stereotype of the communist revolutionary lurking fiendishly under your bed.

I met Peter only once and that was at a press conference at the Hotel Americana that Lyle had organized soon after *The Cookbook* was released. Lyle took me off to the side of the room and introduced me to Peter, a short little Eastern European-looking man, dressed in an ill-fitting and rumpled suit. He looked a little like a cross between Orson Welles playing Harry Lyme in *The Third Man* and Peter Lorre. What I recall most vividly about Peter were his eyes. They darted about the conference room as though on the look out for predators. Given Peter's background as gleaned from the FBI files, he had every right and reason to be paranoid.

Peter Bergman was born to a Jewish family in 1908 in Przeworsk, Austria, which later became Polish territory. He attended Berlin University and studied economics. In the 1930's, Peter became involved in anti-Nazi activities, trade union underground groups, and communist councils.

Peter's political activity during the first years of World War II led to his arrest by the Gestapo on the charges of espionage and treason. He spent some time in Nazi detention before he was ultimately deported from Germany to Czechoslovakia. The FBI files then describe the time that Peter spent wandering in Poland, Norway, France, Sweden, and Switzerland before arriving in California via Russia and Japan. In mid-April 1941, Peter's ship docked in San Pedro, California and he sought asylum as a Jewish refugee. His application form lists his nationality as "stateless."

The FBI launched two Internal Security Investigations focusing on Peter, one in 1943 and one in 1951. Peter was just the caricature communist that Senator Joe McCarthy was so desperately searching for. The files include the following sentences: "Bergman is a self-declared orthodox Marxist who . . . believes in revolution, if necessary, to carry out plans for reforming government. . . . Bergman came to the US in April 1941 stateless. . . . He is contemptuous of the US, refused to fight in the army and has never obtained citizenship."

Had I known about his background before meeting Peter, I would certainly have made more of an effort to get to know him. He unquestionably had some amazing stories to tell.

Lyle Stuart was a brilliant promoter of the books he published. Once, after publishing a novel that featured a chimpanzee, he sent out the author wearing a chimp suit with copies of the book in hand in a Rolls-Royce Silver Cloud, to visit major New York bookstores. Lyle clearly understood that the publication of *The Cookbook* had touched a media nerve and he was ready to exploit it to the maximum. He phoned me repeatedly in Vermont asking me to come to New York for a press conference and some media interviews.

Against my better judgment, I agreed. I had a premonition that I would be a disaster at book promotion—and I have rarely predicted anything so accurately.

There are several reasons why I was so bad at marketing *The Cookbook*. First of all, I didn't have a clue what I was doing. I didn't know what was expected of me; nor what questions I might face from reporters. I simply walked blithely into a media circus.

Secondly, and perhaps most significantly, I had begun to have niggling doubts about the contents of the book. I was still furious with the US Government for waging an unnecessary and brutal war of aggression in South East Asia, and I still fervently believed that the primary moral decision-maker must be the individual—not some anonymous collective that was able to jettison responsibility with a flick of the bureaucratic wrist. However, I was also beginning to question how the advocacy of violence fit with these two ideas. It was a disturbing question that I simply hadn't addressed before. Was violence necessary to reform an out-of-control government?

Is "out of control" a hyperbole to describe the US Government in 1971? The polls at the time indicated that 60 percent of the US population was opposed to the war in Vietnam, and yet President Nixon, in his own words, stated that he would not be swayed by public opinion. Was this the government that Lincoln envisioned—of the people, by the people, for the people? I didn't think so and I don't think so now.

But this begs the question: Was violence a desirable or effective means to constructive political change? I didn't address this question head-on at the time, but it would become an increasing concern over the years that followed the publication of *The Cookbook.*

At the time, I perceived the die to be cast; the book was published and distributed. This wasn't the time to rethink its major premises. I assumed that during my foray into book promotion, I would be expected to explain its contents and justify its existence.

Ultimately, I used the default position of dishonest politicians around the world: I did not address the question, I simply attacked the opposition—American aggression in Indochina.

I drove to New York City for three nightmarish days of being an overnight celebrity.

Following three or four truly uninspired interviews with magazines and newspapers, I drove with Lyle Stuart and his secretary, Carole Livingston to the Hotel Americana where Lyle had organized a press conference. It was here that I met Peter Bergman, the author of *The Cookbook's* unintelligible Foreword. After I had fumbled and stumbled through a few questions, someone in the back of the room hurled a smoke bomb into the midst of the reporters. It spluttered and sparked and smoked. Not knowing that it was harmless, nor what was to follow; I dove behind the lectern where I found myself huddled with Peter Bergman, a collection of journalists and cameramen, and, I assume, at least a couple of undercover FBI agents. It was a fabulous photo op. When the smoke cleared—literally—I became aware that the only people in the room who had remained impassive in the face of the attack were Lyle Stuart and Carole Livingston. If it had only been Lyle, I would have attributed his reaction to nerves of steel—which he most certainly had. However, the nonchalant duet made me suspicious.

Afterwards, they claimed to know nothing about the incident and even suggested that the smoke bomb was probably thrown by rival anarchists protesting the book's "exploitation of the revolution." This was the explanation that *The Village Voice* published the following week. However, given Lyle's proclivity for publicity stunts, I have always suspected that he had organized the "attack."

The second attack was certainly not staged. The nadir of my brief book tour was an appearance with Lyle on a late night radio WOR talk show. The host, whose name I have forgotten, had invited Lyle and myself and a third unnamed person. I should have realized that this was going to be a hostile encounter when the third man greeted us with a scowl. My nemesis was a rabid right-wing, John Birch Society fanatic. He immediately attributed *The Cookbook* to a Soviet/Cuban plot, and exploded into a verbal tirade that went on for almost twenty minutes. I was caught off guard and tongue-tied, and was merely a passive recipient of his abuse. The only moment that I came close to enjoying of the talk show was when Lyle interrupted him and observed that he was actually foaming at the mouth.

As dull as my performance was during my brief tenure as a pseudo-celebrity, I do have to acknowledge that the experience was seductive, exhilarating, and intoxicating. For a brief period of time, it seemed like the attention of the entire world was focused on me. Everyone knew my name and was hanging on my every word. This was a heady brew—far more potent than any drug I had ever experimented with. Fortunately, the temporary notoriety did not last and I soon crashed back to earth and found myself again a freshman at Windham College.

I didn't know it at the time, but the FBI wasn't the only organization that was researching the origins and authorship of *The Cookbook,* and that very soon Lyle and I would be back together—this time in front of a federal court in Denver, Colorado.

CHAPTER 9
Green Mountain Years

I HAD COME TO COLLEGE WITH AN appalling attitude; one that took me years to struggle out of. I was determined to take away from Windham College the very best education possible. I was paying the tuition out of my own pocket and, even then, I recognized that you got out of classes exactly what you put in. I was prepared to put in superhuman effort and I was determined to show everyone, including myself, that I could be a success. I was on academic alpha male trajectory—hyper-sensitive to even the faintest condescension, I would rather fight than eat.

In January, my parents phoned to congratulate me. They had just received my first semester report card. I had achieved straight A's. I had a curious response to their praise. On the one hand, I was secretly pleased that my dad and mom knew that I was doing well. I wanted them to be proud of me, but I was also furious with the college for sending them a copy of my report card. I was twenty-one years old and was paying my tuition fees myself. How dare they send a confidential report card to a third party! I wanted both my parents' approval and my independence from them.

I wrote a letter of complaint to the Dean of Students and received no response. I then wrote to the President of the College, Eugene Winslow, threatening legal action against the Dean of Students—who I thought was a jerk. I did receive a response from President Winslow—a letter of apology stating that in the future I would be the sole recipient of my report card.

In my second year at Windham, I took a course in the modern short story from a young and rather insecure assistant professor. One day he surprised us by handing out an unannounced quiz. I was horror-struck since it was perhaps the only time in my four years at Windham that I had forgotten to read the assignment. I scanned the quiz quickly and announced that it was a stupid exercise of rote memory that required no critical and creative thinking. As such, the quiz was a waste of time and disrespectful to student intelligence. To my surprise and immense relief, the young assistant professor asked us ignore the test. He never gave another surprise quiz again. I have no idea the damage I may have done to the young man's self-confidence, but my persona was intact.

Where did the chip on my shoulder come from?

I'm not entirely sure, because most of my professors were knowledgeable, enthusiastic, and, for the most part, respectful towards me. I actually liked most of them.

I suspect my hostility was borne of insecurity—a nagging sense of limited self-worth that might have been a product of my high school years.

My concern at the time was almost exclusively with myself. I was extremely task-oriented and driven by achievement motivation.

I defined myself in terms of what I achieved. An unfinished project or paper was like an open wound. I worked fourteen hours a day, reading philosophy and long Russian novels while on the graveyard shift pumping gasoline at the Exxon station, or scribbling notes for a term paper outline between drawing mugs of draft beer at the Carriage House Tavern. Accomplishment was a demanding and fearsome deity, leaving little time for anything else—including relationships. I was an obsessive list maker; sometimes adding items to my to-do list solely for the pleasure of crossing them out. But achievement is illusory. Once accomplishment is in your hands, it disappears like the flame of a candle in a shaft of brilliant sunlight.

I didn't perceive others to be as complex as I was. During a philosophy course, I learned that the perception of oneself as the only real person in the world came from Ancient Greece and was called Solipsism. I did not appreciate at the time what a nightmare it was and how difficult it would be to mount an escape attempt from the cell of self. And I had little consciousness of the collateral damage there would be along the way.

Toward the end of my freshman year, I agreed to take on the editorship of the student newspaper, *The Windham Free Press.* Probably not coincidentally, about two weeks later I received a letter stating that I had been awarded a work-study scholarship in the college's public relations department. At the start of my second year, I actually reported for work in the public relations office only to be told by the director, Bruce Dobler, that my job was to bring out a student newspaper that President Eugene Winslow could send to his mother.

Bruce, a rotund and fiercely bearded man who looked like a cross between Bacchus and a garden dwarf, was an aspiring novelist who was also teaching literature courses at the college. Bruce and I rapidly became friends, and I learned a great deal about journalism from him and his wife Patsy.

However, I wasn't about to sell my entire soul for a work-study scholarship, so I set about making *The Windham Free Press* as controversial as I could make it without unduly raising the blood pressure of Eugene Winslow's ninety-year-old mother.

I invited the newly elected student government president to write 300 to 500 hundred words on what he hoped to achieve in his first hundred days. When he failed to respond, I ran a blank column on the front page, with an editorial note hoping that the new student government president would be more responsive to his constituents than he had been to the student newspaper. He wasn't.

Also in the first issue, I launched a "consumer protection" campaign. In 1965 Ralph Nader had published *Unsafe at Any Speed: The Designed-In Dangers of the American Automobile* and this had opened a new chapter in consumer protection watchdog agencies. Why shouldn't, I asked in a newspaper editorial, colleges such as Windham be subject to the same scrutiny? At the time, I don't think anyone saw where this was headed.

For the second issue, I devised a survey that was distributed to students asking them to evaluate their professors and add comments—good, bad, or indifferent. The anonymous survey made a significant stir in the small college community, but the second edition of the paper that published the survey results created a minor tsunami of protest letters to the editor.

It may not have been the height of responsible journalism, but it certainly boosted circulation.

President Eugene Winslow even mailed a copy to his aged mother.

I must have been an enigma to my classmates. First, I was older than most, married, and living off-campus. Second, I had a reputation via *The Cookbook* for being a political radical, but demonstrations and protests against Washington and the War in Vietnam were now secondary to my studies. I did continue to attend protest demonstrations, but I could hardly be thought of as a radical leader. To the contrary, I was an extremely hardworking, straight-A student—what in other circles might have been referred to as a "nerd." And yet I was editing the student newspaper that ran articles that deliberately angered just about everyone, except Eugene Winslow.

In my second year at Windham College, my younger brother Chris also enrolled as a student. We saw each other fairly frequently. In retrospect, I'm not sure Windham was a good choice for Chris. Instead of being under my wing, he found himself in my shadow—not a good place to be.

It was at about this time that I started work on a historical novel that would eventually (eight years later) be published under the title *The First Casualty*. During my time at Windham, I actually took time to travel to what was then called Yugoslavia and do research on the famous assassination.

I wrote *The First Casualty* because I wanted to write fiction and tell what I believed was a fascinating story with huge historic implications. However, the writing was also motivated by a need to try to address the nagging question that *The Cookbook* had raised: At what point is it morally acceptable to use violence as a means to achieve political change?

It is a question that cuts across cultural, moral, political, and religious boundaries, and yet is rarely addressed directly— except in retrospect. We like to think that Lt. Colonel Claus von Stauffenberg was morally justified in his attempt to assassinate Adolph Hitler, but some of us are more ambivalent about Harry Truman's use of the atomic bomb on Hiroshima and Nagasaki.

In point of fact, we rarely address the question of when violence becomes morally justifiable as a means to political change. Instead, we reframe the question in terms of pragmatics: Is it practical? Will force be effective? Will it achieve the desired outcome? Efficiency and efficacy supplants ethical considerations.

When we do address it, our answers are shaped by our own frame of reference. Implicit in every high school American history textbook is the notion that the Sons of Liberty were entirely justified for the violence at Lexington and Concord, but no such justification is offered for the violence of striking workers who led the 19th century American Labor Movement.

So the victors write the history books and the vanquished are compelled to read them.

During my second year in Putney, I received notification from Lyle Stuart that we were being sued by Panther Publications for copyright infringement. Panther Publications (or as they later became known: Paladin Press) was publishing a book by General Alberto Bayo entitled *150 Questions for a Guerrilla.* Alberto Bayo was an extremely colorful character who deserves a short description.

Born in Cuba to a military father, Alberto joined the Spanish military at the age of fourteen. He served as a left-wing republican military commander during the Spanish Civil War, most notable in his attempt to invade Mallorca. Following Franco's victory in Spain, Alberto Bayo took refuge in Mexico where he published a series of short books and pamphlets. The premise behind the books was similar: A small group of passionately-committed guerrilla fighters could defeat much larger traditional military forces. His books came to the attention of a young dissident law student at the University of Havana by the name of Fidel Castro. Later, General Alberto Bayo would set up a training camp in Mexico where Fidel, his brother Raul, Ernesto Che Guevara, and others would learn the strategies and tactics of guerrilla warfare. There is little doubt that the Cuban Revolution would have been a dismal failure without General Alberto Bayo's training.

I had used Alberto Bayo's book in the preparation of *The Cookbook* and had cited it in the text and listed it in the bibliography at the end of the book. Much of what was in Bayo's book was in common domain and I saw no reason to seek permission from Panther Publications. They saw the situation differently.

In 1970, Peter Lund and Robert Brown formed Panther Publications with Alberto Bayo's book as their first publication. The name would change from Panther Publications to Paladin

Press so as to avoid confusion with the Black Panther Party, which was very much in the press at the time.

Paladin Press prides itself in publishing an "action library"; this includes books with titles such as *Silent Killing, The Revenge Encyclopedia,* and *Get Even: The Complete Book of Dirty Tricks.* In 1983, Paladin Press apparently crossed the legal line with their publication of *Hit Man: A Technical Manual for Independent Contractors.* The book portrays itself as a how-to manual for would-be hired hit men. James Perry, a hired killer, actually used the book as a guide. Perry had been contracted by Lawrence Horn to murder his ex-wife, son, and son's nurse. Perry, after being arrested and charged, described how he had used the book as a guide in the triple murder. The families of the victims sued Paladin Press and the US Court of Appeals ruled that *Hit Man* was not covered by First Amendment protection. Paladin's insurance company paid the victims several million dollars and the residual copies of the book were destroyed.

High noon between *The Cookbook* and Panther Publications was again a venture in absurdist street theater; this time played out in the Supreme Court in Denver. Lyle had booked us (we brought with us Lyle's New York lawyer) into the Brown Palace, the second oldest hotel in Denver, which boasted offering accommodation to *The Unsinkable Molly Brown,* Teddy Roosevelt, Warren Harding, Dwight Eisenhower, Dr. Sun Yat Sen, and The Beatles. Since my royalties were paying the expenses, Lyle felt no need to conserve resources.

The night before the trial, we met with our Denver lawyers to discuss strategies. Unlike my brief foray in book promotion, I was determined to be prepared for this spectacle. I had spent hours and hours reading up on Alberto Bayo, the sources he had used, and the translation history of his book.

The trial took a full day and I was on the witness stand for almost four hours. The lawyer who was representing Panther Publications was young and inexperienced and he frequently lost the thread of his own arguments. He also failed to control the questioning of the witness (me). Several times when I had completed answering a question, I added a "furthermore" that undermined his case. At one point, the plaintiff's lawyer asked what I knew about Bangalore torpedoes. I immediately gave him the history, chapter, and verse, about how in 1912 Captain McClintock of the British Indian Army had devised the Bangalore Torpedo as a means of exploding booby-traps and barricades left over from the Boer War and the Russo-Japanese conflict. The intimidation I had felt during the book promotion in New York had disappeared. My thorough preparation encouraged a sense of assertiveness and I remember actually enjoying the verbal combat with the plantiff's lawyer. I felt energized by my time on the witness stand.

At the end of the day, the judge ruled from the bench and threw the Panther Publication claim out of court. Lyle, the legal team, and I went back to Brown Palace for a Rabelaisian celebration dinner—which I paid for from future royalties.

Back in Putney, Vermont, life as an undergraduate went on. I was working three part-time jobs: public relations at the college, bartending on weekends at the Carriage House Tavern, a local watering hole, and working the occasional graveyard shift at the Exxon Station on the interstate. With my studies, there wasn't time for much else. During the summers, I worked as the manager of the Windham Summer Repertory Theater—a job that I thoroughly enjoyed.

My senior year at Windham was an emotional watershed for me. I had come to Vermont to escape the chaos of my life on Manhattan's Lower East Side and I had succeeded all too well. Order had replaced chaos. Safety and stability had taken the place of excitement and danger. The daily routine was comfortable and predictable. Identity was defined through achievement. I was doing very well at school, maintaining a straight-A average, and between my three part-time jobs I managed to balance the monthly household budget. On the surface, everything seemed to be going well—too well.

Beneath the surface, this was not the case. I increasingly felt enclosed and confined by the very order and predictability I had originally sought. Daily life was like the dreary repetition of a single musical note; beautiful and exhilarating when combined with others, but by itself ordinary, isolated, and mundane. There was no variation, no improvisation, no spontaneity. There was no magic.

Some people fear heights or spiders or public speaking, I fear boredom—that dull and spiritless lassitude that hovered like a dark shadow over the emotional wasteland of the future.

During the first semester of my final year at Windham, I couldn't seem to shake the notion that all my undergraduate achievements were hollow and meaningless, my relationships were mechanical and superficial, and what kept me going to class, writing term papers, studying for exams, and tending bar on the weekends, was mere inertia.

Towards the end of the year, I dropped in on the annual awards banquet in the Windham field house. It was a big deal and almost a thousand students attended. I hadn't RSVP'ed and therefore didn't have a ticket that entitled me to a seat at the long rows of tables. I stood at the back of the room. To my confusion and surprise, I was called repeatedly to the stage: Outstanding English Student, Outstanding Senior, Prize for Best Short Story, and Valedictorian of the class of 1974. All of these supposed honors only made me feel even more superficial.

Bruce Dobler may have sensed my despondency as he encouraged me to apply to the graduate program University of Iowa Writers' Workshop. I did apply and sent a sample of my fiction. Soon thereafter, I received a letter of acceptance, followed a week later by an apology that the acceptance had been a mistake. It should have been a rejection letter. I assume that in the interval between acceptance and rejection, they had discovered that I was the author of *The Cookbook.*

Despite my achievements at Windham, I was bored. The daily routine had become dull and repetitive. Engagement and interest had disappeared. For some people, this might be acceptable and even reassuring. For me, it echoed the sound of nails being driven into my coffin. There was nothing new or surprising or exciting: only boundless discouragement.

Such despondency thrives in the absence of any real examination. I felt the tedium and monotony of daily life, but felt unable to look beneath their surface. I didn't recognize at the time that boredom is not a naturally occurring phenomenon, but rather a learned response. I had come to expect to be stimulated, to be engaged, to be thrilled.

I didn't understand it at the time, but the opposite of *taedium vitae* is the search for meaning. We become neurotic, not from frustration, but from the absence of meaning.

The first casualty of that boredom would be my marriage.

I had married Celia four years before more out of convenience than passion. It seemed to me to be a logical and reasonable thing to do. I saw her as safe and stable. For the time that we lived together we treated each other with reasonable kindness and respect, and our disagreements were few and far between. On the surface, the marriage looked fine, but as the years passed, I became aware that there was no emotional depth to it. This emotional depth was not something that I had initially sought after, but over time its absence made itself known. I felt no vulnerability or pain; I felt no joyous intimacy—just a numb sense of repetition. And rather than look deep within myself, I held the marriage responsible. I saw myself as *subject* to the marriage, not one of its architects.

In January 1974, Celia went to Moscow for a month-long intensive course on Russian history and literature. During the time she was away, two individuals came into and changed my life: the English novelist Charles Williams and a young female student named Gretchen.

Just before the Christmas holiday, I found a copy of *The Place of the Lion* in the Windham Library. I devoured it in a single evening and immediately went hunting for other novels by Charles Williams.

Williams was and is one of the most remarkable novelists of the 20th century. He was perhaps the least well known of an Oxford literary group called the Inklings, which included C.S. Lewis and J.R.R. Tolkien. He was also close literary friends with T.S. Elliot, W.H. Auden, and Dorothy Sayers—all who shared his deep spiritual curiosity.

Soon after reading *The Place of the Lion,* I contacted a professor friend at the college with whom I had recently taken a modern intellectual history course and asked if he would sponsor me in an independent study on the novels of Charles Williams. Three days later, he responded that not only would he sponsor such a study, but that there were several other professors interested in joining a Charles Williams' study group.

At about the same time, Gretchen was taking an Introduction to Chemistry Course and was struggling. Like me, she was a humanities major and was taking the chemistry course as a science requirement. We were both seniors and she knew that I had taken the course the previous semester and had done well. She approached me for help. Somewhere in the midst of hydrogen bridges, moles, entropy, and balancing equations, our relationship became intimate.

Unlike Celia, Gretchen was neither safe nor stable, and a stampede of buffalo couldn't have kept her away from the Charles Williams study group. I was soon infatuated with her.

There were five members of our study group. We met in the evenings weekly and would analyze a different Charles Williams novel.

This study group was probably one of the most powerful learning experiences of my life. I was exposed to how fine minds question, inquire, and embrace confusion. These conversations were not about advocating an opinion, but rather about dwelling in the realms of ambiguity, irony, and uncertainty. Someone would take an idea from the text; someone else would elaborate on it or make a connection to something else he had read. Another person would question it or scaffold another idea on top of it. It was literally like building a superstructure of ideas and concepts. The inquiry was intense and yet strangely effortless; time seemed to cease to exist, and some nights it would be after midnight before we finally closed our books and went home.

From Williams' fiction, I turned to his theology, *The Descent of the Dove: A History of the Holy Ghost in the Church*, and to the works of C.S. Lewis—the so-called patron saint of agnostics. I had read Lewis' *The Screwtape Letters* as a child, but now I devoured his adult fiction: *Out of the Silent Planet, Perlandra,* and *That Hideous Strength.* I also read his brilliant essay: *Mere Christianity.*

When Celia returned from her Russian study tour, I told her about my relationship with Gretchen and moved out of the house into a rundown caravan in the middle of a field on the Newfane Road. I was determined that there would not be a repeat of the dishonesty I had exhibited towards Steve over my relationship with Eugenia. I am sure that my announcement surprised, shocked, and hurt Celia deeply. For this, I was and am deeply sorry. She did not deserve to be treated in that fashion.

The relationship with Gretchen was as tempestuous as my marriage had been dull and in mid-March, I asked Celia if we could give the marriage another try. After a hiatus of two months, I moved back in with her.

But I had moved back into what I had tried to escape from. I didn't see relationships as something I had to architect, but rather something that happened to you when the "right" person came along. In the months that followed, it seemed clearer and clearer to me that Celia was not the right person. But far more importantly, I never asked myself, if I was the "right" person.

In May, I graduated from Windham College as co-valedictorian of the class. My dad and mom were in the audience and I gave a short speech. They were proud of me and that meant a great deal to me.

Soon after graduation, Celia announced that she was pregnant. I had strong and very different reactions. The first was shock and surprise. In previous years, Celia and I had actually been trying to have a child. The pregnancy made that relationship more difficult to leave. Rather than bringing us together, Celia's announcement ironically pushed me further from her.

Following graduation, I shared my working life between bartending at the Carriage House and working the graveyard shift at the Exxon Station on the interstate. The idea was that this would give me plenty of mornings to work on my own writing. But it didn't work.

For whatever reason, I was facing a serious case of writers block. I couldn't seem to get words on paper, and even when I did, my prose was mechanical and uninspired. I met resistance with resistance. The more depressed I became about my writing, the more determined I became and the more effort and time I put in, but to no avail. It seemed that the harder I tried, the more effort I put in, the less stimulating and dynamic the results. I began to wonder if I had been fooling myself all along. Perhaps I didn't actually have what it would take to be a writer. Perhaps I didn't have the imagination or the creativity.

I started work on a novel entitled *The Meadow House*—a vast rambling metaphysical and largely unreadable book that spanned several generations of Vermont farmers. I knew as I was writing it that it wasn't any good, but that knowledge compelled me to write more and more in hopes that finally something decent and inspired might emerge. It didn't, and I sunk lower and lower into depression.

The summer of 1974 became a tedious routine of working nights at the bar and gas station and then returning home, fueled by strong black coffee to write drivel. By August I was near despair, but then everything changed in one fateful night.

It was a Thursday evening a week or so before the college year started, and I was tending bar at the Carriage House. There weren't very many customers and I was passing the time of the evening chatting with a few of the usuals who propped up the bar. Then a group of young people entered the bar. Gretchen was among them. I hadn't seen her for several months. They sat at the table and I went over to take their orders. I greeted Gretchen and she seemed pleased to see me.

As I delivered the drinks to the table, I whispered to Gretchen asking her if at the end of the evening I could speak with her in private. Again, she smiled and nodded.

Later that night, I met with Gretchen. She told me what I already knew. Bruce Dobler was going to Alaska to get a job on the trans-Alaska pipe and research a novel using the construction of the pipeline as setting.

What she said next I didn't know. She was going with him—platonically—she quickly assured me. Bruce would be traveling with his wife and two daughters.

"What are you going to do in Alaska?" I asked.

"Have an adventure," she replied. "Seek my fortune?"

"Want company?"

She smiled radiantly, and in that moment I made the decision: I too would seek adventure and fortune in Alaska.

CHAPTER 10
The Last Rush North

THE TITLE OF THIS CHAPTER IS ALSO the title of Bruce Dobler's novel, which is set in Alaska during the construction of the Trans-Alaska Pipeline and in which both Gretchen and I make unflattering, cameo appearances.

Alaska has been subject to a number of "gold rushes"; probably the most famous took place in the years following the discovery of large quantities of gold in 1896. During the years of the Klondike Gold Rush, over a hundred thousand people formed a "stampede," traveling overland to Alaska and the Yukon Territory in the hope of prospecting for gold. There was a sense of urgency, adventure, and competition since gold was scarce and the first to arrive stood the best chances.

The 1974 "gold" rush was similar and different. There was the same contagious hopefulness, the same sense of urgency and competition, but gold was replaced by the lure of high-paying construction work on the Trans-Alaska Pipeline System (TAPS). The lower 48 states were in the doldrums of economic recession and work was hard to find, and so across the country men changed the oil in their rusting station wagons, packed up the family, sometimes sleeping rough under canvas on the bed of the pick-up, and headed north for fortune, if not glory. Unskilled workers could earn a thousand dollars a week; skilled workers could earn up to double or even triple that. Bechtel and Fluor were begging for workers. Accommodation and all the food you could eat were provided.

In the early days of pipeline work, there were three rules: the camps were strictly single-sex—men, and there was to be no alcohol or gambling. All three rules were regularly and repeatedly broken. Poker games were a regular feature of camp life and booze was regularly smuggled into the camps. There was a story told, possibly apocryphal, of a prostitute from Vegas who disguised herself as a man and flew into the construction site of the pumping station near Atigun Pass. Forty-eight hours later she flew out, sixty thousand dollars richer, but in need of a month's rest to recover from exhaustion.

The workers came in human waves. There were rough-and-tumble welders from Oklahoma, skinhead iron workers from East Texas, and long-haul ice drivers from Washington and Oregon. There were tattooed Vietnam vets whose empty eyes masked past trauma, and long-haired college dropouts on a temporary detour from their search for themselves. There were tens of thousands of them—testosterone-driven males, lured by the hope of mammoth paychecks, taking their clapped-out pick-up trucks and braving the week-long day drive up from the lower 48, traversing the fifteen hundred mile dirt Alcan Highway.

But it was not the lure of high-paid employment that caused me to have my Volkswagen Passat serviced and light out for the north. I wanted to escape the dull routine that had become my life in Vermont. Although I felt guilty leaving Celia, it didn't stop me from wanting adventure and a new start. I was truly focused on self.

I left Vermont in early September, spent a couple of days in New York with my dad and mom, and then started the trek to Alaska. I drove between four and five hundred miles a day, curling across New York State, crossing into Canada, rounding Lake Superior and then streaking across the plains into the Rocky Mountains. Just before the beginning of the Alcan Highway, I picked up a hitchhiker—a young Buddhist with whom I shared the three-day wilderness drive. Forty years later he would contact me on Facebook and ask if I remembered him. I did, most notably for his monotonous chanting that drove me close to dumping him in the wilderness to be eaten by bears. Between Whitehorse and Beaver Creek, we ran into our first snow flurries—it was going to be a long, cold, and dark winter.

I arrived in Anchorage nine days after setting out from New York. I had a duffle bag of clothes, a dozen paperback books, five hundred dollars in cash, half a carton of Camel cigarettes and a road atlas of the United States. What more could anyone want?

The first order of priority was to find a place to live. Gretchen and I took the first place we visited, a furnished two bedroom flat in the Linda Arms Apartments—which reduced my working capital by about fifty percent. Later, after Gretchen joined the Anchorage Police Department, we would learn that the Linda Arms Apartment had the highest violent drug-related crime rate in the entire state of Alaska. Ignorance was bliss.

The second order of priority was to find work. We searched the local newspapers. Gretchen was looking for waitress jobs; I was looking for anything that would allow me to write. I queried the local newspapers about vacancies for reporters. None were hiring.

Ten days after arriving in Anchorage with only twenty dollars left in my wallet, I answered a classified advertisement for a bartender at the Black Orchid Nightclub. I was hired on the spot. And while the tips were as ostentatious as the attire of the clientele, I was ready for a change of employment by mid-October.

In the wake of my summary resignation at the Black Orchid, I answered a classified ad in the local paper and went for an interview as a teacher cum cottage parent at the Jesse Lee Children's Home on Abbott Road. Established as a charity by the Lutheran church, the Jesse Lee Home was a residential treatment center for emotionally disturbed children. Some of the youngsters were indeed emotionally disturbed, others were neglected, abused, and abandoned, but many were culturally displaced. These were the children of Native Americans whose tribal collectivist culture had broken down in the face of the oil boom and rampant alcoholism.

Two days after the interview, I received a phone call offering me the job, and so my introduction to special education began with a baptism of fire.

There were five cottages, each housing ten to twelve children. I was to share responsibility for the cottage of twelve ten-year-old boys with Joyce, a six foot African American who was as tough and streetwise as they come. But for all her no-nonsense demeanor, she also emanated a rough maternal warmth that endeared virtually everyone to her. The director always involved Joyce in the intake of new children, many of whom were abusive and sometimes violent. Joyce was oblivious to the verbal abuse, some of which was painfully racial. On one occasion, she actually wound up in the shower fully clothed with a very angry Inuit boy. She suffered the verbal and physical abuse stoically, but firmly made sure the lad was showered, hair was de-loused, and then settled into the room with clean sheets and towels. A week later, she spent half the night listening to the same boy tearfully recount how he had watched his uncle rape and murder his mother.

Joyce was also a brilliant cook. The Jesse Lee Home had an understanding with the Alaskan Highway Patrol that when they discovered roadkill—moose, caribou, or bear—they would radio the center and Joyce would lead a butcher party. She knew her game well and we lived throughout the winter on moose burgers, bear meat loaf, and caribou spaghetti sauce.

In addition to my responsibilities as a cottage parent, I was also a part-time teacher of English and Social Studies. I recall entering the classroom for the first time full of trepidation. First of all, I wasn't a trained teacher and didn't have a clue as to what I should be doing. Second, there was no curriculum to follow or learning outcomes to work towards. Third, although they were only ten and eleven years old, these were tough, streetwise kids—who didn't suffer fools lightly and weren't known for their classroom decorum. I had prepared a lesson on the Lewis and Clark Expedition and I started out showing the class a short filmstrip on the subject. My idea was to have a class discussion after the filmstrip. I had prepared some processing questions, but I hadn't counted on the reaction of Johnny Costa.

Johnny was one of the younger boys in the cottage. He had been removed by court order from an extremely dysfunctional and abusive family relationship. His father had been in the army, but had been court-martialed for manslaughter—the details of which I never knew—but was serving a multi-year sentence in the military stockade. His mother was also violent—often towards Johnny—particularly when she was drunk. Finally, in a fit of rage, she had poured boiling water over his feet and a neighbor had responded to Johnny's screams by calling the police. Johnny had been removed from the home by the Department of Social Welfare and the courts had barred his mother from visiting Johnny at the Jesse Lee Home. On several occasions, usually about three o'clock in the morning, I had the unpleasant duty of trying to explain this to her while suffering her drunken abuse.

Once the Lewis and Clark filmstrip was finished, I asked the class to imagine that they had been planning an expedition like the one that Lewis and Clark had undertaken. I asked what challenges might they have faced.

"Who gives a shit?" Johnny responded. "This is boring."

I hadn't expected such overt resistance and didn't know how to respond. I decided in the moment to pretend I hadn't heard his comment. Mistake.

I repeated the question.

"We heard you the first time," Johnny said. "This is boring. I'm going back to the cottage." He kicked back his chair and rose to his feet.

Johnny was challenging my authority in the classroom. The rest of the class looked on in anticipation. Would the young and inexperienced teacher be able to keep order? Would I set limits or would the students determine what went on in the classroom? Johnny was creating a win/lose situation that had very significant ramifications for my ability to manage the classroom. If I was going to manage the class, I needed to be the winner. Or so I thought at the time.

"Sit DOWN," I instructed him.

Johnny stood still beside his desk and glared defiantly at me.

"Make me!" he snapped back.

"I said *sit down*," I barked at him. The eyes of everyone in the classroom were on Johnny and me. It was a defining moment: If Johnny could get away with being insubordinate, the rest of the class would surely follow suit.

In retrospect, I realize that I had choices, but I didn't see them at the time. I could have asked Johnny what he found boring? I could have paraphrased his response. I could have made a joke. I could have shown him a degree of respect. Instead, I allowed myself to be sucked into a confrontation that Johnny was in charge of. Somewhere in the exchange, I had given him permission to push my hot buttons.

Johnny didn't sit down. He planted his hands on his hips and smirked.

I walked over to where he was standing, towering over him, and glared down at him: "You will sit down now or I will *sit* you down!"

I made the classic classroom teacher error of showing anger while I was feeling it—while I might have been towering menancingly over Johnny, he was clearly in charge. Teacher anger is sometimes appropriate in the classroom, but never when the teacher is actually feeling the anger.

Johnny hesitated for a moment and broke eye-contact. Looking back on it, I suspect he was wondering if I was going to hit him. His psychiatrist later told me that his mother's persistent violence toward him had caused Johnny to perceive the world through a simple dichotomous filter. He saw people in two categories—those people likely to hurt him and those people he could hurt and therefore manipulate.

The expression of defiance returned to Johnny's face.

"If you make me stay in this boring class, I'm going to burn this motherfucking school to the ground!"

"You can burn the school to the ground on your own time!" I bellowed. "This is class time, and you will remain in class and pay attention and listen!"

Johnny sank into his seat and remained in the class until the bell rang, indicating the end of the period: a victory for me and my class management skills.

When the bell rang, Johnny left the classroom with his books. He made his way to the school garages, located a jerry can of gasoline, poured it over the floor, and set fire to the garage. He didn't succeed in burning the school to the ground, but he did a considerable amount of damage to one of the garages.

That afternoon, the director of the Jesse Lee Home called me into his office. I had a premonition of what we might be discussing. The Director led off with a statement.

"Johnny said that you gave him permission to burn the school down."

My explanation was as lame as my reaction to Johnny. Fortunately, the Director, a Lutheran minister, was more concerned with my growth than in retribution. He asked me what I thought might be going on for Johnny—a question that I hadn't, until then, considered. He invited me to consider the perspective of another person—something that I hadn't been accustomed to doing. It would be a few more weeks before I saw another, completely different side of Johnny Costa.

Life as a cottage parent was emotionally arduous. Together with Joyce, we were responsible twenty-four hours a day, seven days a week, for twelve very emotionally-needy boys. Unlike Johnny Costa, some of the rest of them were immediately likeable. They were playful, impulsive, quirky, and funny. But each had his own issues. Victor had ADHD off the charts—he would run up and down the corridor for hours on end making deafening noises that suggested a combination of a jet engine and earth-moving equipment. Abraham was constantly seeking attention and would perseverate, asking the same irrelevant question over and over again. Ozzie wet the bed fairly regularly and his roommate Samuel had to be watched fairly carefully as he had a tendency to set fires—more often than not, in the middle of the night, to Ozzie's mattress.

Did I enjoy my work at the Jesse Lee Home? No, there was nothing enjoyable about it. I found it hard and frustrating, but at the same time meaningful. There was a sense that if I didn't forge a relationship with these kids, no one else was going to do so. I felt needed and it was a new experience.

In the cottage common room there was an antique black and white television. The boys were permitted to watch an hour of TV on school nights, and a little longer on weekends if their behavior had been acceptable. The Skinnerian behaviorists were all the rage and so we teachers talked about behavioral engineering, operant conditioning, and positive and negative reinforcements.

Interestingly, the favorite TV show for all the cottage boys was "The Brady Bunch," which depicted a blended American family coming together to forge for the most part a harmonious union. Certainly there were misunderstandings, squabbles, mild sibling rivalry, and other minor crises in Bradyville, but common sense, parental wisdom, and family values always managed to save the day. I had seen "The Brady Bunch" a few times before coming to work at the Jesse Lee Children's Home and had dismissed it as corny and hackneyed. However, in the Jesse Lee cottage common room I came to see it through different eyes. For ten and eleven-year-old boys, who for the most part had been rejected by their families, this show was a window into what family life could possibly be. It was as though the front of a doll's house had been removed to expose an interior that oozed American middle-class family values. In the Brady household, people drank milk instead of cheap whisky, and used gentle corrective conversation instead of belts and paddles. The dishes were always washed and no one smoked or cursed or stole the rent money. The most sexually daring episode included an extremely tame exploration of dating. It was banal milk-toast at its worst, but it was exactly what the children in Cottage 4 wanted to see. It was poignant watching children who had been abandoned, and in some cases actually tortured, by the adult world sit glued to this thirty-minute fix of a child's American dream. Even hyperactive Victor was mesmerized by it.

One weekend, Johnny started a fight with Samuel and Joyce took away his TV privileges. In reaction, Johnny urinated into the back of the TV and blew out all the tubes. It would be more than a month before we could get it repaired. None of them said anything, but I sensed that the cottage boys grieved for the loss of their weekend window in the Brady household.

During the time I was working at the Jesse Lee Home, Joyce and I shared night duty. She had a full apartment in the cottage, and took most of the nights. However, when she wanted a night off, I would stay in a vacant bedroom at the far end of the corridor. Towards the end of November, Joyce asked me to cover the cottage during a weekend as she wanted to travel down to Homer to celebrate a friend's birthday. I agreed and set about planning activities that would keep the boys out of the more outrageous forms of mischief.

The weekend was going fairly well until four o'clock Sunday morning. I awoke with a start and switched on the bedside lamp. There was a very strange noise in the room with me. It sounded like a subway train was going through the room—a dull rumble that seemed to be coming from the bowels of the earth. Actually, it sounded like a freight train tunneling beneath the room. I was in a large double bed that rested on coasters, and before I was fully awake, I felt the bed start to move and the entire room shake. The walls started to move without relation to each other. I felt frighteningly disoriented. Suddenly, the door burst open and twelve very terrified boys hurtled towards my bed as though they had been shot out of a cannon. Before I could react, I had all twelve of them on the bed with me and the bed was moving around the room banging into the furniture and walls like a bumper car at a carnival. The window shattered, a menacing crack appeared in the cinderblock wall and the large mirror that was hanging above the dressing table did a fandango before careening to the floor. Then the lights went out. At least three or four of the boys were sobbing—I recognized that one of them was Johnny Costa.

Anchorage had just experienced a moderate magnitude earthquake.

After the initial shock, I instructed the boys to evacuate and we all went to the main office building—a wood structure that was much more flexible in earthquake situations than the cinderblock cottages. The fifty plus kids of the home remained in their pajamas in the central office until early afternoon, when a civil engineer declared that it was safe for us to return to the cottage.

I was grateful for the earthquake. It had given me a window into Johnny Costa's emotional life. The tough guy was actually a frightened little boy. His moment of terror had humanized him for me; it was a gift that I would take with me into the future.

One of the tensions I experienced working at the Jesse Lee Home was the constant nagging battle between hopefulness and futility. The statistics were apparent and all the employees of the

Home knew them. When working with severely disturbed children as we were, the majority would end up either in prison or dead. I talked with Joyce several times about this. How could she put so much emotional energy into building relationships with children who, for the most part, were on a road to self-destruction?

I don't think she ever really understood the question or my angst. For Joyce there wasn't the tension. Hope and futility had fused into a kind of immediate spiritual necessity. She actually called it "choosing necessity"; something I found hard to understand.

"Breathing is necessary," I replied to her. "But I don't choose to breath. I just do it."

"Why don't you try it?" she replied.

"Try it? Try what?"

"Try choosing to breathe. You might find life easier."

"I don't understand."

"Lots of folk fight against what's necessary. That's a mistake. Belonging's necessary. Everyone needs to feel a sense of belonging—even Mr. Bill Powell. You can't always be on the outside looking in."

"You think I don't have a sense of belonging?"

"I seen how you look at those kids. You're looking at yourself. Them kids need love. And when I give it to them, I'm choosing necessity."

I was reminded of Charles Williams' exhortion: Rise to embrace the mystery of love.

Joyce understood that she could no more save other people than she could predict the future or get out of life alive, but she had a hunch that she could influence the present—she could be there for them when the cottage boys needed her. She understood that there would be no gratitude or appreciation from these troubled youngsters, and yet their fear and loneliness seemed to energize her. One evening, after lights out for the boys, I asked how she managed emotionally.

"Manage? Shit. Carin' for these boys is like digestin' your food. It's not something you worry about. You just get on with it. It's like swimming in a river. Any damn stroke does the trick. This ain't no Olympic Games, this here's a matter of survival."

I asked if she believed in God.

"Only an asshole wouldn't," she replied.

"But you don't go to church."

"Only an asshole would."

"You don't believe in organized religion?"

"I hate organized religion. It's one of the things that gets in the way of my relationship with the director."

"But your faith sustains your work with the kids. . . "

"I don't know much about faith. But I do know these kids," she snapped. "They've seen things that would curl your hair." Joyce was silent for several moments. Compassion and fury competed for control of her expression. "Last month the cops called through on the radio. They wanted someone from the Home to meet them at the hospital. They'd picked up a thirteen-year-old Inuit girl wandering in a daze on 4th Avenue. Her name was Becky. I met them at the emergency ward. Becky was barely conscious; she'd been beaten and gang raped. She had a concussion and a broken wrist. Cops said that somebody had hit her with a tire iron."

Joyce stared at the surface of the table in front of her. Her eyes were cold and hard and there was deep sadness in her voice.

"Her head and wrist have mended. But there're other, deeper scars. Will she ever trust again? I don't know no answer to that. But I do know that healin' is better than hurtin'—and when I face my Maker in that Great Perhaps, I wanna be able to look that old bastard in the eye and say that I've done more healin' than hurtin'."

As a rule of thumb, Joyce's maxim is not a bad guide.

On December 6th, my birthday, my brother Chris phoned to tell me that Celia had given birth to a boy. I was expecting the news, but was nevertheless stunned by the reality of it. Actually, I should say I was half expecting the news because the rational side of my being understood that pregnancy usually ended with birth, but the emotional part of me was caught unawares. Perhaps even more so, because my son Sean was born on my birthday. It would take several months for the idea of fatherhood to settle, and a lifetime to understand it.

The birth of Sean created powerful emotional confusion for me. Initially, there was a sense of unreality—how could this be true? I tried to envision a baby, but here my imagination failed me. I knew I had a son. I knew I was now a father, but the words were only words; they were devoid of meaning—almost as if they were spoken in a foreign language. Yes, I knew that there was now an infant in Putney, Vermont who shared fifty percent of my DNA, but I had not a clue what it was to be a father. I actually wondered about what I should be thinking and feeling. What did other new fathers think about and feel?

Coupled with the confusion was depression. I sensed that being a father might be a new beginning, a new meaningfulness that lay somehow just out of my reach. In order to be a father to Sean, I knew I would have to deal with my broken marriage to Celia. It was at about this time, or perhaps a little later, that I began to wonder if I had written off my marriage to Celia prematurely.

I also felt a very strong sense of guilt. I had left Vermont—some might say I had run away—abandoning a pregnant wife. My younger brother, Chris, had been a major support to Celia throughout her pregnancy, but I had been absent. I was uncomfortable in recognizing that in some respects I was guilty of exactly the neglect and abandonment that I despised in the parents of the Jesse Lee children.

Somewhere between Christmas and New Year's, Joyce invited me into her apartment for an off-duty beer. After a short while, I told her that I had recently become a father. She knew I was separated from Celia.

"So now you're a confused man?"

I made a grunt of agreement.

"You're wondering what to do?"

"I was thinking of going back to Vermont to visit my son."

"What you be doing that for?"

"I need to figure out what it means to be a father."

"You don't want your kid to grow up like one of our cottage boys?"

I shook my head.

"And you think that by being a father you can make a difference?"

"Something like that."

"So what you gonna do for this baby?"

"I don't know."

"You gonna try and patch up your marriage?"

"Maybe. I don't know. I've got so many questions." There may have been something in my tone of voice, or perhaps my eyes became moist, because Joyce held the silence for a long time, just staring quizzically at me.

"You know what!" Joyce suddenly exclaimed. "I like you when you're confused. You're almost human."

"I just don't know what to do."

"Don't be in a hurry to figure it all out. I like you confused. What's that word that makes men all squirrelly—vul-ner-able. Yes, siree bob, I never met a man who liked to be vul-ner-able. That's when most men get real mean. But being vul-ner-able suits you like a clean shirt and a haircut. Don't be in a hurry. Once you answer all your questions, you'll be just another asshole who thinks he's got it figured out. I get so tired of them arrogant sons a bitches. . . ."

I remember clearly what Joyce said because it was so unexpected and, at the time, inexplicable. She recognized that I was profoundly confused, and she suggested that I savor the bewilderment. "Bewilderment" is my word; Joyce didn't use it. But as a word, it expresses some of what I was going through. "Bewilderment" has the same root as "wilderness." It suggests a journey without a map away from the familiar, orderly, and comfortable routine of daily life. Looking back over forty years, I have now come to understand that the most perilous journey we can undertake is that of self-exploration, and the only thing even more perilous is not to undertake it.

In Anchorage in the sub-Arctic winter darkness, the last thing I wanted to do was "savor" confusion. I was a very linear and dialectic thinker. If emotional confusion was the problem, then the solution should be clarity of thought and feeling, which I assumed would be achieved by decisiveness. You are only confused when you have a choice. Decisions remove choice (the root in the word "decide" is the same as "suicide" and "homicide"—literally meaning "to kill choice"). Therefore, decisiveness eliminates confusion. The logic was glaringly simple and grossly flawed.

Joyce had wisdom born of rough experience. She understood that the remedy for the anxiety and discomfort of emotional confusion was not "clarity of thought and feeling," but personal growth over time. She understood that our most profound learnings are rarely pleasant, and more often than not are nurtured out of trauma. If you ask people about the most significant learning experiences of their life, many people will recount very painful experiences: the death of a loved one, an estranged child, an incident that resulted in deep shame, a ruptured friendship, or a tumultuous divorce. Many times it is out of crisis that new spiritual life emerges. This was what Joyce was trying to tell me, but I didn't understand it then.

In mid-January, I phoned Celia from Anchorage and broached the subject of me visiting Putney to see the baby. The conversation was halting and tentative, but very calm and polite. We were nothing if not civilized; there were no angry outbursts, no recriminations, and no tears. Celia and I had become masterful at masking our emotions from each other, and perhaps even from ourselves. I had no idea what her real thoughts and feelings were, but she agreed to my visit and I went out and purchased air tickets.

The visit to Putney took place not too long after. I flew into Boston and rented a car and drove to Vermont. I was anxious as I anticipated the meeting with Celia. I didn't know what to expect. I had treated her badly and she would have certainly been within her rights to be furious and full of resentment. But I hadn't heard any such bitterness on the phone and there was none apparent when we met face to face.

I stayed at the River Road house and slept on the living room couch. The only subject that we could talk about with any fluency and comfort was the newborn baby. So most of the time we were together we did just that. We talked about feeding schedules, doctor's visits, inoculations, and the milestones in infant development.

I was pleased that she clearly wanted me to have a relationship with Sean. She encouraged me to feed him and to take him out in the car when he was experiencing colic. I didn't know very much about caring for babies, but Celia seemed to trust my instincts because she would leave me alone with Sean for long periods.

Celia and I carefully avoided any talk about ourselves and our ruptured relationship. We went through the week pretending that the past had not happened, and the future would take care of itself.

On the day of my departure back to Alaska, I asked her whether she saw any possibility of resurrecting our marriage. The question clearly suggested that this was something I desired. I braced myself for her anger. She must have perceived me as an incredibly self-serving individual who viewed our relationship only in terms of what benefit it held to me. She would have been entirely justified in venting her resentment, but it was not forthcoming. She listened attentively and then announced that she was as confused as I was. I saw this as an opening and I told her that I could return to Alaska and get a job on the pipeline. Construction workers were making a thousand dollars a week take home. We could save money, and then in six months I would quit and we could go on holiday to Europe, perhaps France or Scotland and rent a cottage where I could write. She seemed open to the idea and we agreed to talk more on the phone and write to each other.

I returned to Alaska determined to become a pipeliner.

CHAPTER 11
From the Icebox to the Cuckoo's Nest

As soon as I returned to Anchorage, I phoned Bruce and asked his help in getting a job on the pipeline. He asked if would be I interested in a job as a timekeeper in Valdez. The pay wasn't quite as much as a construction worker, but there were a number of vacant positions.

I jumped at the opportunity, and within a week I had resigned my position at the Jesse Lee Home (I had very mixed feelings about this, but the salary was volunteer wages) and had given notice to my landlord (about which I had no such regret. There had been a cold snap in Anchorage and the temperature hadn't gone above twenty below for two weeks. The heat in my apartment had failed and a dripping tap had turned my bathtub in a glacial blue sea of ice.)

Two days later, I boarded a bus for the 300 plus mile, nine-hour overland journey to Valdez. The bus made a pee stop in Glenallen and the driver told us that the temperature outside was thirty below zero, with a wind chill factor that made it feel like sixty below.

Valdez is a small town on the Prince William Sound, a deepwater fjord bordered to the north by the heavily glaciated Chugach Mountains. The drive from Anchorage is stunningly beautiful, but in the dark of a late January afternoon, we saw little of the scenery.

On arrival in Valdez, we entered the construction camp and were issued cold weather gear: down parka, heavy duty mittens, down leggings that went over your trousers, inflatable "bunny" boots, and a hard hat with insulated lining. When you put on all the gear, you could barely move. Only on the very coldest mornings did anyone wear the down leggings.

I managed to write three or four letters to Celia each week, and received a number in reply. Celia's letters included information about how Sean was developing, but little about her. She did, however, agree to my suggestion that she and Sean fly to Anchorage in early July and that we take a holiday together in Alaska.

Throughout March and April, Celia and I planned our grand summer tour of Alaska. By July, we would have almost twenty hours of daylight each day, and ten thousand dollars in the bank. For me, this seemed like a small fortune. I wrote to her about the idea of taking six months in Europe, possibly in France, so that I could write. I wanted to finish the historical novel about the First World War, and I had notes for a collection of short stories that I wanted to embark upon. I had a vision of renting a medieval water mill in the Loire Valley and living on cheese, wine, and freshly baked bread. This daydream of an idyllic future held the tedium of timekeeping at bay for most of the time.

On July 7th, I turned in my Arctic gear and my hard hat, picked up my final paycheck and boarded the Fluor bus for Anchorage. My days as a pipeliner were over.

In Anchorage, I picked up my car from Bruce Dobler's house and drove to the airport to meet Celia's flight. Months of anticipation were now coming to fruition.

As her flight landed, I heard my name being paged over the loudspeaker system, asking me to report to the information desk.

At the information desk, I was told that there was a telephone call for me. It was Celia on the line from Vermont. After much thought, she had decided not to join me in Alaska.

I stood so long at the airport information desk that the attendant asked if I was OK. I remember nodding and picking my way back to the car-park.

I sat behind the wheel of the Volkswagen in the airport car-park for a long time before I started the engine. I had a full tank of gasoline, the Rand McNally Road Atlas of North America in the glove compartment, and no obligations to anyone. But still I didn't start the car; I had no idea where to go. I was certainly not going to return to work in Valdez, and I had no inclination to take a holiday in Alaska on my own. I thought about renting a room at the airport motel, but I couldn't stand the prospect of being alone in an empty motel room. So I just sat behind the steering wheel and wondered with an increasing sense of urgency, what on earth my life had in store for me. Thinking back on that moment now—some forty years later—the words of Jean-Paul Sartre come to mind: "You are condemned to be free."

I don't know if I have ever felt so autonomous or confused or lonely. I did feel both condemned and free. Freedom is, after all, about having choices, and we rarely have more choices than when we are confused.

Finally, I started the car and drove out of the airport. In the final analysis, it was more important to launch the ship than have charted out a route to a destination. I drove for three or four hours and found myself on the other side of Glenallen heading south on the Alcan Highway when a revelation hit me—not unlike an emerging from the darkness of a movie matinee into the blinding glare of a summer afternoon. I had a son who I didn't know. Much of my work in Valdez had been to earn money so that I could afford to spend time building a family relationship. Even if Celia was out of the picture, there was still Sean. I wanted to explore fatherhood. Armed with a new sense of purpose, I drove deliberately south.

Six days later, I drove into the driveway of Celia's parents in Boundbrook, New Jersey. Simple arithmetic will reveal that I had driven very long and very hard, sometimes close to a thousand miles a day without a change of driver. I had spoken with Celia a few days earlier and had come to understand that she was still in Vermont, but Sean was staying with her parents in New Jersey.

Celia's parents were civil and welcoming. I spent an hour or so with Sean in their kitchen. I fed him lunch. I wasn't quite sure what would happen next when Celia's mother announced that I would need the car seat. It was the first inkling that I had that she expected me to take Sean with me.

Together, we fastened the car seat in place and folded up the highchair and put it in the back seat. In retrospect, Celia's mother probably expected me to take Sean back to Celia in Vermont. But that was the last place I was going.

We got on the highway and drove to White Plains to my parent's house. I had not a clue about taking care of a seven-month-old baby, but I knew that my mother did. Unfortunately, they were on their summer holiday in Europe when I arrived with Sean. I managed to get the key from the next-door neighbor, and Sean and I went shopping for disposable diapers, baby food, formula, bottles, etc.

If I wanted to explore fatherhood, I had certainly dropped myself in at the deep end.

Sean and I spent a lot of time together during that first year in White Plains. But despite the warmth of the extended family, that first year in White Plains was a dreadfully lonely one for me. Having said that, the little joy that I encountered in that year did come from being with Sean and learning a little about being a father. I was fascinated watching this little guy do all the usual things that babies do—roll over, crawl, pull themselves up against the leg of a chair. It was as if I was seeing these developments for the first time. I was struck with the way Sean would try to make sense out of his world. How his babble would morph into his own idiosyncratic labels for the vacuum cleaner, the bathtub, our dog, and his favorite food—mashed bananas. I was fascinated by how he would show that he could understand even without spoken language.

I recall taking Sean to the playground at the Highlands Middle School. The school was a dark granite, neo-gothic structure that seemed especially oppressive in the watery, late afternoon light.

It was a cold and blustery Sunday afternoon in October and both of us were wrapped up for winter. The playground was in a small depression at the far end of the school building that formed a kind of wind tunnel. What might have been a breeze on the street level became a whirling gale in the playground. From his vantage point in the stroller, I could see that Sean was mesmerized by the leaves that were swirling about in the wind. I unstrapped him and took him out of the stroller. He couldn't yet walk, so I held him in my arms and pointed to the leaves that were being buffeted and tossed about by the wind like small birds in flight. He let out a small laugh. I wondered what on earth he found funny. And then he laughed again. It was contagious and I found myself chuckling. I started to chase after the airborne leaves, darting left and then right, and Sean laughed even harder. We even managed to catch one or two of the leaves in flight. Sean beamed.

When I was finally out of breath, I asked Sean: "Where is the wind?"

It was an impossible question.

However, he pointed to his wind-reddened cheek.

Even without words, we were making contact.

I took long walks with Sean in his stroller. These were times of deep introspection. One crisp autumn morning, I found myself pushing Sean in the stroller in front of St. Bartholomew's Church on Prospect Street. The trees had started to turn orange and brown, and dried leaves crunched underfoot. The church was circa 1920, a large stone structure with arched gothic-style, stained-glass windows. It looked like a church that knows it's being looked at. The novels of Charles Williams came back to me in full flood.

In *The Greater Trumps,* Sybil, an old and spiritually wise woman, asks the young protagonist whether she will "rise to adore the mystery of love?" The question echoed in my head.

Was love a mystery? It certainly was a puzzle to me. But what did Williams mean by mystery? How could you adore a mystery? Weren't mysteries to be solved like problems or dilemmas?

I didn't understand at that time that all we ever have are mysteries and assumptions; the glorious smoke and mirrors of the human sideshow. I didn't appreciate how mysteries make the future worth waiting for. I certainly didn't recognize how grateful we should be to that which we don't understand.

I looked at the cold, impersonal façade of the church and started to turn away. I wasn't really comfortable with overtly religious people—especially those who took it upon themselves to proselytize. I walked to the corner and paused. Sean made a gurgling sound and I noticed that the autumnal air had brought color into his cheeks.

Sean had fallen asleep in the stroller and I pushed him into the darkened narthex. The pews stretched out on either side of the nave like the rib bones of a dead giant. It was a weekday morning and the church was dark and deserted. As my eyes adjusted to the dimness, I began to make out the choir stall, the altar, and the transept.

I wondered what I was doing. Could I get into trouble for trespassing? But I reasoned that pushing a baby in a stroller gave me license. Thieves and vandals rarely brought babies on their incursions.

I passed through the inner doorway that led into the well-lit church office. I knocked on the door and was greeted by a short, chain-smoking, cherubically bald man with a moustache and intelligent eyes. He asked if he could help me and I told him that I had been thinking about coming to church. He responded with a welcoming smile, but made no effort to encourage me, which I appreciated. Perhaps Father Norman Hall sensed my apprehension, because all he did was listen to me talk. It was the beginning of a friendship, one that would last until his death a decade later.

I started to attend St. Bartholomew's Church, and later that year I also attended confirmation classes.

Over the years, my disillusionment with all organized religion has grown. I disagree with the notion that agnostics are simply cowardly atheists. I have glimpsed a few large patterns and sense that there are much greater ones that I am completely unaware of. As my uncertainty has grown, so has my spiritual curiosity. Where am I now? Arthur C. Clarke said it well: "Either we are alone in the universe or we are not. Either way, it's terrifying."

Royalties from T*he Anarchist Cookbook* had dwindled to a trickle. The flash-in-the-pan fad was over (or so I thought at the time), and I had to earn a living. Although stressful, I had found my work at the Jesse Lee Children's Home in Alaska some of the most meaningful I had ever engaged in. I suspect that in a way I had identified with those alienated and misunderstood children. The long and the short of it is that I decided that I would become a special education teacher. I enrolled in a Master of Arts in Teaching program at Manhattanville College, and found—in the Yellow Pages—a school for emotionally disturbed and learning-disabled children that would allow me to do volunteer work in their classrooms. My work at the Hallen School was a life-changing experience on a number of different fronts.

Hallen enrolled students that had been expelled or exited from the nearby public school districts. The student population was a very eclectic mixture—some with relatively mild learning disabilities, others with intensive developmental needs, and still others with serious social and psychiatric disorders. I had come inside the cuckoo's nest, but I enjoyed working with the students and was soon offered paid employment as a teacher.

Hallen certainly was a great learning opportunity, however, it was also very exploitive. The director hired unqualified teachers (I know because I was one of them), paid them a pittance, and provided next to no professional support. There was no curriculum and next to no resources. The school was not accredited and students were enrolled without screening some with mild dyslexia, others with Down Syndrome, severe cognitive and developmental delays, autism, behavioral disorders, and some with full-blown psychoses.

Having said that, Hallen provided a much-needed service in what were the early days of special education. In retrospect, there may be much to criticize, however it was one of the very few schools at the time that would accept students, who for whatever reason, had been declared "unfit" for the regular classroom. Of course, these were not easy children to work with. Many of them had years of repeated failure in schools with all the attendant damage to their self-esteem. Many of them no longer believed in themselves. They were often defensive, withdrawn, angry, and sad. Each of them carried great challenges for themselves and their teachers. I sense that my own cultural and social alienation may have drawn me to work with these children.

One very positive aspect of Hallen was the dedication of the teachers. Even without inspired leadership, the staff had a sense of mission. They understood that for many of our children, Hallen was the last resort. If the kids didn't achieve some sense of success, their future was a dead end.

At the start of the 1976-1977 school year, I was the high school English teacher and assigned fifteen students. Some of the students had learning disabilities. Ralph W. was one of them. An African American eighteen-year-old, Ralph was severely dyslexic and was reading at a first grade level. For years and years, Ralph had been fed a steady diet of remediation—dreadfully boring workbooks and well-meaning teachers who attempted "to remediate his deficits." The workbooks focused on reading skills that were taken out of context and were clearly designed for much, much younger students. They were demeaning and represented an assault on Ralph's already-damaged self-esteem. Disillusioned with school and learning, Ralph was apathetic and cynical.

I took a different approach. I knew intuitively that beneath the sullen exterior, Ralph had considerable intelligence that was waiting to be ignited. My hunch proved correct one Wednesday afternoon. I had just read Alfred Noyes' poem "The Highwayman" aloud to the class. Ralph's eyes lit up. He loved the rhythm and the music of the language. On only one recital of the poem, he had managed to memorize a significant piece of it. He was reciting it to himself as he boarded the school bus to go home.

The moon was a ghostly galleon tossed upon a cloudy
sea.
The road was a ribbon of moonlight over the purple
moor,
And the highwayman came riding—
Riding—riding—
The Highwayman came riding, up to the old inn-door.

The following day, Ralph asked if there were other poems like
"The Highwayman." I explained the ballad genre and introduced
him to the work of Robert Service. He loved "The Cremation of
Sam McGee" and the corridors of Hallen echoed with ". . . *The
Arctic trails have their secret tales that would make your blood run
cold. . . .*"

We then moved on to Vachel Lindsay's controversial poem
"The Congo." Again, Ralph loved the music of the language, but
had reservations (as I did) about the racial stereotyping. The
sullenness disappeared.

During this time, I was doing my student teaching, which
meant that I was being regularly observed by my supervising
professor. During one such observation, I read Yeats' "Second
Coming" aloud to the class, and Ralph responded with a very
insightful and sophisticated interpretation. My supervisor was
very impressed, but criticized me for not providing Ralph with a
written copy of the poem. I tried to explain that doing so would
have interfered with his understanding. He would have tried to
read the poem—and that effort would probably have rendered
the words incomprehensible to him. At eighteen, the prognosis

of Ralph learning to read wasn't good, but that didn't mean he couldn't enjoy literature and even excel at interpreting it. Ralph was finding success, and this was what truly mattered.

The director's indiscriminate admissions insured that there were some severely emotionally and behaviorally disturbed students in all our classes. For example, on the first day of school, I took class attendance. I read the names aloud and students dutifully raised their hands when their names were read. When I came to the end of the list, I realized that I had fifteen names on the list and fifteen students in the classroom, but no one had responded to one of the names on the list.

"Martin Ferman," I repeated the name. "Is Martin Ferman here?"

No answer, but a girl in the back of the classroom was shaking her head fairly adamantly as if to say that Martin Ferman was definitely not there.

"So," I said to the young man whose name I hadn't called, "what is your name?"

"Ronald Bamforth," he replied.

Dutifully, I added the name to my class list assuming that he was a late admission whose name had not yet been entered on the roll.

However, after class the girl who had been shaking her head in the back of the classroom came to me and told me that the boy who claimed to be Ronald Bamforth was actually Martin Ferman. I wondered if he had been playing a joke. I soon found out that it was no joke.

Two days later, Ronald Bamforth answered to the name of Martin Ferman. I am not sure whether the two personalities were aware of each other, but they were stark opposites. Ronald was a diligent, obedient student who did his homework and was reasonably polite in class. Martin Ferman was a hellion— abusive, foul-mouthed, and itching for a fight with other students and me. When I sought advice and support from the principal and director about the Martin/Ronald duo, I was told that I was exaggerating the situation. Several weeks later Martin/Ronald disappeared. He simply stopped showing up for school. I asked about it, but no one seemed to know why or where he had gone. Several months later, we heard a story (possibly untrue) that he had murdered his mother.

At Hallen, I tried to connect with the students on both a professional and personal level; sometimes more successfully than I had imagined. One Saturday night, three of the boys in my class came to visit me at home. After several minutes, I looked out the window and became aware that there was a strange car in the driveway. None of the boys were old enough to drive, but I had other more serious concerns.

"Where did you get the car?" I demanded.

"We sorta borrowed it," Jimmy said sheepishly.

"Does the owner know that you've 'sorta borrowed it'?" I demanded.

"Not exactly. But we're gonna return it," Danny added.

"Damn right you are. And you're going to do it right now!" I bellowed. I could have been talking to a younger version of myself.

It was a second grade student, Ramy, who introduced me to Ochan, albeit in an unintentional and rather unusual manner. Ochan was doing her student teaching in Ramy's class. It was towards the end of September and Ramy had had a particularly bad day at school. She had started the day by withdrawing from interacting with the other children. During self-directed play time, she isolated herself in the dress-up corner. She appeared sullen and angry.

A little later in the morning, Ramy was at the painting station when her tablemate accidently spilled the water that they had been using to wash the paint brushes. Some of the water splashed on Ramy's dress. The young girl lost all control and attacked her classmate, nails flailing and teeth barred. The teacher managed to pull Ramy off her classmate and ascertain that no serious harm had resulted. However, Ramy remained furious for the rest of the day.

That same afternoon while on bus duty, I caught sight of a small, elementary school girl with pig tails, jump off the curb and run out into moving traffic. She proceeded to attack the side of a moving bus.

I then heard a shout "Ramy! Ramy! Come back here this instant!"

Seconds later, a small Chinese woman dashed into moving traffic after the young girl. This appeared to be good sport, so I followed suit.

The child was rescued without injury, but the three of us did end up rolling around in the gutter. Once the dust settled,

I introduced myself to the young Chinese woman. Her name was Ochan Kusuma and was a student teacher in grade two. We discovered that we were both graduate students at Manhattanville. I offered her a ride to the college during which we discovered that both of us were third-culture kids (children who had grown up outside the culture of Mom and Dad), and that both of our fathers worked for the United Nations.

Although I certainly didn't know it then, Ochan was destined to be my wife, best friend, and closest professional collaborator. As I write this, we have been together for more than forty years. In the weeks and months that followed, I saw quite a bit of Ochan and I felt as though I was awakening from a stupor.

We shared our globally nomadic childhood (her's was much more extensive than mine—Jakarta, New York, Bangkok, Addis Ababa, Beirut, and even short stints in Amman and Cairo. We enjoyed talking about education and philosophy, and the puzzling and demanding students that we both worked with at Hallen.

Both Ochan and I enjoyed our work with the students at Hallen, and it was not long before we decided to start an afterschool drama club. We started casting for a December production of A Christmas Carol. I seriously doubt that a more bizarre production of Dickens' classic has ever been produced. We built the set on weekends in the back garden of my parent's house, and for many of the students, the manipulation of hand tools was quite a challenge. Roger, a teenager with severe cognitive delays, was unable to understand that to hammer in a nail, you have to keep your eye on the nail. His vision focused on the movement of the hammer. Laura painted the canvas flats, her classmates, and herself.

The rehearsals were equally challenging. Many of the students had great difficulty memorizing their lines, and the blocking was next to impossible. However, a couple of the students exhibited real understanding and talent. For Teddy, the play was the first time he had succeeded in something at school, and so he took his part very seriously.

We cast Adrienne as the ghost of Christmas past. Adrienne was an eighteen-year-old girl well along on the autism spectrum with a logic that was entirely her own. She was convinced that ghosts did not wear clothes and we had to assign a teacher to stay with her in order to be sure that she didn't appear on stage naked.

We cast Andy as Ebenezer Scrooge. Andy, a red-haired fourteen-year-old with an obsessive compulsive disorder, was also seemingly incapable of speaking without whining. On the night of the performance, Leslie, the speech and language pathologist, volunteered to help costume the students. We specifically asked her to help Andy with his makeup. We needed to age Andy by tinting his hair grey. Leslie worked on Andy's hair for more than a half hour without any appreciable success. His red hair showed not a hint of grey. Finally, she gave up and Andy went on stage as . . . well, Andy.

The next morning, Andy's mother was waiting for us when I arrived at school. I don't think I have ever seen anyone as enraged as she was.

"WHAT HAVE YOU DONE TO MY SON'S HAIR?" she demanded.

Andy was standing by her side and was an astounding sight. His long red hair was standing up straight into a bizarre cockscomb. I reached out and touched it. It was solid and hard. Andy looked like a terrified woodpecker.

"WHAT HAVE YOU DONE TO MY SON'S HAIR?" she demanded again, but in even a louder voice.

On investigation, we discovered that Leslie had inadvertently used photo-mounting glue on Andy's hair instead of grey highlighter.

Despite the follies and the mistakes, the production was a great parental success and we did a musical melodrama as a spring production.

As Leslie's faux pas with the photo mounting glue illustrates, we all make mistakes, but that in no way excuses the really stupid ones. Leslie's mistake was careless, mine, however, was really stupid and had dire consequences—consequences that I regret to this day. Towards the end of my second year at Hallen, I inherited a seventeen-year old student by the name of Richard L. Richard who had a condition called hypoglycemia, which meant that periodically his blood sugar would suddenly drop to very low levels. The low blood sugar would result in headaches, a racing pulse and pounding heart, profuse sweating, and trembling. Richard would also become anxious and irritable. It was during one of these hypoglycemic episodes that Richard had hit a teacher at his previous school: thus his enrollment at Hallen.

Richard was also a bodybuilder who worked out at the gym daily and took real pride in his physique. He was not someone to mess with physically.

When Richard was placed in my class, we had a long conversation about his condition. Richard had a great deal of self-knowledge. He was acutely aware of the symptoms associated with the onset of low blood sugar and knew exactly what was needed: He needed to eat. However, he was self-conscious about his condition and didn't want the other students to know about it. While the rule at Hallen was no eating in the classroom (an absurd rule), an exception was made for Richard. He carried a jelly sandwich with him wherever he went. On several occasions in class, Richard would make eye-contact with me. I would nod my assent and he would surreptitiously withdraw the sandwich and proceed to eat it.

At the beginning of November, I came down with the flu. I soldiered on with my class, but all day the symptoms got worse until just after lunch I decided I had to go home. A colleague covered my classes for the rest of the day. That evening, I called the substitute teacher who would cover my classes the following day to go over each class' lesson plan. I explained where the substitute could find textbooks and other resources. I covered everything, except I forgot to mention Richard's condition.

Needless to say, the following day Richard felt a hypoglycemic episode coming on and started to eat his jelly sandwich. The substitute teacher knew that eating wasn't allowed in the classrooms, so he snatched the sandwich from Richard and threw it in the trash can. Richard then proceeded to deck the substitute teacher, run out of the classroom and down the hall to the director's office, and then hurl a bookcase at him.

The police were called and the last thing that anyone at Hallen saw was Richard being carried to a waiting police car in a straitjacket.

If only. . .

All during this time, Celia and I were going through the legal rigmarole of getting a divorce. Over the four years that Sean and I lived in White Plains with my parents, Celia visited Sean perhaps four or five times, and each time it was only for a couple of hours and was very traumatic. Sean would refuse to see her. He would have temper tantrums and even try to hide in cupboards and under the bed.

As time passed, I became increasingly certain that the only thing I would not negotiate on with respect to the divorce was the custody of Sean. The divorce was finalized in early 1979. I had custody and Celia had visiting rights.

In the spring of 1978, I resigned from the Hallen School. I needed to earn a proper living. I interviewed for and was offered a year's contract at Westlake High School in Hawthorne, New York, to cover high school English classes for a woman on extended maternity leave. I was sorry to leave the kids at Hallen, but the prospect of doubling my salary was more than incentive enough to make the move.

As a result of a conversation that Ochan and I had, we visited White Plains High School, where I had spent a couple of pretty miserable years as a student. The purpose of our visit was to take advantage of the Freedom of Information Act, and look into my high school records. Once I had produced a photo ID, these were made available to us. In between the letters of complaints about my behavior in school and some dismal report cards, were two documents that were of interest: two IQ tests—four years apart using different instruments. Both provided a common profile—a thirty-five plus point discrepancy between the verbal subtest and the performance subtest. This, coupled with the great difficulty I had had learning to read, suggested that I was what is referred to as "twice exceptional"—being gifted in some areas and learning disabled in others. This seemed to bear out the findings of the US Army test of mechanical aptitude.

Within a week of my divorce coming through, I asked Ochan to marry me, and to my enduring delight, she agreed. My brother, Chris, was the best man and Sean served as the ring bearer. Ochan's sisters were her bridesmaids. Ochan's mom organized a wonderful reception in the garden of their house in Rye, and I was especially pleased that nine of our Hallen students attended the wedding.

Bill at 6 years, in school uniform in England.

With the publisher, Lyle Stuart, at a press conference in New York city after the publication of *The Anarchist's Cookbook.*

In the back garden of the Powell family home in White Plains, NY, 1978. This was the photograph used for the dust jacket of The First Casualty (1979).

With Julius Nyerere, first president of the United Republic of Tanzania, in the garden of Nyerere's home in Dar es Salaam, circa 1987. As Secondary School Headmaster at the International School of Tanganyika, Bill had taken a delegation of students to meet the president.

With Ochan at their home in Jakarta. Bill had recently been appointed High School Principal at Jakarta International School (now Jakarta Intercultural School). Photo by Colin Powell.

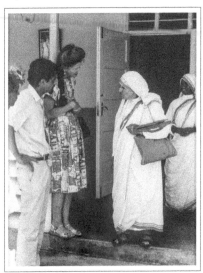

With Mother Theresa in Dar es Salaam, circa 1988. As Secondary School Headmaster, Bill accompanied a delegation of high school students from the International School of Tanganyika to talk to her about their service learning projects.

At home in Massat, France, at Christmas time, circa 1997, with sons Sean (L) and Colin (R).

Kindwitwi Leprosy Village, located on the south bank of the Rufiji River, about 120 miles south of Dar es Salaam, circa 1998. As Secondary Head and later as Head of School of the International School of Tanganyika, Bill accompanied student trips to the village, and served as a Trustee for the Rufiji Leprosy Trust until his death.

United Nations Day, October 2005. Bill served as the Headmaster of the International School of Kuala Lumpur.

Luala Lumpur, Malaysia, 2006, with Malaysian Prime Minister Abdullah Ahmed Badawi and Frank Whiteker, then Chairman of the Board of Directors of the International School of Kuala Lumpur.

Bill with his friend, Bruce Dobler, working on the Trans Alaska Pipeline.

In Halifax, Nova Scotia, shortly before his death in July, 2016.

Part Three: My Life as an Expatriate

CHAPTER 12
The Yeast Never Sleeps

OCHAN AND I HAD THE FIRST disagreement of our married life at the circus at Madison Square Gardens. In between a performance of a tango by four elephants and a troupe of monkeys riding unicycles, Ochan and I disagreed about our future. The subject was my job prospects. It was the spring of 1979 and my one-year contract with Westlake High School was rapidly coming to a conclusion. I was married to Ochan and had a three-year-old son to provide for. I interviewed widely. To my surprise and delight, the Greenwich School District had offered me a full-time high school teaching position. Greenwich was one of the highest paying school districts in the country.

However, I sensed that the prospect of suburban Greenwich didn't sit well with Ochan. She had been the product of international schools and she had an itch to work outside the United States. So she discovered an advertisement in *The New York Times*: The University of Riyadh in Saudi Arabia was looking for lecturers in English. Would I apply?

I really didn't want to. The job in Greenwich was a dream. Why would I want to go to a desert theocracy that prohibited women from driving and banned red wine? But, Ochan argued, there was no harm in applying. So I sent in a resume and was promptly invited to Houston, Texas for an interview.

"But I don't want to go to Houston, Texas for an interview."

"It can't hurt. You aren't agreeing to anything. It's all expenses paid. You're gathering more information. . . .   "

The interview in Houston was absurd. It lasted four minutes. The interviewer, a Saudi professor, appeared completely disinterested. I left the Saudi Consulate relieved that I had failed the interview and would likely hear no more about the University of Riyadh.

A week later, a letter arrived on University of Riyadh letterhead: "Congratulations on your appointment as a lecturer at The Center for European Languages in Translation." In the heyday of the oil boom, that was the way Saudi organizations did business.

It was somewhere between the hareback riders and a scantily clad trapeze artist that I gave in. Saudi Arabia it would be.

In retrospect, it was one of the best decisions that Ochan and I ever made.

We arrived in Riyadh in the middle of the night at the end of August. We were part of a cohort of new hire lecturers with whom we were soon trading recipes for beer and wine. Alcohol is prohibited in Saudi Arabia, and possession can lead to deportation and even in some cases a prison term. This, however, didn't stop the expatriates from making wine and beer. The recipe for wine was fairly simple. You needed several twenty-liter plastic jerrycans, a length of thin plastic tubing, good quality grape juice (without preservatives), sugar, and yeast. The grape juice was then mixed with the yeast and sugar and decanted into the jerrycan. As the yeast began to "work," the fermentation process released carbon dioxide. The gas escaped via the tubing into the bottle half filled with water and generated something akin to New Age music. We brewed our wine in the bedroom cupboard, and it was rather pleasant to drift off to sleep to the sound of bubbling water. The yeast never sleeps.

When I came into the university to work, the head of department, an eccentric English gentleman, was working on the master schedule of classes and asked me when I liked to teach.

"When?" I repeated, puzzled by the question.

"Are you a morning or afternoon person?"

"Morning. The earlier the better."

"You would be OK with a class starting at 7 a.m.?"

"That would be fine."

When the teaching schedules were finalized, I was assigned a class that started at 7 a.m. and finished at 8:30 a.m.

"Where's the rest?" I asked.

"That's all there is," he replied. "The university is so overstaffed that most of us are only teaching one class a day."

The autumn of 1979 had several highlights. In October, Lyle Stuart sent me a contract for my historical novel The First Casualty. I had been working on the manuscript off and on for almost a decade, and I had come to wonder if it would ever see the light of day. It tells the story of Gavrilo Princip, the assassin of Archduke Franz Ferdinand.

The second highlight of the autumn of 1979 occurred on the morning on November 20th. Actually, November 20th is the date in the Western calendar. In the Hijri (Islamic) calendar, it was the first day of the year 1400. This, it would turn out, was significant. At five in the morning, between 400 and 500 heavily armed Jihadist insurgents took over the Grand Mosque in Mecca and held almost 100,000 pilgrims hostage. Led by Juhayman al-Otaybi, the insurgents proclaimed that Mohammed al-Qahtani was the revealed *Mahdi*—the redeemer of Islam. Juhayman was a Sunni extremist who wanted a return to the origins of Islam—a repudiation of Western influences, an end to the education of women, abolition of television, and the expulsion of all non-Muslims from the Kingdom. Juhayman also called for the ousting of the Royal Family.

This was a historically significant event, under-reported at the time, at least in the West. A number of historians trace the origin of Al-Qaeda and the so-called Islamic State to the 1979 Siege of Mecca. One reason that it was under-reported was that the Saudis wanted a complete news blackout until they secured control of the Grand Mosque—a bloody process that took over two weeks and at the cost of several hundred lives.

I was made aware of the siege by my students. We stood at the lecture hall window and watched a steady flow of C-130 Hercules flying overhead, carrying troops and arms to Mecca and bringing back the dead and wounded. It was all my students at the university could talk about, and speculation was rife. At first, there was widespread suspicion that the Iranians might have been behind the attack. Saudi relations with Iran have always been tenuous at best. My students were all Sunni, and for them it seemed absolutely logical for this to be a nefarious Shiite plot. The US State

Department reached the same erroneous conclusion and issued a press statement on the insurgent take-over of the Grand Mosque, pointing the finger at Ayatollah Khomeini, who only hours later went on the radio and blamed the Americans, Jews, and Zionists for the attack on the Holiest Site of Islam. Both accusations were absolute nonsense, but Ayatollah Khomeini's assertion resulted in violent demonstrations throughout the Islamic World with the US Embassy in Islamabad being burnt to the ground.

While there was an official ban on talking about the events in Mecca in university classrooms, you couldn't have stopped my students. My role was to insist that they spoke in English. As the days passed and it became evident that this was not a Shiite plot, but the work of Sunni extremists, my students became increasingly troubled. For Muslims, The Grand Mosque in Mecca is sacred ground where no violence can take place. No animal is killed or injured within the mosque, and even the uprooting of plants is forbidden without permission from the ulema, the Islamic leadership.

The Siege of Mecca and the conversations with my students at the university made me aware of how little the West knew or understood about the desert Kingdom. At the end of November, I wrote a letter to Lyle Stuart asking whether he might be interested in publishing a non-fiction book about Saudi Arabia, tentatively entitled *The Palm and the Scimitar*. Even before receiving his response (positive), I went to work on an outline.

Following the Siege of Mecca, I sensed a change in my relationship with my students. There was an openness that had not been present previously. I made no mention of the book on

Saudi Arabia that I was working on, but made it clear that I wanted to learn about their country from them. Without exception, they were graceful and gracious hosts who quickly volunteered to take me on tours of old Riyadh, Diriyah, and Ain Heet—an oasis some hundred kilometers south of Riyadh. They were keen to share their family histories and provide a window into Saudi Arab culture. I learned about Islam and listened to descriptions of their experience with the Hajj. One student was brought to tears as he recalled an elderly man reciting the Koran at dawn on Mount Arafat. The music of the language danced in the air with the shafts of early morning sunlight.

The big family highlight of the fall of 1979 came in early December when the doctor at our local hospital confirmed what Ochan had suspected for some time. She was pregnant. We were both delighted with the news and made plans for the baby to be born in the United States in mid-July.

In May, Ochan left with Sean for the United States on the last day that the doctors would allow her to travel. I stayed behind in Riyadh to finish the term at the university.

I joined Ochan and Sean in New York, and on July 6th, Ochan went into labor. After more than fifteen very painful hours, she delivered Colin.

The second year of my contract with the University of Riyadh was similar to the first. The organization was so overstaffed that I again taught only one class from 7 a.m. to 8:30 a.m. Ochan was working a real job at the international school and didn't get home until after four in the afternoon.

I filled my time by caring for Colin and working on the Saudi book.

About this time, I encountered one of the worst experiences of my life. It was towards the end of the university year and I was assigned to proctoring final examinations. The cheating was rife and I was running around the room instructing students not to talk to each other, confiscating cheat sheets, and actually expelling several students from the exam.

Then, quite suddenly, I started to feel strangely cold. The air conditioner was on, but no one else seemed to be feeling the dramatic temperature drop. Then, I began to feel anxious, but was unable to pinpoint the source of my anxiety. I thought about all the things that could cause me to worry, making a mental inventory of them. I thought that by locating the source of my concern, I would gain control over it. The opposite turned out to be the case. The list of worries became overwhelming. I knew intellectually that none were really pressing, but still the anxiety grew, and I felt colder and colder.

My hands began to tremble. I clamped my jaw together to stop my teeth chattering. It was unrealistically cold. No one else was shivering, no one else seemed aware of the drop in temperature. It was only me. What was happening to me?

I became very self-conscious and was determined that the students not become aware of my condition. The anxiety increased in intensity and I felt truly frightened. But still I couldn't locate a source for my fear. Something very threatening was happening. I was definitely at risk, but by what or whom, I had no idea. I broke out in a cold sweat and wondered if I had contracted some exotic disease. What if I had come down with some tropical disease—dengue or malaria? What if I were to die in Saudi Arabia?

I don't know how I made it through to the end of the examination. I had now moved beyond thinking that I had contracted a disease, to wondering if I was going mad. There was no rhyme nor reason to what was happening to me. I became hypersensitive to light and sound. Even small noises made me jump. The hum of the fluorescent lights was like a dentist drilling inside my head. The sound of a raised voice made me cringe. I knew this wasn't a normal reaction. Something was terribly wrong. I was losing my mind. By the time the students were handing in their papers, I was in a full-blown panic attack. My heart was palpitating and I was drenched in cold sweat. My hands were shaking so violently that I could barely hold onto the exam scripts that I was collecting.

One of my students noticed my condition and asked me if I was all right. I shook my head. He asked what was wrong.

"I'm cold and frightened."

"What are you frightened of?" he asked, very sensibly.

"I'm frightened that I will forget to breathe," I whispered. It was the first thing that came out of my mouth. I felt that I desperately needed a reason to be so frightened. I was experiencing abject terror and I had no idea of the source of the fear. By this time, I was shaking so badly that I could barely walk. My student half carried me to his car and then drove at breakneck speed to the local hospital. If I had been terrified before the ride, I was petrified by the end of it—literally petrified—unable to move. When we pulled up in front of the hospital's emergency ward, I was unable to get out of the car, and a nurse had to come and collect me with a wheelchair.

Several hours later, the doctor diagnosed a severe, free-floating panic attack, which he said was a result of stress. It was the first of several that would span more than a decade. I would have serious panic attacks in Dar es Salaam, which would actually make me wonder if I could continue working. I came close to resigning for mental health reasons. And I would also have panic attacks in Jakarta. Like many people who have strange and irrational things happen to them, I kept my panic attacks a secret from all but Ochan and my mother. I was ashamed of them, as though they somehow represented a weakness that I needed to conceal. My mother was a phobia therapist and sent me a great deal of helpful material with respect on how to respond. Being too embarrassed, I did not seek professional help. However, I received an enormous amount of strength and support from Ochan.

Over the years, I became sensitive to the signs that a panic attack was starting. I knew the physiological signs—the surge of adrenaline in my stomach, the hypersensitivity to light and sound, and the growing sense of dread. Over time, I also came to know that these panic attacks were not lethal. Despite the heart palpitations and cold sweats, I would not have a heart attack and die. I slowly came to understand that I could "ride out" the panic attack—the way a ship rides out a violent storm. I didn't fight the panic or try to deny it. It was real and needed to be addressed, but not by resistance. Brute psychological force, the proverbial British stiff upper lip, only increased the fear. I sought out the rhythm of the terror and tried to bring myself inside its tidal flow, so that I was a part of it and it was a part of me. As my confidence in dealing with the panic attacks grew, they became less frequent and milder in intensity. I was developing resilience. The last panic attack I had was in Jakarta twenty-five years ago.

What did I learn from these panic attacks?

The crippling effect of the attacks was humbling. Humility is seeing things as they really are. I began to see myself differently. I recognized that I was an emotionally and psychologically fragile person—much like everyone else. The acute discomfort also helped me to develop empathy for others, particularly others who had similar experiences. If I previously had a tendency towards stoicism, the panic attacks opened a window into the remarkable complexity of other people. Slowly, I came to appreciate that other people were as awe-inspiringly complex and frail as I was.

The Saudi book was finished by Christmas, and I smuggled a copy of the manuscript to Sri Lanka in February where we met my mom and dad. My dad carried it back to the US and mailed it to Lyle Stuart. In general, the book is a very positive portrait of Saudi Arabia.

However, the book did contain a heresy—not a religious one, a political one. I wrote that the Saudi Royal Family manipulated their "custodianship" of the Holy Sites of Mecca and Medina in order to stay in power. It was clear to me then that it would be unwise for the family to be in the Kingdom when the book was published. So the search for new jobs began.

CHAPTER 13
Mop Heads, Chinese Pickles, and Konyagi

IT WAS 1981 BC (BEFORE COMPUTERS) and applying for jobs was a tedious affair. Each letter had to be typed separately. We applied to 128 international schools in Europe, the Middle East, Africa, Asia, and South America. We received 127 rejections. The biggest obstacle was that expatriates working in Saudi needed an exit permit in order to leave the Kingdom. This permit was virtually impossible to acquire during term time, so we couldn't travel for interview. However, we did receive one response that offered a ray of hope. Mr. T. Michael Maybury, Headmaster of the International School of Tanganyika (IST) in Dar es Salaam, requested a telephone interview with us.

Mike Maybury offered us jobs: Ochan was to teach in Elementary School and I was to be the Head of the English Department in the Secondary School. After a brief discussion, we accepted.

Our decision to take a young family (Colin was just over a year old and Sean was seven) to Dar es Salaam was either incredibly bold or the height of foolhardiness—probably both. We had read about the game parks, the unspoiled beaches, the hill stations around

Kilmanjaro, and the exotic and mysterious island of Zanzibar. The more we thought of the prospect, the more excited we became.

The first inkling that everything might not be paradise in Dar was the receipt of a two-page typed, single-spaced letter from the wife of the Headmaster listing what we should bring with us. The list included a year's supply of the following items: toilet paper, cooking oil, laundry soap, light bulbs, sugar, flour, cloth nappies (read diapers), prickly heat powder, sunscreen, tampons, and birth control pills. There was also masses of advice about clothing: "stick to cotton or it will stick to you," booze ("stock up at the duty free"), and sports equipment ("bring them with you—nothing available locally"). The advice on other things to bring for the kitchen was quaintly British: Marmite, Coleman's Mustard, Bovril, a tin of Christmas Pudding, and Jacob's water biscuits.

My first response was to question the author's mental health: a year's supply of flour, cooking oil, and sugar? What did the local Tanzanians do for staples?

The answer, we later discovered, is that they did without, but we didn't know that sitting in our apartment in Riyadh. With bravado that bordered on idiotic, I threw the letter away and packed a steamer trunk full of books.

After a summer visiting Morocco, London, and Barbados, we flew to Dar es Salaam from Charles De Gaulle Airport in Paris, armed only with a large leg of dried ham and an even larger bottle of whisky.

I realized the gravity of our mistake during the first shopping trip that the school organized. The shops in Dar were virtually empty. One of the largest shops, Patel's Stores, had the following inventory: mop heads, cutting boards, a few dusty tins of Chinese pickled cabbage (left over from when the Chinese built the Tazara Railroad to Lusaka), tins of a putrid margarine substitute called "Tanbond," and copious quantities of Konyagi—a gin substitute that was manufactured in a plant that on alternative weeks produced fluid for duplicating machines. Rice, flour, sugar, and cooking oil were simply not available. Gasoline was rationed and there was a Sunday driving ban in place. Bread was sold under the counter.

Fortunately, there were a number of open air markets that sold a variety of tropical fruits and vegetables. The paw paws, mangos, and citrus were outstanding. Potatoes, onions, tomatoes, and garlic were just about always available. There was also a wonderful, if smelly, fish market on the beach near the Kigamboni Ferry where you could buy fresh tiger prawn, lobster, sole, and kingfish steaks.

We learned to sleep under mosquito nets, to iron our underwear to prevent *washa-washa* (an incredibly itchy reaction to hairy caterpillars that might have crawled over the laundry drying on the clothes line), and to boil for ten minutes and then filter all of our drinking water.

There were a number of challenges to learning how to live in Tanzania. One of the most pressing was the need to come to understand the economy—it operated on principles that were completely opposite to everything we had come to understand. First of all, there were actually two economies in Tanzania—the official one (which virtually no one used) and the black market. The Tanzanian shilling was a soft currency, and you could not trade it for hard currency. The official rate of exchange when we first arrived was six shillings to the dollar. The black market rate was close to thirty-six shillings to the dollar. During the next few years, the black market rate of exchange would soar to ten times the official rate.

This created an economy where nothing was as it first seemed. The *apparent* cost of living in Tanzania was so astronomically high, that for the first few months Ochan and I rationed meat to ourselves and our children.

The local currency was devaluing faster than the value of commodities, so that there was no incentive for shops to stock their shelves. In fact, shopkeepers actively tried to avoid selling their merchandise. Strict import and export restrictions prohibited them from re-stocking their shelves anyway. Whatever merchandise the stores had, they hoarded and hid. Price controls were in place on virtually everything. Selling above these limits constituted economic sabotage and could earn you a lengthy stay in a Tanzanian prison.

We came to Tanzania and IST in August 1981 with the intention of staying for our two-year contract and no more. However, that two-year commitment readily morphed into a sixteen-year love affair with the school and the country. This didn't happen overnight, and many factors and people influenced our growing affection for IST and "the Land of the Thorn Tree."

In our third year in Dar, there was an economic crackdown by the government. This meant regular nightly raids on individuals and businesses who were suspected of dealing in black market goods (flour, sugar, coffee, etc.), or who might be in possession of illegal foreign currency or imported goods. It was a scary time, particularly for the Asian business community. In those Wild West years, it was impossible to do business in Tanzania legally, and everyone was "on the fiddle"—some with remarkable imagination and creativity. Daily, we received reports of members of the IST parent community being arrested and jailed.

During this time, basic consumer goods (laundry powder, cooking oil, flour, rice etc.) became increasingly hard to find. This was the focus of a conversation I had one evening with Charlye Woolman, the Head of the Science Department over several glasses of Konyagi and lime. We knew that not only were the shops in Dar empty, but that the black market, which teachers had previously relied upon, was also drying up. The risks were no longer commensurate with the gains. Why risk several years in prison for selling a loaf of bread or a crate of Fanta? Charyle, well into his third or fourth Konyagi, made an astute observation: "It is much easier to purchase one 50 kilo sack of rice, than to purchase 50 one kilo sacks of rice." His point was clear: It would be much easier to buy commodities in bulk on the black market. The risk of exposure and arrest diminished dramatically.

Out of this conversation, Charyle and I founded IST's Group Resource Allocation Bureau (GRAB)—a school cooperative shop. Charlye and I would scout out black market commodities that could be purchased in bulk, and then set up a rota of volunteer teachers to bag and serve in the school shop. The shop was open for two hours every Thursday afternoon. It was an exciting and nerve-wracking time. In Graham Mercer's history of IST, he quotes Charlye as saying, "Bill and I used to see if the police were waiting for us whenever we returned to the campus."

Tanzania and IST grew on me. In terms of the dramatis persona, probably the most influential in my growth and development were three transplanted Englishmen: Ernest Pollack, Robin Lamburn, and Nick Bowley. Each were very different, but shared strongly held values, quiet philosophical determination, a strenuous work ethic, a humane but realistic view of the world, and a wonderfully playful sense of humor.

One of the earliest influences was Ernest Pollack, the Secondary School Principal. Arguably, the most significant of Ernest's adventure was his journey south into the remote Rufiji District of Tanzania to find Father Robin Lamburn, the elderly Anglican missionary director of Kindwitwi Leprosy Village. Like David Livingstone before him, Robin Lamburn wasn't actually lost and didn't need "finding." Robin knew exactly were he was.

Ernest wanted to establish a meaningful community service project for secondary school students and had heard that there was an ex-British missionary priest who was running a leprosy village south of the Rufiji River in one of the most remote and inaccessible parts of Tanzania. And so, armed, Ernest set out in a twenty-year-old Land Rover, with a couple of jerrycans of extra diesel and a Marmite sandwich to "find" Kindwitwi Leprosy Village and Canon Robin Lamburn. He succeeded, and that began a long-term relationship between the school and Kindwitwi.

The history of Kindwitwi begins in about 1911 when Tanzania was German East Africa. The German colonial administration designated it as a "Leper Colony," and it was essentially a dumping ground for those unfortunate enough to contract the disease. The "Leper Colony" status continued under the British administration of Tanganyika, and Kindwitwi emerged as one of the most squalid and dangerous places on the face of the earth. The stigma surrounding leprosy was so strong that outsiders avoided the village at all costs. Kindwitwi earned a reputation for lawlessness, banditry, and widespread drunkenness. The "lepers" at that time didn't think of leprosy as a physiological disease. They perceived themselves as the "accursed of Allah" and had an understandably large chip on their shoulders. This was the state of affairs that Canon Robin Lamburn found when he walked into Kindwitwi in 1964 with nothing but the clothes on his back and a Bible.

Robin Lamburn, who had degrees from Cambridge in both theology and medical pathology, came out to East Africa in the early 1930's as a medical missionary. He worked in Masasi in Christian education and was very active in the Tanganyikan Boy Scouts. During our sixteen years in Dar, Ochan and I made numerous trips to Kindwitwi and came to know Robin well— although as Archbishop Trevor Huddleston said in his eulogy: "Like most missionaries, Robin Lamburn was a loner." Robin himself was characteristically more direct. He told me: "It's no fun being my friend." And it wasn't. Sometimes things which are truly meaningful aren't much fun.

After breaking his hip, Robin spent nearly three months living with us in Dar. During this time, he told us about the early years in Kindwitwi. In early 1964, Robin met with his Bishop, Trevor Huddleston. Robin was set to retire from his position in Masasi and the conference was focused on what he might do next. According to Robin, Huddleston suggested that he might consider taking on the directorship of a leprosy village in the Rufiji District. The village was in a desperate state and the challenges would be enormous.

The Rufiji District was, and is, the poorest and most remote area in Tanzania. There was no electricity and no running water. It borders the Selous, an uninhabited game reserve the size of Denmark. The District is named after the enormous Rufiji River, which meanders through it. The river is full of hippos, crocodiles, and gigantic catfish. There was a public ferry, but it was so often out of operation, that most of the time we were forced to cross the river in dug-out canoes. During the rainy season, the river flooded and the District was entirely cut off from the outside world.

The Rufiji District is a solidly Muslim area of Tanzania. Having said that, Islam in that part of the country is inexorably mixed with witchcraft and magic. At the time of Robin Lamburn's arrival, Kindwitwi was controlled by witches. Witchcraft remains to this day a very powerful force in Tanzania. Robin's presence was an immediate threat to the witches' power. His first house was burned to the ground by the witches and his first convert to Christianity was murdered, his heart removed from the chest cavity. Robin told me that he suspected it was eaten by the witches.

At first glance, in the October of 1983, Kindwitwi seemed to be just another African bush village eking an existence out of growing rice, cassava, maize, and cashewnuts. The villagers lived, as most Tanzanians did, in huts built of dried mud. Water for the village was delivered through three standpipes, which the villagers queued up to use. There was no electricity. Nor were there any indoor toilet facilities.

This was not an accident. For the previous twenty years, Canon Robin Lamburn had been working to make Kindwitwi as typical as possible. Almost immediately upon arrival, Robin changed the policy of providing the villagers with all their needs, and instead emphasized self-reliance and self-sufficiency. In 1965, he gave the villagers one year's notice that in the future no beans would be brought into Kindwitwi from outside. A year later, the villagers were self-sufficient in beans.

On one occasion, I had been in the village godown helping Robin inventory the sacks of dried maize. In the far back corner of the store, I discovered a coffin that was so termite eaten that when touched it exploded into a fine cloud of red dust. Robin explained that a few years before, a carpenter had found his way to Kindwitwi and had asked the village elders for refuge. He had gone blind as a result of leprosy and was no longer welcome in his home village. In order to get the carpenter started in Kindwitwi, Robin commissioned his own coffin. He said he hadn't needed anything else, and then added, with a twinkle in his eye, that he was the only man he knew who had outlived his coffin.

My friendship with Robin Lamburn would last a decade—until his death at eighty-nine in the October of 1993. Occasionally, Robin would come to Dar and stay with us at our home on the Msasani Campus, but I sensed that he was like a fish out of water outside of Kindwitwi. This was, to some degree, confirmed when in 1985 he won the Albert Schweitzer International Prize for the Humanities. The prize was organized by the University of

North Carolina in Wilmington and consisted of a medal, a check for $5,000, and a return air ticket to the United States. At first, Robin was very reluctant to go to Wilmington to accept the prize, however, Ochan and I encouraged him to go. He donated the prize money to Kindwitiwi.

In September 1982, Ernest announced his decision to resign from IST as Upper School Principal at the end of the school year. Africa, he declared, was a young man's continent. Soon after his announcement, I wrote to Mike Maybury enclosing an application for the principal's position. I knew I was a long shot. I was not qualified and had no administrative experience.

To my enormous surprise, Mike offered me the principal's position, which although unqualified and completely inexperienced, I immediately accepted.

My first year as a school principal did not get off to a good start.

At the close of the previous school year, Mike had suggested that John Clayton, the Head of the Mathematics Department, help me with the construction of the master timetable of classes. I embraced this offer, as manual timetabling (we didn't have computers then) is very complex and demanding work. John said that he would work on the timetable over the summer holidays. I was relieved and very grateful.

On my return to Dar, Salus Fernandes, a chemistry teacher, appeared rather breathlessly in my office.

"Have you heard?" he asked. "John Clayton's dead. He died in Liverpool ten days ago of cerebral malaria. The British doctor said he had the flu and sent him home with a bottle of aspirin. They never tested for malaria. In twenty-four hours he was in a coma and two days later he was dead."

My response was the predictable, initial shock of hearing that someone you know has died suddenly. The shock was compounded by the fact that he had died of malaria. He didn't get malaria in Liverpool; he had clearly carried it with him from Dar. Tanzania was becoming a more dangerous place and I had a young family.

My next reaction was to think of the wretched timetable—the construction of which would now become m*y sole responsibility*. Please note the hubris in the previous sentence. My unwillingness to ask for help would become a central flaw in my early years as a school leader. Like the writing of *The Anarchist Cookbook*, the construction of the timetable would be a self-imposed DIY job.

The manual construction of a master timetable of classes is a complex affair. A single decision in one arena of the timetable can have all sorts of unexpected ramifications in another area. I literally locked myself in my office for three, fourteen-hour days and managed to produce probably the worst master timetable in the history of international education. Even this dreadful product had required intense concentration. I worked through both lunch and dinner. The result was urgent. Teachers were beginning to arrive back at school and wanted to know what and when they would be teaching.

A curious episode occurred during the construction of the timetable that would become a harbinger of personal learning for me in the years ahead. Despite the fact that I had left strict instructions with my secretary that I was not to be disturbed, there came a knock at my office door.

I did not know then that on the other side of the door was Nick Bowley, a British teacher, newly arrived in Tanzania, who would become one of my most trusted colleagues, a very good friend, and a mentor. My friendship with Nick would come to span more than three decades.

Nick introduced himself as the new Head of Geography. He said he had heard of John Clayton's death, and asked if I needed any help with the timetable.

My response begs examining. I thanked Nick sincerely for his offer, but told him that everything was going well (although I knew that it wasn't) and suggested that he focus on getting his family settled into their house.

Why would I reject the offer of help when I knew that I desperately needed it?

I suspect there were two reasons—neither made much sense, but being sensible has never stopped me from leaping into the abyss. The first is that I didn't want to appear inexperienced and incompetent. The irony of this was that, ultimately, the master timetable would have to be a public document. Teachers needed to know what, where, and who they would be teaching. And the mistakes (large and small) would also become glaringly apparent. It's hard to hide the screw up when two teachers arrive in the same classroom to teach different subjects to the same students at the same time.

The second reason for my "go it alone" stance was even more insidious and ultimately self-destructive. I had a largely unexamined assumption that the simplest and most straightforward approach to a difficult challenge was to attempt to handle it alone. The timetable was urgent, and I managed to convince myself that I didn't have time for group work or collaboration. If it was to be, it was up to me.

The solo construction of the timetable also produced an immense amount of personal stress. And so, it was perhaps not surprising that I suffered a massively debilitating panic attack at the end of September that knocked me out of work for three or four days.

The first year as a principal was a humbling experience. The panic attacks brought home how vulnerable I actually was. Slowly, over the course of that painful year, I began to appreciate and understand the need for interdependence.

For Christmas in 1985, we met up with my mother and father in New Delhi and then flew up to Kathmandu for New Year's. It was a delightful trip, but I noticed that my dad seemed a little less stable on his feet, and seemed to tire more easily than I had remembered.

In January, back in New York, my father complained about a prolonged sore throat, which after some investigation turned out to be a malignant tumor in the throat. He was operated on in May, and a tumor the size of a small grapefruit was removed from his throat. In order to try to remove all of the cancerous tissue, the surgeon also removed part of Dad's tongue, which made speaking very difficult. For a man who was as highly verbal as my dad, this must have been a particularly difficult cross to bear.

The operation appeared to go well, and the surgeon was confident that he had removed all of the cancerous cells. Dad had speech therapy and was still planning on meeting us in Mallorca for a holiday together in the summer. However, in June it was decided that he was not well enough to travel, and Ochan, the boys, and I planned for a holiday in White Plains instead.

In August, Dad suffered a set back and developed lower back pains and appeared to lose some of the energy that he had previously had. My dad visited his oncologist and received confirmation that the cancer had spread to his spine. We all knew what that meant. Spinal cancer is inoperable. Dad was dying. But none of us anticipated how fast the cancer would spread.

On October 10th, my mom telephoned me in Tanzania. The news was grim. Dad had been given two or three days at most. I called the airlines and got us booked on the flight out that night. We flew through Amsterdam and then on to New York. I felt frightened and unprepared. Ochan and I read Elizabeth Kubler-Ross' book *On Death and Dying* on the plane to New York. We only had one copy, so Ochan, being the faster reader, read ahead and then tore out pages so that I could follow behind her. In retrospect, it was a curious exercise: It allowed me to intellectualize my emotional state. By thinking about and analyzing my feelings, I found a way to avoid their full and awful impact.

As we started our descent into JFK, I gathered up what remained of the book: a mass of torn, crumpled, and disassociated pages bound with a blue rubber band. The pages were no longer in order and the chaos of the decimated book seemed an accurate reflection of my state of soul.

When we disembarked from the plane and were going through immigration and customs, I wondered who had come to the airport to meet us. As we came through the sliding glass doors and I saw my mother, I knew instantly that we were too late. My mother would never have left my dad's side if he had still been alive.

My dad passed away on October 11, 1986, the night before we arrived in the United States. While it was not the first time I had experienced a death in the family, it was unquestionably the most immediate and emotional. As an adult, I had come to love my father deeply, respect his work, and share his passion for history, literature, and good conversation. I felt empty and bereaved, as though this was not just his death, but also the death of part of me.

By the mid-1980's, *The Anarchist Cookbook* was dead-in-the-water. Lyle Stuart had written to me that he had sold his publishing company and the new owner did not want to continue to publish *The Cookbook*. This was fine with me. My interests had moved from anarchism to special education and school leadership.

I was aware that something called the Internet was emerging as a cyberspace reality, but had no idea that it would serve as a catalyst for the resurrection of *The Cookbook*.

In 1989, we decided that it was time for a change and began the process of applying for new jobs. I was appointed High School Principal at Jakarta International School and we spent two years in the Indonesian capital. I developed a perverse affection for this bustling metropolis. Ochan did not. As a Chinese Indonesian she was very much aware of the virulent prejudice that rested just beneath the surface of day-to-day affairs.

So when our two-year contracts were up, we didn't hesitate to apply to return to IST in Dar es Salaam.

CHAPTER 14

The Return of *The Anarchist Cookbook*

MY APPOINTMENT AS CEO of the International School of Tanganyika was a controversial one. The board made the appointment on a split vote, essentially down racial and ethnic lines with the Europeans and Americans voting against me, and the Asians and Africans voting in favor.

The IST that I inherited in July 1991 was quite a different place than I had left two years before. The school had become highly politicized, and generally accepted boundaries had become blurred. A small group of teachers had become socially and politically close to a handful of board members. While the administration was attempting to lead the school during the daytime, the teachers and a rump board were leading it in the evenings at their ad hoc meetings in local bars and clubs around town. It was a very unhealthy situation.

Schools are organic, and they either improve or deteriorate depending on the leadership and quality of the teaching staff. The senior leadership that was in place when I returned to Dar was uninspired, self-serving, and nondescript. The school had deteriorated, and student learning was not a priority.

I needed a new leadership team that I could rely upon, and in early 1992, I had an opportunity to recruit. I made several outstanding appointments. Nick Bowley, a trusted man of great integrity, returned to IST from Jordan to become the secondary headmaster, and Areta Williams, a forthright and courageous educator with whom I had worked at JIS, accepted the Junior High Principal's position.

As I saw it then, the greatest need facing IST was dynamic, engaging, and academically rigorous teachers in every classroom. I made no secret of this. The senior leadership team and I spent many, many hours analyzing the present state of affairs at IST, and talking about individual teachers who needed either to be put on an improvement plan or counseled out of the school.

These were very frank and candid conversations that were held in the strictest confidence. I trusted that as a senior leadership team we could speak openly with one another. At the time, I had no idea that the contents of these conversations, particularly my concerns about some of the elementary teachers, were being regularly reported back by the Elementary Head to his friends on the teaching staff. Over time, a perception developed among a relatively small group of elementary teachers that I had a "hit list" of teachers. Understandably, this resulted in a climate of fear and anxiety.

Ochan refers to the 1993-1994 school year as the "Year from Hell." It was a year packed with tragedy, trauma, and conflict.

The year began with an IST graduate from the previous year's class dying of malaria. The start of school was an understandably somber affair. Not a month into the school year, another secondary student died as a result of a very severe asthma attack, and by October, IST suffered what was possibly the worst school tragedy: A tenth grade British student successfully committed suicide. After the second death, I remember standing with Nick and a large group of students at the graveside. The school had been in the process of rehearsing the musical *Coming of Age* and we had made black T-shirts for the cast and crew. Since these T-shirts were the only item of black clothing that many of the students owned, they wore them to the burial. The poignancy of looking at thirty or forty young adolescents paying their last respects to a classmate wearing *Coming of Age* T-shirts was not lost on me.

In the late October of 1993, I received the news of Father Robin Lamburn's death. Several days after my return to Dar, I received the last almost-illegible letter from Robin, written two days before his death. Hastily scribbled in a spidery hand, the letter instructed me to clear through customs a consignment of wheelchairs donated to Kindwitwi by a church group in Germany. There was no supporting documentation, no bill of lading, no estimated date of arrival, and no mention of which church group in Germany. There was also no "please" or "thank you," just Robin's characteristic closing line: "Pray and serve and leave the rest to God"—these are the words that are inscribed on his headstone.

As if Robin's death was not enough to deal with, something else transpired during this time period. *The Cookbook* was coming back from the grave.

After leaving school on a Thursday evening, Ochan telephoned through to me in Botswana with an odd and very disturbing piece of information. On arriving at work, my secretary had found a pile of large envelopes on her desk for delivery to individual board members. Since the envelopes had not been there the night before and I was out of town, she opened one. Inside she found a photocopy of *The Anarchist Cookbook* and a two-page cover letter that threatened that unless the board of directors terminated my employment, the authors, the so-called "anonymous group" (of unhappy teachers) would publicize the fact that I was the author and thereby bring the good name of the school into disrepute. The letter threatened to inform the entire IST community, the Ministry of Home Affairs, the Prime Minister, the Ministry of Education, the European Council of International Schools, the US State Department, and, curiously, the German magazine *Der Spiegel*.

So how had the blackmail letters gotten onto my secretary's desk?

Both my office and my secretary's office were locked, but there was a connecting door between them. The only people with keys were my secretary, myself, and the Elementary Head.

Ah, the plot thickens.

When the full Board of Directors met in early November, they collectively denounced the letter as "a clear form of blackmail." However, they also decided that the underlying "discontent" should be investigated. The Anonymous Group had got the ear of at least a few of the board members.

In the meantime, the "Group" made good their pledge to distribute further poison pen letters. Copies of the original letter and photocopies of *The Cookbook* were sent to various diplomatic missions, local newspapers, and government ministries. There were few mornings that we didn't receive a telephone call stating that such and such had received a copy of the letter. At this point, the entire community knew about *The Cookbook*, and so the blackmail threat had actually been realized and, in effect, neutralized. *The Cookbook* was no longer the issue. The focus of the attack had shifted to my leadership style.

While the attacks from anonymous teachers and individual board members took a toll on me, I was also deeply concerned about the effects of this crisis on Ochan and Colin. Both were emotionally involved, but impotent to effect change. We were particularly concerned about Colin. He had the children of board members in his class who had obviously overheard their parent's dinnertime conversation. In at least one situation, he was ridiculed and ostracized by the son of a board member because of the political situation.

My main professional concern during this period was the fragmented and confused leadership team. The Elementary Head isolated himself from most of the rest of the team, and even attempted to turn some of the other administrators against me.

I spoke at considerable length with Nick Bowley about the situation, but put off making a decision for several weeks. During the time, I had a one-on-one meeting with the Elementary Head and asked him point blank whether he wrote the anonymous letter or whether he had assisted in the distribution. He denied both.

The situation with the Elementary Head and the board went from bad to worse. The distribution of the blackmail letter had continued, and a sixth grade teacher, who clearly felt threatened by me, had hired a lawyer who was writing incomprehensible, menacing letters to the Board Chair.

On the evening of December 1st, Areta Williams dropped by the house for a drink. The topic of the conversation turned, as it was wont to do, to the Blackmail Affair. As she was leaving the house, Areta called over her shoulder what she may have meant as a rhetorical question: *Why don't you just fire the Elementary Head?*

I didn't treat it as a rhetorical question. I fully believed that the Elementary Head was centrally involved in the blackmail attempt, and that he thought he had sufficient board support so that he would be appointed CEO after my departure. The leadership team was unable to function with him present. Why didn't I just fire him?

The reason was that I didn't have that authority. According to school policy, I could suspend a member of the leadership team and I could recommend dismissal to the board. The actual decision to fire was one that the full board would make.

So the next day, I suspended the Elementary Head and wrote to Madeleine Stockell, the Board Chair, saying that I would be formally recommending that the board terminate his employment with immediate effect. Madeleine was a highly intelligent and very compassionate woman, who was clearly unused to the stress of this kind of situation.

The board meeting of December 15th that considered the question of the Elementary Head's dismissal must have set a duration record. It began at 4 p.m. on December 15th, and ended after 9 a.m. the following morning. Prior to the board meeting, I had shared with the leadership team my draft memo to the board explaining the rationale for the Elementary Head's termination. At the end of that meeting, Nick had asked me to leave the room, and the leadership team took a secret ballot as to whether they wanted to co-author the memo. The result was unanimous, and the entire administration ultimately recommended the dismissal.

The board was split, and the outcome of the meeting was a stupid compromise—the product of exhaustion rather than clear thinking. The board determined that the evidence against the Elementary Head, with respect to the authorship and distribution of the anonymous letter, was circumstantial. However, they recognized that trust had been very significantly eroded and that he could no longer function as part of the leadership team. They determined that he would be placed on "sabbatical" (on full salary) until the end of his contract in August. However, the board also had concerns about my leadership and determined that my contract would not be renewed beyond August, when it was due to expire.

This was an unacceptable outcome. Accordingly, the next day, I tendered my resignation effective August of the following year. I stated my reason as an absence of support from the board. Nick Bowley and Areta Williams immediately followed suit. Most of the remaining leadership notified the board that they would also be leaving IST, unless their concerns were addressed. The board now faced the prospect of losing virtually all of the leadership team the following August.

The IST leadership team went off on the Christmas holidays. I suppose at that point we were all engaged in updating our CV's. I know I was. As soon as I got to France, I contacted the recruitment agencies and started applying for other jobs.

A couple of days after Christmas, Ochan took a telephone call from Mark Talbot, a parent at IST and the father of Colin's best friend, Timothy. Curiously, Mark wanted to speak to Ochan, not me. He wanted Ochan to find out whether I would accept another contract at IST if the board were to offer it. I was confused. The board had already determined that my contract was not to be renewed. Mark had implied to Ochan on the phone that Nick, Areta's and my resignation had caused concern in the parent community. We would later learn that Mark Talbot and Vinoo Somayia, a sitting board member, were in the process of circulating a petition amongst the parents that would call for an Extraordinary General Meeting, and a vote of no confidence in the board of directors. The petition they ultimately submitted to the Chairman had over four hundred signatures. The message was clear: A very significant portion of the parent community was opposed to any move to force me out. The votes were there to replace the entire board. In early January, the Chairman telephoned to informed me that the board would have a retreat at the Bahari Beach Hotel on the weekend before school opened, and that Nick Bowley and I were invited to the final session on the Sunday afternoon. Would we attend?

I called Nick and we agreed that we would attend.

The meeting was brief and to the point. Would Nick and I accept contract renewal offers from Board?

We agreed that we would, and both of us served IST for another five and a half years.

I wrote in an early chapter of this book of "flashbulb moments." These are sudden incidents with strong emotional connections that become etched upon the memory. I had such a flashbulb moment on the morning of August 7th, 1998. I had been back in Dar for about a week following the summer holidays, and was engaged in preparing for the orientation of new hire teachers.

I had arranged a meeting in my office with the new Board Chair, John MacKenzie, at 10 a.m. I wanted to give him an overview of how the new school year was shaping up. John was late for the meeting and we had barely poured our cups of coffee when there was an enormous boom. My office door flew open, the building shook, and the windows rattled furiously. It was an enormous explosion. Both John and I were on our feet instantly.

"What the hell was that?" John demanded.

I didn't bother to reply. I ran downstairs and out into the parking lot to see what I could discover. Everyone else in the Admin. Block had had the same idea, and the stairwell was jammed with people asking exactly the same question that John had posed.

From the parking lot, we could see a plume of dark, black smoke rising from the far end of the Selander Bridge, probably about a kilometer and a half from the school.

"A Tanesco sub station must have blown," someone suggested.

"I hope that wasn't my lunch," I quipped. The plume of smoke was in the general direction of our house on Msese Road.

It was not until about thirty minutes later that we came to know what had happened. My secretary, Mwamy Sykes, had a friend who worked at the American Embassy in Nairobi who phoned her.

"It's a terrorist attack on the American Embassy," Mwamy announced. "There was also a bomb in Nairobi. The damage is terrible in Nairobi. They are estimating 50 or 60 people died."

As we know now, that was a gross underestimate; there were over 200 people killed in Nairobi and 11 in Dar.

I immediately called Ochan who was at the Indonesian Embassy having her passport renewed. She had also heard the blast and informed me that the Tanzanian security forces had closed the Selander Bridge. Emergency services were arriving at the scene of the blast.

Fortunately, school had not yet opened, so we did not have to deal with frightened children and panicked parents.

Several days later, I was invited to a US Embassy security briefing at Marine House (the Embassy had been all but destroyed). There were predictable questions from American parents about the safety of their children at IST. The Regional Security Officer announced that the school was not perceived as American, and therefore would not be, in his estimation, a terrorist target. At the time, his words seemed reasonable and comforting. They were exactly what the parents and I wanted to hear. However, in retrospect, they now seem very naïve. Welcome falsehoods are often embraced as truths.

Soon thereafter, Ochan and I decided that the school year 1998-1999 would be our last at IST. It was a difficult decision. Tanzania was a country that we had become very fond of, and

IST was a school we had come to love. However, Colin was set to graduate, and so it seemed time to start another chapter in our lives.

I didn't know it at the time, but the shadow of *The Cookbook* would continue to haunt us. There were individuals from the 1993-1994 school year who made our search for new employment extraordinarily difficult.

CHAPTER 15
Time out of Time

DURING THE 1998-1999 SCHOOL year, I applied for seven or eight heads of school positions around the world. I was not short-listed for any of them. I had made no secret of the fact that Ochan and I were leaving IST, and I suspect that my detractors from 1993-1994 were at work with anonymous emails to schools that had director vacancies. I know this was true a year later when I was actively interviewing for positions. Portions of *The Anarchist Cookbook* were sent anonymously to almost every school that had invited me for interview.

So Ochan and I embraced the prospect of unemployment. We celebrated Colin's graduation from IST in grand style (the graduating class elected him to speak at the ceremony, and the class had their graduation dinner in our garden at Msese Road), and then flew to rural France for an enforced sabbatical.

The title of this chapter is "Time out of Time." It is a Kiswahili expression for which there is no adequate translation in English. I first heard it on a return trip to Dar from Kindwitwi. I arrived at the south bank of the Rufiji River and found the ferry landing thronged by people. The ferry had been out of commission for the best part of a day and half, and a crowd of would-be passengers had gathered, which in turn had attracted vendors of drinking coconuts, pineapples, hard-boiled eggs, and deep-fried cassava chips. There was almost a carnival atmosphere.

"How long will it take them to fix it?" I asked an elderly man dressed in a brown *kanzu* and a white Hajji cap. I was thinking of all the appointments I had the following day in Dar and how to get in touch with Ochan and my secretary. The Rufiji was far outside the cell phone network.

The old man shook his head to suggest that he had no idea.

"It's time out of time," he murmured, and offered me a banana. "It's a gift from God."

"Time out of time" is some enforced interruption in our busy lives where everything that is routine, planned for, or obligatory comes to a sudden stop, and we have thrust upon us an unexpected opportunity for developing friendships, personal reflection, and meaningful growth.

Wazungu's (the Kiswahili word for foreigners—specifically white people) are not very good at recognizing and appreciating "time out of time." Like me on the day I was stranded on the south bank of the Rufiji, we tend to live in the future tense, and worry about the next day's appointments or next week's obligations. We are impatient and become easily frustrated. We worship the twin Western deities of efficiency and punctuality, as though there were something inherently moral in each. The empty hour often fills us with dread.

Our year in France was in many respects "time out of time," and very much an unexpected gift from God. It was a time for reading

and writing, quilting for Ochan, and for us to cook together—
something we were especially keen on. Ochan learned to make
dumplings and focused on extending her repertoire of soups. I
worked on mastering the finer arts of making crispy Chinese roast
pork. We put in a vegetable garden and experimented with growing
different herbs. We explored new recipes and even ventured into
the tricky business of baking. We started a file that we hope will
one day become *The Massat Cookbook*—This cookbook will contain
recipes that you can actually eat.

I had wanted to write fiction for many years, but had not
found the time. Now, I had that opportunity and threw myself into
writing a novel set in Dar es Salaam.

Ochan and I also threw ourselves into a joint professional
project. Ochan had written a grant application to the Office of
Overseas Schools, which is part of the US State Department, to fund
the writing of a book that would support international schools in
becoming more inclusive of students with special learning needs.
We used our "time out of time" to write *Count Me In! Developing
Inclusive International Schools.* The book proved so popular that it
went into four printings.

In addition, during our "time out of time," Ochan and I
began to prepare and present material that focused on teacher
professional learning. In the September of 1999, we spent a week
in Northern Nigeria in Kaduna working with the teachers at Kaduna
International School on differentiation, and meeting the needs of
children with specific learning issues.

From Kaduna, we spent three weeks on the AISA Conference
circuit, presenting workshops in Accra, Harare, and Kampala.

In December, Ochan and I flew to Istanbul so that I could interview for the directorship of the Enka Schools. It so happened that a teacher that I had hired in Dar es Salaam was then employed by Enka, and she was the one who told me that an anonymous email had been received during the interview process linking me to *The Anarchist Cookbook*. We left after a week of interviews and never heard anything more from Enka Schools—not even a polite rejection.

After Christmas I was notified that I was a shorted-listed candidate for the headship of the American School of Paris. Two days later, I was notified that the board had just learned of *The Anarchist Cookbook* through an anonymous email, and were withdrawing the invitation to interview.

It was at this point in time that I recognized that I needed to make a public statement disavowing *The Cookbook*. I did so using the Amazon website, and a number of wire services and newspapers picked it up. I then telephoned Ralph Jahr, a senior associate for International School Services who was the consultant for a number of the head searches that I was interested in. I gave Ralph the background details and asked him whether I should actually list *The Anarchist Cookbook* as a publication on my CV, along with a note explaining that I no longer agreed with much of the content. Ralph counseled me not to do so. His reasoning was that we don't need to include all the stupid things we did as adolescents on our resumes some thirty years later. The advice seemed to make sense at the time, but it was bad advice that would come back to bite both Ralph and me.

In February, Ochan and I flew to Senegal to interview at the International School of Dakar. We both liked the school, but no offer was forthcoming. A couple of weeks later, I flew to Accra, Ghana to interview for the director's position at the Lincoln School. I met with the board, the present administration, the faculty, and the students. The interviews went extremely well and the chairman of the board all but indicated that I was the board's first choice, and an offer of employment would be forthcoming. I was packing my bags at the hotel when she arrived at my hotel room door clutching faxed pages from *The Cookbook*.

Was it true that I was the author?

We had a ten-minute conversation, at the end of which it was clear that she and the rest of the board did not see me as a viable candidate. The board was understandably angry that they had paid to fly me to Accra for interview, and the information about *The Cookbook* had been withheld from them. I told them about my conversation with Ralph Jahr and they responded by threatening to sue ISS. I don't know how that conflict resolved itself, but I vowed from then on I would list *The Anarchist Cookbook* prominently on my CV with an appropriate disclaimer.

Still unemployed and without jobs for the next year, Ochan and I set out to visit Colin at Simon Fraser University and attend the annual conference of The Association for the Advancement of International Education in San Francisco.

Money was tight. We did have some savings to draw upon, but we were loath to do so. We really did need to work.

Then came the phone call from Search Associates. My papers had been forwarded to the International School of Kuala Lumpur in Malaysia. This was exciting news, but I didn't get my hopes up. There had been a string of previous disappointments.

I was invited to Kuala Lumpur for interview. I had decided to pre-empt the possible question of *The Anarchist Cookbook* by bringing it up myself during the interview with the board. They didn't seem to care. World War III was going on in the school and *The Cookbook* seemed a trivial matter to them.

So if "time out of time" has the potential for personal growth, what did I take away from this period of unemployment?

Our year out of work was a hiatus in what had become for me a rapidly accelerating, and largely unexamined, career trajectory. I had become a head of department at thirty-one, a principal at thirty-three, and a CEO at forty. I had passively adopted a definition of professional success that was already in the public domain. I held a high position at a fairly prestigious school, and I was publishing professional articles fairly frequently. I was also presenting workshops at international conferences. I had been elected as President of the Association of International Schools in Africa and had served as a co-opted member of the International Baccalaureate Representative Committee of School Heads. In addition, I was a board member of the Academy of International School Heads, and the president-elect of the Association for the Advancement of International Education. By almost anyone's definition, I was successful, and therein lies the rub. It was by *almost anyone else's definition*, but not necessarily my own.

It was as if I was on one of those thrilling rides at an amusement park where you sit strapped into a little car that hurtles you through a darkened tunnel. During the ride, adrenaline pumps and you find yourself gripping the edge of the seat. However, after the ride is over, you start to wonder what those sensations were actually all about.

Another question I wrestled with during my "time out of time" was a sense of belonging. I grew up in both Britain and the United States, and I was now equally uncomfortable in both countries. Home had ceased to be a geographical location. I was most comfortable where I knew that I didn't belong, in a culture that was alien; or perhaps more correctly in a culture in which I was the alien.

So I was no stranger to a sense of detachment, but our "time out of time" took that sense of disassociation in an unexpected direction. Slowly, over our months of retreat in the French Pyrenees, I sensed a change in myself. I was still curious and craving to learn about the world, and yet there was a new distance between external experience and me. I was no longer trapped within an incident and subject to its turbulent weather. This detachment in no way diminished the richness of experience or its intimacy. To the contrary, the new flexibility allowed for a multitude of perspectives, empathy was enhanced, patterns—both large and small—became more obvious, and the environment seemed richer and more complex.

Apprehending the larger patterns in our social, emotional, and spiritual environment is the first leg of our journey into embracing the mysteries. And it is the mysteries that are our greatest gift; the reason why each sunrise is an intrigue; and the reason why I have come to think of Hell as a place in which all questions have answers.

During the summer of 2004, Ochan discovered a lump on her left breast. We were in France at the time, and she visited two doctors. Both told her that it was probably a benign cyst and nothing to worry about. Fortunately, Ochan and I did worry about it and sought a third opinion when we returned to Malaysia. A biopsy followed. I recall that we were shopping for furniture at a store on Jalan Ampang when Ochan's cell phone rang. It was the doctor and all he would say on the phone was that he wanted to see Ochan in his office the following morning, and that she was to bring her husband along. Both Ochan and I were filled with dread and neither of us slept that night.

As we had come to expect, Ochan had breast cancer: a particularly aggressive, estrogen-negative strain. Immediate surgery was required, followed by both radiation and chemotherapy. Ochan handled the situation remarkably well and was an inspiration for me. Other than the time that she was in hospital for the surgery, she didn't miss a single day of work. This was by design. Ochan knew that she needed to keep herself busy and, more importantly, her mind occupied. She made no secret of her cancer and women from all over the world contacted her offering moral support.

I accompanied Ochan to each of the radiation and chemotherapy sessions. Life-threatening diseases have a way of quickly clarifying our priorities. Our relationship perched itself on the front burner of my consciousness. I wanted more than anything else in the world for her to survive. Mortality had thrust itself into our midst and made each day together a prize of a lifetime, and the thought of tomorrow a chilling terror. I said to myself that I couldn't imagine a life without Ochan, and yet that was a lie. In my darker moments, I allowed myself to drift into the nightmare of a life without Ochan. I suppose this may be a natural response to a life-threatening disease, but it often found me locked in the bathroom in tears.

Before Ochan started the chemotherapy, we went shopping for a wig. The idea was that Ochan would take the wig to the hairdresser and have it shaped into the way her hair was naturally so that most people wouldn't notice that it was a wig. Having said that, Ochan made no secret that she was wearing a wig, and actually announced that she had cancer and was wearing a wig to her 8th grade classes. Her students, without exception, were wonderfully empathetic and kind. Ochan wanted to bring cancer out of the closet. She wanted to give other people permission to talk about it, and therefore promote early detection. She was very brave, very determined, and very compassionate.

Ochan became a cancer survivor who proudly wore the crossed pink ribbon and sought out opportunities to provide support for other women going through the cancer journey. I was, and am, extraordinarily proud of her.

However, Ochan's battle with cancer wasn't over. We celebrated the five-year all-clear milestone and year six and seven and eight. The statistics were looking ever so positive. As each year passed with Ochan cancer-free, the likelihood of a recurrence diminished dramatically. Unfortunately, statistics are only that— statistics. And in 2012, the doctors found another lump in her left breast. Again, there was a biopsy and again, the result indicated an aggressive, estrogen-negative cancer. This time, Ochan had a mastectomy.

We had to face the fact that Ochan was not actually cancer-free, but in remission. We live with that and treasure every day we have together.

Ochan and my decision to leave ISKL in 2006 was unquestionably the most difficult of our respective careers. The school had a hardworking and outstanding faculty, supportive parents, and the most collegial and effective board that I have ever had the pleasure to work with. Ochan was team teaching with outstanding colleagues, and we were getting a great deal of fulfillment from our work.

Everything was going well, so why leave?

According to Professor Mihaly Csikszentmihalyi, the Shushwap Indians of the Pacific Northwest lived in a environment that was very rich in game, fish, and edible roots and plants, and yet every twenty years the elders would decree that the tribe move from their familiar surroundings to a new location where the rivers and the game trails were unknown. Food was unquestionably important, but so too were new learning challenges. Without them, our spirit atrophies and dies.

Like the Shushwap Indians, we wanted to explore new game trails.

CHAPTER 16
The Year My Brain Caught Fire

OCHAN AND I LEFT ISKL'S EMPLOYMENT and established a tiny, mom-and-pop organization called Education Across Frontiers. I did some back-of-the-envelope calculations and figured that we could put bread and wine on the table if we earned about thirty thousand dollars a year. I was cautiously optimistic that we could reach this target.

We continued with our writing projects. *Making the Difference: Differentiation in International Schools* had become an underground bestseller, and from that we wrote *How to Teach Now: Five Keys to Personalized Learning in the Global Classroom.* We became fascinated in the connection between teacher emotional intelligence and student learning, and as a result co-authored *Becoming an Emotionally Intelligent Teacher.*

The school year 2006-2007 was kind to us. We had work in Europe, Africa, South America, and Asia. We developed some highly interactive workshops that were very well-received by teachers. Schools started to ask for multiple year commitments. We shared our time between France and Malaysia.

The year 2007 was not kind. It was the year that my brain caught fire. Or, in the words of bestselling author Susannah Cahalan, it was my months of madness. Susannah Cahalan is the author of *Brain on Fire*. We had the same autoimmune condition and communicated afterwards by email. It was my descent into hell—psychosis and near death.

I became aware that something was wrong in August while Ochan and I were working with teachers at the American School of The Hague. At first there was a general sense of malaise, insomnia, and a lack of appetite. We then returned to France for a week before flying to Brussels to work with the teachers at the International School of Brussels. I visited doctors in both Massat and Brussels, but to no avail. My health continued to deteriorate during the week in Brussels, and Ochan and I made the decision to return immediately to Kuala Lumpur to seek medical attention. We needed doctors who could speak English.

Three or four days after we had returned to KL, I found that I was unable to urinate. My body was not behaving itself. Although I would not appreciate it for many months to come, this was a blessing in disguise.

Ochan rushed me to the emergency ward at Gleneagles Hospital, and I was admitted with a catheter in place. This was the end of August. I didn't know it at the time, but I would be hospitalized until the first week in December.

On the wall of my hospital room in KL was a watercolor painting of a colorful, tropical orchid. One afternoon, as I was staring at the painting, the orchid changed into an elephant. The petals became the elephant's ears and the stamen became its trunk. As I looked at the painting, I knew that it was supposed to be an orchid, but all I could see was an elephant. I found this worrying because I knew that there wasn't an elephant in the picture, but still that was all I could see. I mentioned the strange picture to Ochan and she said something to the effect that the orchid did look a bit like an elephant. The trouble was that for me, the orchid didn't look a bit like an elephant: *It was an elephant.*

Neither of us understood that this was the beginning of a series of psychotic hallucinations that would dramatically increase in frequency and intensity.

I was subjected to a massive battery of tests, but nothing was conclusive. The lead doctor of the team was Dr. Sng, who had the worst bedside manner of any doctor I have ever encountered. He didn't listen, didn't answer questions, and constantly interrupted.

Dr. Sng became convinced that my condition was related to tuberculosis. I had had a suspected case of TB some years earlier and had been treated for it. Dr. Sng ordered another massive battery of tests that would show conclusively that I had some strand of TB—and all of the tests came back negative. Finally, Dr. Sng had to admit that he didn't have a clue what was wrong with me, and advised that we go to a hospital with greater expertise. Within twenty-four hours, I was in an ambulance on my way to National University Hospital (NUH) in Singapore.

Enter Professor Einar Wilder-Smith, a remarkable doctor to whom, along with Ochan, I owe my life and what little sanity I still possess. Professor Einar was everything that Dr. Sng was not. He was a superb listener, highly intelligent, compassionate, and methodical with a cheerful and often wry sense of humor. He filled Ochan and me with confidence.

However, my medical situation in Singapore continued to deteriorate. I suffered from severe short-term memory loss and apparently engaged in bizarre facial movements. My circadian rhythm became very confused, and I had trouble knowing whether it was day or night. I lost control over bodily functions and became subject to intense bouts of perspiration that left my hospital gown and bed linen drenched. I virtually stopped eating and needed to be fed intravenously. I also became subject to seizures and spent a good portion of the time comatose. When I was conscious, the hallucinations became more intense. The pictures on the walls mysteriously transformed themselves into snakes, and at one point, became a larger than life Malaysian Flag. Apparently, I heard and responded to voices that no one else could hear. Professor Einar wrote in an article about my case that appeared in *Lancet,* that I saw messages written on the wall that I claimed were only written for me, and that I conversed with a neighbor that no one else could see.

As you might imagine, this was a very difficult time for Ochan.

I do recall becoming convinced that the acoustical tile ceiling of my hospital room was composed of fragments of antique maps and I spent hours attempting to read and understand them. One of the more bizarre hallucinations was when I saw that each light fitting in the ward had a piece of toast or a croissant stuffed into it. This was puzzling to me as I knew that bread wasn't usually stored in light fittings.

In October, my condition had deteriorated to the point where I was placed in the Intensive Care Unit. I had stopped talking and was more often than not blessedly unconscious. I also had stopped eating and had to be fed through a large tube that was inserted into my nostril. The tube must have been physically irritating, because I am told that several times I ripped it out. This resulted in my being restrained. My wrists were tied to the bed rails with rubber straps. If there is anything that is guaranteed to encourage paranoia, it is tying someone to a bed and sticking a large tube up their nose.

One night in ICU, I died. This may sound like an odd thing to say, given that eight years later I am writing this book. Nevertheless, I was certain at the time that I had gone into death and it was a gently swirling, downward whirlpool into a darkened peacefulness. It was a particularly attractive alternative to my miserable and very painful existence in ICU.

Soon after, Ochan phoned our sons and asked them to come to Singapore, which they did immediately. My condition was touch and go. We had no diagnosis and my condition was worsening by the day. Ochan also called my mother, who wanted to know whether Ochan knew my final wishes. The next day during a brief interlude of lucidity, I confirmed that I wanted to be cremated.

All this time, Professor Einar was working through all possible causes of my condition. He had taken an extensive statement from Ochan about our recent travels and was testing for everything from Lyme Disease to West Nile Virus. Slowly, he was coming to the conclusion that the condition was probably autoimmune. The body was attacking itself.

In November, Professor Einar sent a sample of my blood to Professor Joseph Dalmau at the University of Pennsylvania. Dalmau had been doing extensive research on autoimmune diseases. Professor Dalmau did respond several weeks later and formally typed my condition as NMDA antibodies negative, an autoimmune form of brain stem encephalitis. It was a very rare condition: I was number 65 worldwide and only the third recorded male to have the condition.

In the interim, my condition had continued to deteriorate, and Professor Einar felt that we could not wait on Dalmau. He proposed what he called a "risky" treatment: a massive series of doses of steroids. It was a kill or cure treatment. Both Ochan and I had confidence in Professor Einar and told him to go ahead with the treatment. Professor Einar suggested that Ochan call our two sons back to Singapore . . . just in case. And return they did for the second time.

Two days after the first pulse of cyclophosphamide, I was fully conscious and, for the first time in several weeks, I was able to speak. The torturous road to recovery had begun.

I wrote earlier that my inability to urinate at the onset of the disease was a blessing in disguise. While painful and frightening to me, it made it clear to the doctors that my condition was physiological, not psychological. For many patients who suffer from NMDA negative, they are first misdiagnosed with psychiatric disorders and in some cases committed to mental institutions causing dangerous delays in appropriate treatment. NMDA negative has a thirty percent fatality rate, which is obviously exacerbated by faulty diagnosis.

I was discharged from NUH on December 4th. After almost four months in the hospital, I had no muscle strength left. I had had some physiotherapy in Singapore, but still could not walk or even stand by myself.

It took a full year for me to recover physically, emotionally, and mentally.

My illness in Singapore and Ochan's repeated bouts of breast cancer were poignant reminders of our mortality. There were times when each of us wondered if we would survive, and what on earth we would do without the other. For me, the experience in NUH brought home as never before the importance of relationships. Ochan had been my steady companion for four months in hospital. My sons had traveled halfway around the world TWICE in order to say goodbye to their dad. Friends had also traveled great distances to visit. And many, many had written emails saying that Ochan and I were in their thoughts and prayers. All this was, and is, tremendously humbling.

Both events and conversations can be life changing. One such conversation took place in the early darkness of a November afternoon in 2012 when Ochan and I found ourselves together with Kristen Pelletier sitting in Kevin Bartlett's office at the International School of Brussels. Kevin was then the headmaster of International School of Brussels, a school that had a well-deserved reputation for being inclusive of students with learning disabilities. The conversation was transformational.

We were talking about how international schools around the world were often reluctant to accept children with special learning needs, children with learning disabilities, ADHD, autism, or Down Syndrome. Kevin framed the question in moral terms: "By what right do international schools think they have the right to cherry-pick only the students who are easiest to educate?"

For several years, Ochan and I had perceived the inclusion of children with special learning needs as a human rights issue: "Within my lifetime, schools in the south of the United States thought they had the right to exclude African American students. Even today, some international schools are discriminating against children and young adults who have learning issues."

Two remarkable hours later The Next Frontier Inclusion was born. I am credited with naming it NFI over Kevin's objections (in Australia NFI stands for "No fucking idea"). The four of us hammered out a series of belief statements including the idea that international education should be redefined as being inclusive of children who are not only racially and ethnically diverse, but also learning diverse. We also framed the audacious goal of having at least one inclusive international school in every major city of the world.

The Next Frontier Inclusion started with two small "conversations" at the International School of Brussels. At each "conversation" we had about thirty participants who had come to learn more about inclusive education, and to see it in operation at

ISB. We particularly targeted heads of school and board members, as these individuals tend to be the change agents in schools. These first two events were so successful that the second one generated a waiting list. The NFI Conversations grew in number and were widespread geographically: Cambodia, the Philippines, the Netherlands, South Africa, Mexico, France, India, Hong Kong, Kenya, and Thailand. As of this writing, NFI has about a hundred member schools.

Each year, the NFI Design Team, Kevin, Kristen, Ochan, and I spend a weekend in our farmhouse in Massat developing new materials and products designed to support international schools in becoming more inclusive. Little by little, NFI is changing the world. It is demanding, but meaningful work.

CHAPTER 17
Aging for Dummies

THERE IS A WIDESPREAD ASSUMPTION that people are reasonably well-equipped to handle the inevitable stages of life: childhood, puberty, middle age, the aging process, and, of course, death. I'm not convinced.

For many of us, life happens—ready or not.

Over the last decade, there have appeared a series of "For Dummies" books. The idea is that even very complex ideas and situations can be addressed in a simple (but not simplistic) and accessible manner. And so you have books entitled *The Middle East for Dummies* or *Quantum Physics for Dummies*.

I have been looking for one entitled "Aging for Dummies." Unless our lives are prematurely cut short, we all age. Some do it with a degree of grace, wisdom, and joy, and others with loneliness, unfulfilled dreams, anger, and bitterness. Aging is not just coming to grips with physical deterioration—not being able to hike the twenty miles that you had done twenty years before. It is also coming to grips with that relentless journey towards oblivion.

I'm not sure that I have been the architect of most of my life. I have probably been more reactive than proactive. But now in my seventh decade, I want to age by design, not by default.

2011 represented the 40th anniversary of the publication of *The Anarchist Cookbook*, and a very intrepid Tony Dokoupil from *Newsweek* was determined to write a story. Under the so-called Freedom of Information Act, the FBI files that had to do with *The Cookbook* were to be released that year. Tony contacted me by email and I politely declined his invitation to interview. This was for two reasons: First, I had disassociated myself from *The Cookbook* years before, and had nothing more to add. Secondly, publicity surrounding *The Cookbook* made Ochan anxious.

However, earlier that year I had declined an interview with the magazine *Wired*, and the result was a fairly inaccurate article.

I assumed that if I just ignored Tony Dokoupil and *Newsweek,* they would simply go away. Not so. Tony was on the phone virtually daily, and I came to realize that the article would appear with or without my involvement. And so, I agreed to answer his questions. Tony ended up writing an accurate and reasonably balanced article. He ended the article describing how Ochan and I had just received a lifetime award from the Association for the Advancement of International Education as a result of our work in special education.

I assumed that would finally put an end to the interest in *The Cookbook.* Not so. The British paper, *The Guardian*, contacted me and asked whether I would write an Op-Ed for them. I did so. And the BBC asked for an interview, which I granted.

In the summer of 2014, Gabriel Thompson contacted me and stated that he was working on an article for *Harper's* on *The Cookbook.* My refrain was the same: There is nothing new or newsworthy. However, Gabriel proved to be as tenacious as Tony Dokoupil, and in February 2015, the article appeared. There was nothing really new, but Gabriel had done his research thoroughly and included a multitude of details that had escaped previous publication. The on-going interest in a forty-five-year-old book continued to puzzle me.

A week or so after the publication of the article in *Harper's*, I received an email from a gentleman from California who introduced himself as an Oscar-nominated documentary filmmaker who might be interested in working on a film about *The Cookbook.* After several long conversations with Ochan, I agreed to a Skype conversation. I hoped that the film might be an opportunity to promote the work of The Next Frontier Inclusion.

The film crew descended upon our farmhouse in Massat in mid-June 2015, and we underwent four days of intense filming (Ochan refers to it as a "home invasion.") The experience was not what we had expected. The previous Skype conversation had suggested a more collaborative approach.

I also hoped that the process of making the film would help me understand my life and myself—so that I might age by design and not default.

Perhaps the most perplexing question about *The Anarchist Cookbook* is why it continues to be in print almost fifty years after it first appeared. It certainly seems to have tapped into the turbulent zeitgeist of the 1960's and 70's, and to some extent, captures the petulantly enduring and supremely self-confident voice of rebellious adolescence.

I have come to see the process of writing *The Cookbook* as a period of self-radicalization. Given the rise of Islamic extremism, I have become interested in how radicalization takes place. During the period that I was writing *The Cookbook,* I came to formulate and believe that the world was to be seen in terms of black and white, good and bad, oppressor and oppressed, friend and foe. It was a simple place and I came to believe that there were simplistic answers to complex issues. It worries me now that I was so easily manipulated by myself.

Historically, schools have also been places of manipulation where indoctrination and compliance were the order of the day, and opinions were forced upon young minds. This has started to change, and international schools are increasingly thoughtful and humane places. Of course, schools are about learning stuff (math, science, and history), but they are also about developing values, cognitive processes, and relationships; they are about learning empathy and developing compassion. This is why the work of The Next Frontier Inclusion is so critically important. In the words of Kurt Hahn, the purpose of education is to make the brave gentle and the gentle brave.

Almost fifty years after writing *The Anarchist Cookbook,* I ask myself what I have learned. What messages do I want to give my grandchildren?

First, cultivate a healthy skepticism of all governments and other autocratic organizations. Most are filled with knaves who will not hesitate to lie, cheat, steal, and kill to accomplish their self-serving goals. Do not be deluded by democracy—overnight it can morph into the tyranny of the majority. Having said that, it's probably the most benign form of a necessary evil.

Secondly, extend trust before it has been earned. You will inevitably be burned in the process, but the risk is absolutely worth it.

Third, mistrust all dogma—especially simplistic solutions to complex problems. Avoid people with poor listening skills, they are a waste of time.

Fourth, have faith in individuals and small groups to change the world for the better. This is the way the world has become a more humane place.

And fifth, know that cruelty is the failure of the imagination and love is its triumph.

These are the messages that I want to give to my grandchildren.

A WORD FROM THE PUBLISHER

I had the rare opportunity to work with William Powell for many years, both for his fiction projects as well as the development of his memoir, *The Cookbook*. I always found him introspective, charming, and intelligent. I hope that by publishing this book, we bring to light just who William Powell was as a person, not just the author of *The Anarchist Cookbook*. His true legacy was to help others, not hurt them. He was a true light in the world.

Reputation Books

CPSIA information can be obtained
at www.ICGtesting.com
Printed in the USA
BVHW071542080819
555425BV00001B/53/P